PRAISE FOR

Although of Course You End Up Becoming Yourself

A National Public Radio Best Book of the Year

"Lipsky's transcript of their brilliant conversations reads like a two-man Tom Stoppard play or a four-handed duet scored for typewriter."

—Lev Grossman, *Time* magazine

"Crushingly poignant . . . The rapport that [Lipsky] and Wallace built during the course of the road trip is both endearing and fascinating. At the end, it feels like you've listened to two good friends talk about life, about literature, about all of their mutual loves. . . . A startlingly sad yet deeply funny postscript to the career of one of the most interesting American writers of all time."

—Michael Schaub, National Public Radio

"Lipsky is not telling us about Wallace's life: He is showing Wallace living his life. . . . One thing is certain: If you didn't already love Wallace, this book will make you love him. . . . Wallace's humor, his pathos, his brilliant delivery—his tendency to explore the experience of living even as he's living it—make this book sing. If art is a way of caring for others, Wallace cares for us through the novels, short stories, and essays he left behind. And Lipsky, in the wake of Wallace's death, gives us a narrative that does the same."   —Alicia Rouverol, *Christian Science Monitor*

"For readers unfamiliar with the sometimes intimidating Wallace oeuvre, Lipsky has provided a conversational entry point into the writer's thought process. It's odd to think that a book about Wallace could serve both the newbies and the hard-cores, but here it is. . . . You get the feeling that Wallace himself might have given Lipsky an award for being a conversationalist. . . . We have the pleasure of reading two sharp writers who can spar good-naturedly with one another. . . . What we have here is Wallace's voice."   —Seth Colter Walls, *Newsweek*

"Exhilarating . . . All that's left now are the words on the page—and on the pages of *Although Of Course You End Up Becoming Yourself,* too, with the voices they conjure of two writers talking, talking, talking as they drive through the night."

—Laura Miller, *Salon*

"Compelling . . . The conversations are far-reaching, insightful, silly, very funny, profound, surprising, and awfully human. . . . Ultimately, the only person who can talk about David Foster Wallace is, apparently, David Foster Wallace."

—Menachem Kaiser, *The Atlantic*

"A gift . . . Even though officially Lipsky was the interviewer and Wallace the subject, they became pals, talking about movies, music, craft. . . . The reader, hanging out with Wallace vicariously, gets the sense of jogging along with a world-class sprinter. The jogging is very fine. . . . Wallace's writing illuminates the painful truth that life can be unbearable. But we owe it to him not to let those passages eclipse the vitality that made his prose, and his readers, come alive."

—Michael O'Donnell, *Washington Monthly*

"Insightful . . . Lipsky seems at ease with Wallace, despite being awed by his fame and talent. More importantly, Wallace seems relatively at ease with Lipsky. The two men drive through the raw and icy Midwest, all the while trying to make sense of art, politics, writing, and what it means to be alive."

—Lee Ellis, *New Yorker* Book Bench

"A victory, albeit a brief one, over time . . . Wallace's voice, with its mixture of extraordinary erudition and occasional homespun folksiness, is one of the most distinctive in contemporary American writing and this undertaking represents a desire by Lipsky to capture the cadences of a personality now lost. Heartfelt and devastating."

—David Herring, *Journal of American Studies*

"The reader goes inside the cars, airports, and big-portioned Midwestern restaurants with the two men and, ultimately, inside Wallace's head."

—Steven Kurutz, *Wall Street Journal*

"It's a road picture, a love story, a contest: two talented, brilliant young men with literary ambitions, and their struggle to understand one another. I can't tell you how much fun this book is; amazingly fun. . . . You wish yourself into the back seat as you read, come up with your own contributions and quarrels . . . the wry commentary of the now-mature and very gifted Lipsky, is original, and intoxicatingly intimate. . . . It's exhilarating."   —Maria Bustillos, *The Awl*

"Full of everyman details. . . . Throughout the book, astonishingly profound things are said in airport parking lots and rental-car cockpits. . . . As Lipsky writes, the author's singular achievement, especially in his nonfiction, was capturing 'everybody's brain voice'; Wallace's writing sounds the way we think, or at least the way we like to *think* we think. . . . We may never have a better record of what it sounded like to hear Wallace talk. . . . *Rolling Stone* sent the right guy."

—Zach Baron, *Bookforum*

"Sent by *Rolling Stone* to interview Wallace, David Lipsky recorded, over the course of the last five days of Wallace's *Infinite Jest* book tour, their conversations, and the details are achingly and beautifully human."

—Eden Andres, *Oxford American*

" 'Suicide is such a powerful end, it reaches back and scrambles the beginning,' David Lipsky writes in an introductory note. That's well put, but it won't prepare you for the experience of reading the conversation that follows. . . . One thing that the book makes clear is that Wallace's vigor and awe-inspiring writing was, in some ways, part of a deeply intricate personal effort to beat death. . . . The book has some elements of good fiction: blind spots, character development, and a powerful narrative arc. By the end, no amount of sadness can stand in the way of this author's personality, humor, and awe-inspiring linguistic command. His commentary reveals how much he lived the themes of his writing; all of his ideas about addiction, entertainment, and loneliness were bouncing around in his head relentlessly. Most of all, this book captures Wallace's mental energy, what his ex-girlfriend Mary Karr calls 'wattage,' which remains undimmed." —Michael Miller, *Time Out*

"A hauntingly beautiful portrait of Wallace as a young artist, a raw and honest account of a writer struggling with what it means to have all of his dearest dreams come true. . . . As readers, we're given unfettered access to Wallace's incredible wit. . . . Although haunted by it, this is not a book about his death; it's a book about his life. Lipsky has given us a true gem: Wallace in his own words, in a voice that remains vibrant, hopeful, and frank even after its speaker has been silenced. We all may know how it ends, but *Although Of Course You End Up Becoming Yourself* takes us back to where it all began." —Stephanie Hlywak, *Flavorwire*

"Twelve years before his suicide, David Foster Wallace shared his inner self . . . Lipsky kept everything in. So we are voyeurs to this raw conversation between two young writers. . . . I loved it." —Susan K. Perry, *Psychology Today*

"Wallace was the next great voice of a young generation. But he wasn't a dweeb-child shut-in hiding with books. He was a big handsome dude who played football and tennis, chewed tobacco, cussed, watching action movies and ticking off references to Hobbes and Dostoevsky while mixing in Stephen King and Alanis Morissette. . . . A trip into the mind of a writer who owned a dazzling style and a prescient view of modern culture." —Mike Kilen, *Des Moines Register*

"Lovely." —Sam Sacks, *Wall Street Journal*

"Three hundred magnificent pages that are the closest we'll get to an autobiography of the writer. . . . [Wallace] is lucid, entertaining, self-critical, constantly self-reflective, and to read this book is to meet this personality . . . These talks changed [Lipsky's] life, gave him phrases that have stayed with him forever. This poignant book will do the same thing for many readers." —Edmundo Paz Soldán, *El Mostrador* (Chile)

"Required reading. . . . Lipsky not only got the local color of a book tour. Wallace, who committed suicide in 2008, let loose with his life story in the week-long conversation." —Billy Heller, *New York Post*

"Editor's Choice . . . David Foster Wallace was, to many, *the* writer of his generation. . . . An in-depth rendering of a writer whose effect on his generation was matched by few others. . . . It is candid, intimate, personal, exploding with culture—pop and otherwise—and now, probably essential to the David Foster Wallace bookshelf." —Jeff Simon, *Buffalo News*

"A portrait of the artist as newly famous. It's part biography, part road trip; we hear [Wallace] at his most conceptual, expounding on his theories on writing, but also get a glimpse of him as a self-described 'normal guy.' . . . He answers Lipsky's questions in an infectious mixture of academically precise terms and peppery slang. The gravitational pull of Wallace's charm is on full display, as is his hyper-intelligence, electric sense of humor, and staggering self-awareness . . . almost unbearably heart-wrenching. . . . *Although of Course* offers a glimpse of Wallace in his prime for those of us who weren't lucky enough to know him outside of his books."

—Margaret Eby, *The Brooklyn Rail*

Fascinating . . . entertaining . . . funny. . . . It will likely be seen as a treasure trove—a hero's words and thoughts, unedited and unfiltered, put down on paper. . . . *Although of Course You End Up Becoming Yourself* ultimately provides a unique portrait of a unique talent at a unique time in his creative life."

—James D. Watts Jr., *Tulsa World*

"A remarkable book . . . A heartbreaking and surprisingly intimate visit with a giant talent. . . . Lipsky is a skilled interviewer and a terrific writer and so what we end up with is far, far beyond what might be expected. One of the great literary minds of his generation speaking frankly and at length with an award-winning journalist who, himself, has a great deal to say. . . . I doubt, however, we'll see another portrait that cuts quite this close to the bone. . . . You hear Wallace's amazing voice on every page. And your heart breaks all over again."

—Linda Richards, *January Magazine*

"Brainy and passionate . . . incredibly poignant . . . Lipsky vividly and incisively sets the before-and-after scenes for this revelatory oral history, in which Wallace is at once candid and cautious, funny and flinty, spellbinding and erudite as he articulates remarkably complex insights into depression, fiction that captures the 'cognitive texture' of our time, and fame's double edge. Wild about movies, prescient about the impact of the Internet, and happiest writing, Wallace is radiantly present in this intimate portrait, a generous and refined work that will sustain Wallace's masterful and innovative books long into the future."

—Donna Seaman, *Booklist*

"A rollicking dialogue . . . Wallace discusses everything from teaching to his stay in a mental hospital to television to modern poetry to love and, of course, writing. . . . The format produces the kind of tangible, immediate, honest sense of its subject that a formal biography might labor for. Even as they capture a very earthbound encounter, full of common road-trip detours, Wallace's voice and insight have an eerie impact. . . . [C]ompellingly real . . . [with] observations as elegant and insightful as his essays. Prescient, funny, earnest, and honest, this lost conversation is far from an opportunistic piece of literary ephemera, but a candid and fascinating glimpse into a uniquely brilliant and very troubled writer."

—*Publishers Weekly* (starred review)

"Highly recommended. A glimpse into the mind of one of the great literary masters of the end of the twentieth century. . . . What shines through even more is [Wallace's] deep passion for writing and ideas and his kind, gentle nature. . . . Many fans of Wallace's writing come to think of him as a friend—by the time they have finished Lipsky's moving book, they will undoubtedly feel that even more strongly."

—*Library Journal*

"Part biography, part autobiography, and part meditation on what it means to be a man in modern-day America." —Rachel Syme, *NPR*

DAVID LIPSKY

*although of course you
end up becoming yourself*

A ROAD TRIP WITH DAVID FOSTER WALLACE

B\D\W\Y

BROADWAY BOOKS

NEW YORK

For Lydia and Sally James
And for their mother and grandparents

Copyright © 2010 by David Lipsky

Published in the United States by Broadway Books, an imprint of the
Crown Publishing Group, a division of Penguin Random House LLC, New York.
www.crownpublishing.com

BROADWAY BOOKS and its logo, B \ D \ W \ Y, are trademarks of Penguin
Random House LLC.

A portion of this work was previously published as part of an article titled
"The Lost Years & Last Days of David Foster Wallace," which originally
appeared in *Rolling Stone* on Oct. 30, 2008.

Library of Congress Cataloging-in-Publication Data

Lipksy, David, 1965.
Although of course you end up becoming yourself : a road trip with David
Foster Wallace / David Lipsky—1st ed.
  p.   cm.
1. Wallace, David Foster—Interviews.   2. Authors, American—20th
century—Interviews.   3. Self-actualization (Psychology)   4. Creative
writing—Psychological aspects.   I. Wallace, David Foster.   II. Title.
III. Road trip with David Foster Wallace.
PS3573.A425635Z46 2009
813'.54   2009045018

ISBN 978-0-307-59243-9
eBook ISBN 978-0-307-59244-6

Printed in the United States of America

Design by Elizabeth Rendfleisch

10

Also by David Lipsky:

Three Thousand Dollars
The Art Fair
Absolutely American

If writing had a logo, it'd be the anchor, the quicksand easy chair, but from the minute I shook David's hand we didn't stop. We hit his class, then rolled into the car keys, sodas, strangers, and hotel rooms of a road-trip movie. Airports and taxis and the eerie sensation of knowing your feet have stood in different cities in the morning and afternoon.

This introduction is the Commentary track—which nobody goes in for until they've loved the DVD—so I'd recommend a quick select back to Main Menu and Play Movie. The road trip was the end of David Foster Wallace's *Infinite Jest* book tour, when, as a reporter, I asked and he told me the story of his life. David had a caffeine social gift: He was charmingly, vividly, overwhelmingly awake—he acted on other people like a slug of coffee—so they're the five most sleepless days I ever spent with anyone. (The last day, we crossed three states by air, shot down another 140 miles of highway, and I thought it was still midnight. "That's what your watch says?" David snorted. "It's two *twenty*, dickbrain.") Then it was over, and we were standing still again, and it was hard and sad to leave. And you'll see me trying to cook up reporting jobs in order to hang around.

It has the feel of a highway conversation. Late at night, the only car in the world, on icy morning roads, yelling at the other drivers. It has the rhythms of the road: grouchiness, indefensible meals, and

the sudden, front-seat connections—reciting high points from movies, the right song and a good view sending the radio into soundtrack,
a statement that gives you the bright, runway lift of knowing that another person has experienced life the way you do—that are the stuff
you go on trips for.

When you skip ahead, you should know it's early afternoon,
March 5, 1996. The air has the gray, erased-blackboard quality of
weather tightening itself for a storm. David has just stepped out of
his little brick one-story house. He has his hands in his jean pockets, his two black dogs are running thrilled tours of greet and pa-
trol. He's wearing round glasses. The look beneath them says two
more or less clear words: *now this.* I've got some treasured beliefs
about my own emotional tone. I'd like to think it's grittily complex,
penetrating, understanding, and deeply individual. It's pretty obviously: *please be impressed by me.* At our first big conversation—our
first stunning meal: Chicago-style pizza, the cheese mound and top-
ping landslide—he'll tell me he wants to do a profile of the reporters
who've come stamping through, doing profiles about him. "It'd be
a way for me to get some of the control back," he'll say. "Because if
you wanted—I mean, you're gonna be able to shape this essentially
how you want. And that to me is *extremely* disturbing." It would
have been one of the deluxe internal surveys he specialized in—the
unedited camera, the feed before the director in the van starts making cuts and choices. The comedy of a brain so big, careful, and kind
it keeps tripping over its own lumps. That's what this book would
like to be. It's the one way of writing about him I don't think David
would have hated.

So it's two in the afternoon. I've just dropped my bag on his living
room carpet, which is a mess, but the mess feels hospital cornered,
curated. (Whatever reassurance and encouragement the decorations give him is going to be tagged and sifted, for what it might
explain publicly.) We've addressed the two women's magazines on
his counter. (David is a *Cosmopolitan* subscriber; he says reading
"I've Cheated—Should I Tell?" a bunch of times a year is "fundamentally soothing to the nervous system.") I've also been surprised

to find the towel of Barney, the purple dinosaur and befriender of children, subbing as a curtain in his bedroom, and the big poster of complaint singer Alanis Morissette on his wall. I've just unpeeled and loaded a Maxell cassette into my recorder. Always a pleasant, blameless moment to the journalist; a round in the chamber, boots polished, reporting for duty. I got up at five this morning, hailed a cab at the New York hour when the city is still drifting through sleep, the streets rolling over and steam drizzling upward out of the manholes. Then I flew two hours to Chicago, signed and initialed for the rental car, drove another two here: If you were putting us in a comic book panel, you'd draw motion lines coming off my body. And there'd be black scrunches over David's head. He's been touring for two weeks, reading, signing, promoting. He's walking toward me over the clumps and vines of unsorted travel memories, signaling from behind the hurricane fence of someone who's become bewilderingly famous.

I'm thirty years old, he's thirty-four. We both have long hair. I've just placed the tape recorder on top of his magazines. He's made a request. What with all the travel, he'd like the right to retract anything that might come off awkward or nasty. (He's about to say a hundred unbelievably honest, personal things. The one place he'll get cold feet is where he feels he's been a little uncharitable to poetry. The form will touch readers again once it focuses on nine-to-five and couples who spend a marriage in the same bed. The verb he used was meatier.) Otherwise, this book runs from the minute I turn on the recorder, through five days of diners, arguments, on-ramps, friends, a reading, a faraway mall, his dogs, up to the last word David said to me. It's a word that meant a great, complicated amount to him. After he died, I read through this week again. I was surprised and moved—it seemed very much like him—to see that he used it in the context of a dance.

preface

Because I'd like to clear the set as quickly as possible, the rest of what I have to say about David I've put in the afterword—important stuff: what he looked like, how he died, how his friends saw him, the people we both were when we met. He'd just come off a success so giant-sized it was going to shade and determine the rest of his life, and we're going to talk a lot about that. (Four years later, after reporting on the 2000 election, he'd ask his agent to send the piece to his editor, to show that "I'm still capable of good work [my own insecurities, I know].") I've published two books, am about to publish another, but I've never had a success (the experience has been all near misses, standing in a crowd while people around me are pegged by golden bullets), and that professional position has led to an interesting social approach: I believe that if I can't impress people by how much I've accomplished, I can maybe be impressive with how practical my ambitions are, how little I expect. So I'm always reminding David—while he jumps ahead to big and speculative things—about the small reliable pleasures. A good night of TV, a closed deal, a morning coffee. That's one of our arguments: He wants something better than he has. I want precisely what he has already, and also for him to see how unimprovable his situation is. That's all in the afterword. David will make a funny remark about how books work toward the end of our time together. Re *Infinite Jest,* he'll say, "It's divided into chunks, there are sort of obvious closures or last lines—that make it pretty clear that you're supposed to go have a cigar or something, come back later." When you hit one of those cigar breaks, read the afterword. Because I love David's work, what I like best about these five days is that it sounds like David's writing. He was such a natural writer he could talk in prose; for me, this has the magic of watching a guy in a business suit, big headphones, step into a gym and sink fifty foul shots in a row. This is what David was like at thirty-four—what he calls "all the French curls and crazy circles"—at one of the moments when the world opens up to you.

And here's a guide to the people he's going to be talking about. Bonnie Nadell is his agent—cool, motherly, though she's only a year older than he is. (Visiting David at the hospital in 1989, the first thing she did was track down scissors and cut his hair.) Michael Pietsch is his editor on *Infinite Jest*. (Pietsch is now the head of Little, Brown, David's publisher, and is a very nice guy.) Jann is Jann Wenner, the owner and editor of *Rolling Stone*, and so the person I report to. And I think that's it, all you need to know. David has written two books before *Infinite Jest*: They're called *The Broom of the System* (another freeway of a novel) and *Girl with Curious Hair* (short stories). Yaddo is an artists' colony, whose seat cushions have borne the imprints of a lot of famous writers. David talks in the universal sportsman's accent: the disappearing G's, "wudn't," "dudn't" and "idn't" and "sumpin'." His two dogs are named Drone and Jeeves.

afterword

David was six feet two, and on a good day he weighed two hundred pounds. He had dark eyes, soft voice, caveman chin, a lovely, peak-lipped mouth that was his best feature. He walked with an ex-athlete's saunter—a roll from the heels, as if any physical thing was a pleasure. He wrote with eyes and a voice that seemed to be a condensed form of everyone's lives—it was the stuff you semi-thought, the background action you blinked through at super-markets and commutes—and readers curled up in the nooks and clearings of his style. His life was a map that ends at the wrong destination. He was an A student through high school, he played football, he played tennis, he wrote a philosophy thesis and a novel before he graduated from Amherst, he went to writing school, published the novel, made a city of squalling, bruising, kneecapping editors and writers fall moony-eyed in love with him. He published a thousand-page novel, received the only award you get in the nation for being a genius, wrote essays providing the best feel anywhere of what it means to be alive now, accepted a special chair to teach writing at a college in California, married, published another book, and hanged himself at age forty-six.

Suicide is such a powerful end, it reaches back and scrambles the beginning. It has an event gravity: Eventually, every memory and impression gets tugged in its direction. I was asked to write about David's death and spoke to friends (all writers, all called away from keyboards, all stunned) and family (who were smart, and kind, and nearly impossible to talk to). One thing they struggled with was how alive, how delightful, David could seem. I talked with a professor of psychiatry at Harvard Medical School, who spoke in quick, lucid, emphatic phrases, as if facts were neutral but could turn sad if handled for too long. The professor did what experts do. Reminded me he hadn't treated David personally, but could illustrate the basic principles. Which are: nobody likes to take medications. "I mean, I sympathize," the doctor said. "I don't like to take any medicine myself." I told him what I'd learned: that from 1989 on, David had been prescribed a powerful first-generation antidepressant called Nardil. It came towing a boxcar of 1950s-era side effects, the worst of which was a potential for very high blood pressure. In 2007, he'd decided to stop taking the drug. The doctor made the kind of quick silence that's the telephone equivalent of nodding. "There's a pattern. When an agent has worked particularly well, people can't possibly imagine getting depressed again. So there's this false security. They feel like they're fine, they're cured, it'd be great to get off the medicine. Unfortunately, it's quite common to see people can and often do experience a recurrence of symptoms. And then they might not respond the same way to previously effective treatments."

Here's how it happened for David. Nardil comes with a long interdicted menu—chocolate, cured meats, certain cheeses, for some reason overripe bananas. And then there are off-book ingredients waiting in dishes, to combine and catalyze. The previous half decade of David's life, everyone agrees, was the happiest. Marriage, tranquility, California—the sunset, happy-ending coast. In late spring of 2007, David; his wife, Karen; and his parents, Jim and Sally, sat down at a Persian restaurant. Something in the food took him wrong. Terrible stomach pains, for days. Doctors were surprised to hear how long he'd been taking Nardil—a workhorse medication, from the predigital era of leaded fuels and antenna TV. They suggested he go off the drug, try something new.

"So at that point," his sister, Amy, said, her voice sounding sober, bruised, "it was determined, 'Oh, well, gosh, we've made so much pharmaceutical progress in the last two decades that I'm sure we can find something that can knock out that pesky depression without all these side effects.' They had no idea that was the only thing keeping him alive."

The course David followed is called a washout; David would slowly taper off the old drug, then taper onto a new one. "He knew it was going to be rough," Jonathan Franzen told me. Franzen's novel *The Corrections* won a National Book Award; he was the best friend of the second part of David's adult life. "But he was feeling he could afford a year to do the job. He figured he was going to go on to something else, at least temporarily. He was a perfectionist, you know? He wanted to be perfect, and taking Nardil wasn't perfect."

It's something Franzen wanted to stress. (Franzen, interviewed, had a writer's not quite off-duty quality; part of him wanted to shoulder me aside and tell the story himself.) David had a level of self-criticism that sometimes made him the one person whose company he didn't enjoy in a pleasant room; now he was happy. He loved his marriage, his life. "This is the main narrative, it's reason number one among the nine. It was from that position of optimism and happiness and strength that he tried to take another step. All the signs were pointing in the right direction. Because things were going well, he thought he was in a strong enough position to make some fundamental changes. And he had bad luck, it didn't work."

Doctors began prescribing other medications, each one a failure. By October, David's symptoms had landed him back in the hospital. He began to drop weight. That fall, he looked like a college kid again: longish hair, eyes intense, as if he'd just stepped off the Amherst green.

When Amy talked to him by phone, he was sometimes his old self. She said, "The worst question you could ask David in the last year was, 'How are you?' And it's almost impossible to have a conversation with someone you don't see regularly without that question." David was very honest. He'd answer, "I'm not all right. I'm trying to be, but I'm not all right."

The year ran good and bad, fast then slow, ascents with sudden pits, the sky looking very distant overhead. In early May, he sat down at a café with some graduating seniors from his fiction class. He answered their jittery, writer's-future questions. At the end, his voice went throaty, he choked up. Students assumed he was joking—some smiled, a memory that would cut later. David sniffled. "Go ahead and laugh—here I am crying—but I really am going to miss all of you."

No medications had worked. In June, David tried to kill himself. Then he was back in the hospital. Doctors administered twelve courses of electroconvulsive therapy, a treatment that had always terrified David. "Twelve," his mother repeated. "Such brutal treatments," his father said. "And after this year of absolute hell for David," his mother said, "they decided to go back to the Nardil."

Franzen, worried, flew to spend a week with David in July. David had dropped seventy pounds in a year. "He was thinner than I'd ever seen him. There was a look in his eyes: terrified, terribly sad, and far away. Still, he was fun to be with, even at ten percent strength." David could now make skinny jokes: he'd never before noticed, he said, "how hard certain chairs in the house were." Franzen would sit with David in the living room, play with his dogs, the two would step outside while David lit a cigarette. "We argued about stuff. He was doing his usual line about, 'A dog's mouth is practically a disinfectant, it's so clean. Not like human saliva, dog saliva is marvelously germ-resistant.'" When he left, David thanked him for coming. "I felt grateful he allowed me to be there," Franzen told me.

Six weeks later, David asked his parents to fly west. The Nardil wasn't working; the great risk with taking time off an antidepressant. A patient departs, returns, and the medication has boarded its doors. David couldn't sleep. He was afraid to leave the house. He asked, "What if I meet one of my students?" His father said, "He didn't want anyone to see him the way he was. It was just awful to see. If a student saw him, they would have put their arms around him and hugged him, I'm sure."

The Wallaces stayed ten days. David and his parents would get up at six in the morning and walk the dogs. They watched DVDs, talked. Sally cooked David's favorite dishes, heavy comfort foods—pot pies, casseroles, strawberries in cream. "We kept telling him we were so glad he was alive," his mother said. "But my feeling is that, even then, he was leaving the planet. He just couldn't take it."

One afternoon before they left, David was very upset. His mother sat on the floor beside him. "I just rubbed his arm. He said he was glad I was his mom. I told him it was an honor."

In the middle of September, Karen left David alone with the dogs for a few hours. When she came home that night, he had hanged himself. "I can't get that image out of my mind," his sister told me—and said another smart, kind, impossible thing. "David and his dogs, and it's dark. I'm sure he kissed them on the mouth, and told them he was sorry."

Writers tend to have two great topics, on heavy internal rotation, a very abbreviated playlist. Their careers, their ailments. There's a famous story, about the party where James Joyce ran into Marcel Proust. You expected heavyweight-champion banter. Joyce said, "My eyes are terrible." Proust said, "My poor stomach, what am I going to do? In fact, I must leave at once." (Joyce topped him: "I'm in the same situation, if I can find someone to take me by the arm.") David wasn't like that. For one thing, he never told anyone, beyond the tiniest audience, that he'd been diagnosed as a depressive. For another, he didn't much look the way you imagine a writer; he looked like a stoner, a burner. (The writer Mark Costello was the best friend of the first part of David's adult life; the Illinois term David taught him, he said, was "dirt bomb." "A slightly tough, slightly waste-product-y, tennis-playing persona," Costello said.) David looked like someone who'd played a little varsity, then proceeded to too-cool his way off the squad. A big guy, with the bandanna and flop of hair, someone who was going to invite you to play Hacky Sack, and if you refused, there was a possibility he was going to beat you up.

Which was on purpose. As a student, David had been put off by the campus-writer look—creamy eyes, sensitive politics. He called them "the beret guys. Boy, I remember, one reason I *still* don't like to call myself a writer is that I don't ever want to be mistaken for that type of person."

Which didn't prepare you for the company—which was astonishingly ample, gentle, comic, overflowing. It makes sense. Books are a social substitute; you read people who, at one level, you'd like to hang out with. Chapters, pages, novels, articles are the next best thing. Even when it's just a good factual writer, you want to hang around them to get the facts, the way you'd sit next to a brainy kid at a test to copy off their answer sheet. David's writing self—it's most pronounced in his essays—was the best friend you'd ever have, spotting everything, whispering jokes, sweeping you past what was irritating or boring or awful in humane style.

Mark Costello met David at Amherst. They became friends through the housing lottery. "Dave had figured out all the math for how to get the best room, the best game theory way to do it. Go in with one other person. Ask for a double, because no one else was going to do that. And then we proceeded to draw the worst number in western Massachusetts. We lived in a single that'd been forced into a double, right over the Dumpsters." The roommates walked the campus; crossing a green, it became the Dave Show. He would grab and imitate how people walked, talked, angled their heads, pictured their lives. "Not to mirror what they did, but to sort of capture them. I can't think of anybody else I've met in my life who could do that," Costello said. "Incredibly quick, incredibly funny. Dave had this ability to be inside someone else's skin."

The writer Mary Karr dated David in the early 1990s, when he was coming back from the worst period in his life. The ground must have still had a postconvalescent wobbliness underfoot—but there was David, big-booted, pocketing everything, happy, a man on an information safari. "Data went into his mind, and it would just shoot off sparks. Wildly funny, unbelievable wattage, such a massive interest in and curiosity about his place in the world. He had more frames per second than the rest of us, he just never stopped. He was just constantly devouring the universe."

This was the time when David began publishing his stuff in *Harper's* magazine. When a piece ran, staffers "would be walking in the hallways trading lines," Charis Conn told me. "Or if people had any conversation with him about any part of it, they would *tell* each other. It was just the thrill of this writer—everything he had to write and everything he had to say." Conn, a *Harper's* editor and writer, had pulled David into the magazine; when David visited the city, they'd go on rounds, a full-screen version of Amherst Dave. "Him in New York City—that was a show on its own. Sort of gee-whizzing everything, amazed by everything. He was so much smarter than anyone, including you, and yet his attitude was, he was genuinely pleased to be wherever he was, most of the time. If he was with a congenial companion. Amazed and interested in everything. How could he write what he wrote if he wasn't looking at everything all the time? And you got to be in his senses, so you got to see more. He's using all six and a half senses at once, which can drive you crazy. But he shared it with us, which was nice of him to do. Talking to him was (a) a delightful social experience, and also a literary experience."

Just knowing him could land you in some funny spots, make the world turn Wallace-ish—embarrassing, surprising, alive. When David finished *Infinite Jest,* he enrolled Conn in a tiny band: product testers, the literary focus group he mailed the manuscript to. She read back-and-forthing to work on the subway. The stack of book, the pile of novel, riding next to her in its own seat. Commuters would look at it, at her, laugh. "It was a spectacle, it was ridiculous. People thought it was funny. I was very proud of it, I loved it. Nobody knew what it was. But it was a nice feeling."

David met Jon Franzen in the most natural way for a writer; as a reader, as a fan. He mailed Franzen a nice letter about his first book, Franzen replied, they arranged a meet. And no David. This was right in the middle of the bleak period, when simple calendar stuff turned challenging. "He just flaked," Jon recalled. "He didn't show up. That was a fairly substance-filled period in his life." By the middle part of the '90s, Franzen found an easy valuation for David's company: "I would always use any opportunity to hang out with Dave." In 1995, banging together a big piece on the reasons for writing and reading, Franzen boarded a train for Connecticut and David. "We met in a parking lot and we hung out for about three hours, just sitting on the edge of the parking lot. I kept saying, 'I need quotes for the piece, I need quotes for the piece!'" It's nice to imagine them there, these two writers who would someday write famous books, talking for hours among the fast-asleep cars and concrete dividers. What they decided—David proposed it—was that the point of books was to combat loneliness.

In New York on publishing trips, David bunked with Franzen. This was the just-before-fame moment, when a writer is still picking up his own expenses. "When he used to come stay with me—this was before he got his diet sorted out—as far as I could tell, he subsisted on those cellophane-wrapped Blondies from delis and chewing tobacco. The first thing he did when he got to the apartment would be to select the biggest tomato can from my recycling bag and appropriate it. You know, he was very good about only spitting *in* the can. And about washing the can out very carefully and putting it back into the recycling. So the apartment would always have this faintly wintergreen smell of the can after he left."

Franzen tried, a single time, to haul David to a literary party. They trooped through the front door together; by the time Franzen hit the kitchen, David had vanished. "I went back and proceeded to search the whole place. It turned out he had walked into the bathroom to lose me, then turned on his heels and walked right back out the front door. To my apartment, where I returned an hour and a half later, to find him trading stories that embarrassed *me* with my then-girlfriend."

Meetings and departures were fraught; for one thing, David always had the ability, in conversation, to hear a few extra steps down the hall. David put a great examination of departures—half in text, half marooned on a footnote—in the essay he did about spoken English. Four nights after he died, I pulled out the book and read it over the phone to a friend, to show her how awake and funny David had been. Halfway through I started remembering how unenthusiastic I'd been about getting out of his hair; it wasn't about me, but it had the queasy feeling of a photo taken before you could pose, suck in the cheek and chin gut. "Suppose you and I are acquaintances," he writes, "and we're in my apartment having a conversation, and that at some point I want to terminate the conversation and not have you be in my apartment anymore. Very delicate social moment. Think of all the different ways I can try to handle it: 'Wow, look at the time'; 'Could we finish this up later?'; 'Could you please leave now?'; 'Go'; 'Get out'; 'Get the hell out of here'; 'Didn't you say you had to be someplace?'; 'Time for you to hit the dusty trail, my friend'; 'Off you go then, love'; or that sly old telephone-conversation-ender, 'Well, I'm going to let you go now' . . . in real life, I always seem to have a hard time winding up a conversation or asking somebody to leave, and sometimes the moment becomes so delicate and fraught with social complexity that I'll get overwhelmed . . . and will just sort of blank out and do it totally straight—'I want to terminate the conversation and have you not be in my apartment anymore'—which evidentially makes me look either as if I'm very rude and abrupt or as if I'm semi-autistic . . . I've actually lost friends this way."

When it came to work, he was sharp and modest, with a contractor's strategic sense of what types of projects he could build well. People who set out to be writers are as glutted with careers and lifetime stats as athletes in training or the people who join fantasy baseball leagues. It's just that the numbers and ballparks are so much more domestic: age at first publication, age at first award, first marriage, first crisis, and sometimes age at first, second, or third divorce. (David will make fun of me for memorizing this stuff. Feel free to join in.) When we met, David had the confidence of having just published *Infinite Jest,* which is the confidence of knowing he'd pushed everything aside and practiced his trade the hardest he could. This is a generous confidence. I kept thinking of what Hemingway wrote about F. Scott Fitzgerald, before they headed on a train to Rouen to pick up a car. Fitzgerald had just written his best novel:

He asked questions and told me about writers and publishers and agents and critics [and] the gossip and economics of being a successful writer, and he was cynical and funny and very jolly and charming and endearing, even if you were careful about anyone becoming endearing. He spoke slightingly but without bitterness of everything he had written, and I knew his new book must be very good for him to speak, without bitterness, of the faults of past books. He wanted me to read the new book, *The Great Gatsby* . . . To hear him talk of it, you would never know how very good it was, except that he had the shyness about it that all non-conceited writers have when they have done something very fine . . .

A few months after his death, David's sister Amy wrote me. Interviewers were coming, asking what David was like, but the questions always circled back to the same anxious ground. His phobias, low points. "My own anxieties are many," she wrote. "My brother was a hilarious guy, a quirky, generous spirit, who happened to be a genius and suffer from depression. There was a lot of happiness in his life. He loved to be silly, he made exquisite fun of himself and others. Part of me still expects to wake up from this, but everywhere I turn is proof that he's really most sincerely dead. Will he be remembered as a real, living person?"

That's the other thing this book would like to be: a record of what David was like, when he was thirty-four and all his cards had turned over good, every one of his ships had sailed back into harbor.

In February of 1996, I'd been assigned to write about David, I was sitting at a party, when a friend plopped down next to me on the sofa. "Poor David Foster Wallace," she said. "It's not his fault, this kind of attention, it's weird, it can be hard to synthesize unless you're very strong. Meanwhile, all these relationships are being screwed up by David Foster Wallace." She flicked her face to people at the compass points of the room. "All these men—because they secretly want to *be* David Foster Wallace—they flip out whenever he's in the paper.

All the girls are like, 'David Foster Wallace, he's really cool.' So the guys are like, 'I *hate* David Foster Wallace.' Every anxious writer I know is obsessed with him, because he did what they wanted to do." I shrugged and blinked, to say I wasn't sure what she was talking about. At thirty, you put lots of faith in misunderstanding and the magic of ignorance: it's as though admitting to gravity means you're going to fall, or saying the word "tuberculosis" means immediate fever and a cough.

In fact, a personal hardship, my own girlfriend had been reading only him, steadily, languorously. One afternoon, she took a cigarette with her to the kitchen to cool off, and I found this e-mail on her computer. She'd sent questions to an editor friend, who'd written back:

> Mr. Wallace is cool-looking. A big hulking guy with long stringy hair. Looks sort of like a rock star. Perspires freely. Wears a do-rag, and participates in the urban American experience thusly. Is un-married, I believe. What were your other questions?

Life is the accumulation of flukes. (A passionate belief in the re-verse was what I was abandoning at the time I met David. I believed a really good person could make everything in their lives *on purpose*.) I ended up on this story because Jann Wenner, the vigorous and interesting and fast-acting man who owns the magazine I work for, happened to open *The New York Times* to a photo of David. In early 1996, David's picture had become an everywhere fact: the tiny box, the tilted head with bandanna, stubble, long hair. "Oh," Jann said. "He's one of us. Send Lipsky."

And here's me—career and ailments. (It's not that David was immune to the glossy, braggy parts of a writer's life; he called them the greasy side and had this fear that he'd end up a party fixture, one of the rotating, nonworking famous who horn in on other writers' photos. I told this to Mark Costello, who laughed: "Yeah, but by then he was sober, so you know you're knocking out a whole strut from under the literary engine." He paused, then deadpanned, "And I also don't know to what degree Dave would like to spend time at events where other people were the centers of attention.") Actually, just to put that off for a second, let me tell you about my tape recorder. The one I placed on the magazines in David's living room. When you meet someone for the first time, they mostly seem a perfect ambassador for their job. It's the impossible remarks that carry and strand a person in specificity. David looked like a young writer having a pretty easy ride of it. To him, I was simply a reporter—whatever snazzy cultural box that opened—with expensive props, and he got a kick out of my repeating especially sharp things he said into the tape. I was a wily, seasoned professional, somebody who'd bagged lots of celebrity game, and had crashed into the Illinois wilds on the hunt for one more.

Actually, David was only the third famous person I'd ever interviewed, and the first writer. Buying the tape recorder—it cost $320—had made my palms sweat and sent my heart up to my mouth and throat on a brief walking tour. When I met David, I was only twenty-eight months past an almost perfect financial collapse. That was my ailment. It turned out spending time in college, waking up each morning to statues and gardens, had not been especially good preparation for sidewalks and billing statements. Every week our mailboxes got stuffed with fresh offers for Visa and Discover cards, so I came out of college going great guns in the credit world. A classic romance—flashy courtship, accusatory divorce. I lost credit cards, telephone numbers, basic cable channels, apartments. Depositing money into my pocket was like releasing it into a nuclear whirlpool: I'd reach back a second later, and instant disintegration. I stopped carrying a wallet. It seemed nostalgic. ATM visits turned impossibly dramatic. Cruxes: a man meeting his fate. I became the kind of customer who shies away from his on-screen balance, the way good-hearted drivers will avert their eyes from a wreck. This continued to happen for years, until I lost the bank account too. In 1994, I went to apply for a New York lease. I filled in my social security number. I have no idea what flashers and alarm bells this set off. But when I showed up the next morning, the landlord—a big Eastern European, a man building a respectable life on a far-off shore—told me he was controlling himself from wanting to kick my butt. He came and stood very close to me. "Do you know what your credit report looks like?" "No," I said. "Well, I am not going to tell you."

I'd steered by that movie-ish American idea about ambition and arrival: to get to a place, the best route is to live like you're there already. It's a magic idea, and it's also the way a language lab works. Hear and speak French only, eventually your language improves. (It's also what college preps you for, the columns and rolling grounds; you'd become an Athenian, or you'll be loaded.) If you think and speak only novels, eventually the world will bookstore around you. Lowering your sights isn't sensible—it's bad luck, an invitation to a more general sinking. I'd lived for seven years only like a fiction writer, published two books, and verified absolutely that this approach doesn't work.

I got a job at *Rolling Stone*. And suddenly having money was like stepping out of a storm, shaking the damp from your umbrella in a bright quiet auditorium. All at once, no dark, no wet, no noise. The Lewis-and-Clark, the financial explorer's sense of your early twenties, when every day and billing cycle is a river forded, pasture mapped, a flag planted, I got to relive it in my late twenties. First bank account, first newspaper home delivery, first credit card (secured). People would guess the best part of journalism was the travel. Not the tray meals or the exchange of skylines. The being included, the knowing that somebody had taken the trouble to book a flight, reserve a car and a hotel bed, because in the whole world they needed only you to complete the assignment. Every boarding pass—every flight crew, with the hushed smiles and nighttime lighting—felt like an amazingly tactful compliment.

I recovered from being poor the way you do from a virus: suspiciously, gratefully, not wanting to test my luck. It was such a relief to pay for the bus, to sit down at a restaurant without the menu changing into italics and exclamation points, that for years I didn't disagree with anything anybody said who could pay me a salary. (Disagreement might return as a possibility in my thirties. No, the late twenties were going to have to be the compliant years.) I rented part of a giant, dusty apartment—long hallways and barn rooms—across the street from the Museum of Natural History. I had a private entrance, my roommates were an old, not terribly well-matched couple called the Bechsteins. The fights were noisy, endless, wrenching. Anna Bechstein, when she watched TV, wanted to be joined at the set by her husband, Arthur. His wish was even smaller, and easier to grant. He wanted to be left alone. She'd moan, "You knew, you knew, how could you, you *cheated* me of something I could have watched with you. And it was *funny!*" And I'd take notes. During the day, I'd go hang around the desks and windows and blue-ribbon bathrooms and great jackets and buzz of the magazine, everybody cool and the feel of an interesting future tingling over every head like an upstairs party or the runs of excellent weather you get in California. Then I'd go home and listen to the Bechsteins heartbreakingly argue. I liked to try to imagine the two worlds coming into contact. Jann Wenner, all stubble and glamour, dropping by with a folder I'd left at the office. The four of us meeting in the doorway—Jann, me, Arthur, Anna—and me explaining dreamily, "Jann, these are my roommates. The Bechsteins. They're *married*."

But everything had worked, slow and steady. All you had to do was lower the temperature in your eyes, the heat and the need. All you had to do was be willing to adjust, slightly, what you wanted, tuck your head down and provide the stuff other people asked for on a dependable schedule.

And then David—with stuff he'd only asked himself for—earthquaked the city. Crowds, applause, a full-on city anxiety attack. His cruise ship piece ran in January of 1996; it cleared the landscape, cut the runway for his novel. People photocopied it, faxed it, read it out loud over the phone. He'd done a thing that was casual and gigantic; he'd captured everybody's brain voice. The talk show with its solo guest; the yammer while you're commuting the office halls, kissing, musing in the bathroom. All the different thought categories—books, *Jurassic Park,* weird business terms of art, curses, how things could suddenly make you depressed or happy for no reason at all—it was the way you flattered yourself your brain really might sound, if you'd just devote the time to shelving and organization. Then the novel arrived. His photo ran in *Time, Newsweek. Esquire* went ahead and called it a work of genius. (That scary, special-case compliment which can excite resistance, since the unspoken second half is: "Not you.") *New York Magazine* made the tame suggestion that the year's fiction prizes be escrowed in a safe-deposit box with his name. Even the name—you had to say all three parts—was overflowing. A special case, a burger deluxe: David Foster Wallace. The *Times* rolled the months into a clinical, prescription-pad voice, a resident toting up symptoms. David was "the first young novelist in several years to pique such intense curiosity."

And then David arrived in the city. February, that handicapped month, with squashed daylight and the sidewalks trickling. There were rumors. Who he was dating, how he'd turned down *Charlie Rose* and the *Today* show (to a city that refines and exports media, this felt misplaced but gallant, like declining a knighthood). His first reading, at the East Village bar KGB, was as crowded as a rush-hour subway. Women in the front rows batted their eyelashes, men at the back huffed, scowled, envied. The second reading, at Tower Books, was publishers' night, executives who never came out nodding tautly to each other as if from across battlements. Then the thronged book party, with the inevitable people wearing black—it looked like the cheeriest possible wake—and David stood in the hallway near the lavatories, while people with stars in their eyes came to shake his hand, congratulate him, just stand close tilting drinks and *look* at him—he was pumping out glamour like a reactor. I watched him closely. I couldn't imagine what he felt. This was more than it would ever have occurred to me to ask the world for. No, this was precisely the request I'd trained myself to stop making. He looked abashed and excited and comfortable, like someone on a personal water slide. At intervals, he'd excuse himself to hit the bathroom. I imagined (another mistake you make at thirty: you believe that everyone, beneath the disguises of last name and background, remains basically you) he was going to consult the bathroom mirror, to remind himself that all this had happened because of him.

Then he left for his book tour. (I identified. I'd gone on book tour myself a few years earlier. I traveled seventy blocks and signed bookstore copies. Then, tour complete, I grabbed a subway home, unpacked, recuperated.) He remained a city microclimate, fogging the reading zones. I told my girlfriend it'd be great if she got the book finished while I was out of town. Then I flew to Chicago and drove to Bloomington. The strange reporter's experience, dunked into another person's life. Questions you approach your friends with on tiptoe (romance, parents, money, grudges) it was my salaried duty to plant my feet and ask. To dilute his feeling of being reported on—to make me seem more like an unbelievably inquisitive houseguest— David invited me to sleep in his second bedroom. "My spare blanket is your spare blanket," he said. I woke up in the middle of the night. One of the dogs on a cycle: howl, pause, repeat. Then I heard David, sleep as the crust in his voice, say, "Jeeves—*enough.*" I felt all the strangeness of it. Two a.m., this person I didn't know—I was listening to David Wallace in negotiations with his dog.

In our talks, you see me always giving the wised-up, padded-shoulder advice. Endorse the check, take the deal, get seconds, put your feet up. This was the payroll doctrine eight years of my life had trained me to spread. David keeps talking about the largest things, I keep countering with the smallest: You're doing great, don't over-think, the simple pleasures are a job and your morning coffee. It's like a younger brother trying to impress an older one with the rough schooling he's picked up in the lower grades. I think it was on the airplane that I finally relaxed. OK, he was quicker than me—also funnier than me. I could enjoy him and quit trying to match him. I think he did in the car, by the Henry Ford road-trip equation: two men will become comfortable if they have to travel any distance in excess of forty miles.

Then I had to leave, but when I got home, it turned out I'd wanted to keep a foot in his world. David sent me a giant box a week later. One of my loafers traveled inside, plus a note on Chicago Bears stationery, which he'd signed with a smiley face. "Yours, I presume?" I felt like a barefoot idiot.

I never, thank God, had to write the piece. I tried to write it, and kept imagining David reading it, and seeing through it, through me, and spotting some questionable stuff on the X-ray. And then Jann changed his mind. I was sent to Seattle to find heroin addicts (who were after all in lots hotter water than I was), and it was much, much easier. I phoned Bonnie Nadell, David's agent. David had mixed feelings about publicity, and I asked her to pass along the good news. (His sister told me later David had no hard feelings. "He said you were a decent guy—that, for about five years, was his praise word—and that I would have liked you." Typing this makes my stomach go hollow, it snags at the inside of the chest. He had that casual, urgent social gift: You wanted to be liked by him.) I felt even more barefoot than before.

In a few years, I'd get my taste of the things I'd wanted—TV, contracts, bestseller list. Then I'd be embarrassed for how much I'd tried to extract my experience of them from David. It seemed hungry and ungenerous. I wrote many e-mails in my head, and one or two on the actual computer, and one I finished and e-mailed to myself to see what it'd read like to open, and decided it looked a little loopy and that I'd been the right person to open it after all. I read him, thought about him, and I never saw him again except on television once.

About a year before he died, I pulled out the days here and read them again. We were back in his crapped-up living room, in the Pontiac, sitting at Denny's. One thing kept touching me: We were both so young.

But here we are. When I think of this trip, I see David and me in the front seat of the car. It's nighttime. It smells like chewing tobacco, soda, and smoke. (The smell of chewing tobacco is like a muddy lawn you've just fed a truckful of cough drops to.) The window is letting in a leak of cold air. R.E.M. is playing. The wheels are making their slightly sleepy sound of tape being stripped cleanly and endlessly off a long wall. On the other hand, we seem not to be moving at all, and the conversation is the best one I've ever had. We cover everything. David's life was harder than I would have guessed. It was smarter. I recognized it, it was different from mine; every area of it was completely occupied by feeling. Neither of us knows where our lives are going to go, we're both trying to decide who we'll be at various points of arrival. We talk about what matters to any person. What to want, how to be a good person, how to read, how to write, how to think about others. There are things he said to me that shifted my life, that joined my talk show, that are in the list of quotes I recite to myself. *Give me twenty-four hours alone, and I can be really, really smart.* His moment with Michael Ryan, which is everything about what ambition can do to you. What he guessed about my own personality. What a person has every right to expect from you, what you ought to expect of yourself. David thought books existed to stop you from feeling lonely. He'd come by this idea talking to Jonathan Franzen. Franzen said a sad, moving thing to me. He said losing David had been like watching a science fiction movie, when a small figure gets sucked out of the airlock. An abrupt, absolute, quiet disappearance. A little while later he said, "Does it look now like David had all the answers?" I don't think the fact that David would be dead twelve years later changes what this meant to me. John Updike—and you're about to watch or have watched already us argue like crazy about John Updike—once wrote that temporariness, the nature of things being provisional, shouldn't disqualify them. He wrote—another of the lines that's stuck on shuffle in my brain, and plays at odd, uplifting moments—that "all things end under heaven, and if temporality is held to be invalidating, then nothing real succeeds." So I'd say to David, if I could, that living these days again with him was a great pleasure. I'd thank him, I'd say I was grateful for his letting me be there. I'd tell him it reminded me of what life was like, instead of being a relief from it, and I'd say it made me feel much less lonely to read.

FIRST DAY
DAVID'S HOUSE
TUESDAY BEFORE CLASS
IN THE LIVING ROOM, PLAYING CHESS
HIS DOGS SLINKING BACK AND FORTH OVER CARPET
3/5/96

You were saying about the tour that while we travel, "I need to know that anything that I ask you five minutes later to not put in, you won't put in."

Given my level of fatigue and fuck-up quotient lately, it's the only way I can see doin' it and not going crazy.

[Drone—he's got two dogs—is chewing on the chair David sits in. He now has an unlisted phone number, because of fans.]

I don't know if "fan" would be the right word . . .

[Looking at bookcases . . . He had a board out, and is eager to play. So we are playing chess.]

I think when I was twenty-five this was what I wanted. But . . . I don't mind it now. I mean, I'm proud of the book, I'm glad the book is getting attention. Stuff about me is (a) makes me uncomfortable and (b) is bad for me, because it makes me self-conscious when I write. And I do not need to be more self-conscious. Oh, fuck me! It takes a while for me to get in a groove. I honestly don't know what's gonna sort of eventuate here. Well, fuck! (Looking at the board)

Little, Brown bought both the hardcover and the softcover rights at the same time. I think I could make a lot if I took an advance for the next thing, but I can't do that, so . . .

[He's not interested in money for next novels, which friends have said is the wisest course. I talk about my own friends—people he knows too—who arranged deals while touring for successful books.]

That's incredible. I've got this thing where I just can't take money for something till it's done. So I'm sort of *screwed* about that stuff. (Slow, Southernish voice) I've been burnt on this before, I just can't do it.

I had no choice on this book, it was sort of under way. There was so much research I had to do, that I literally could *not* teach and do it at the same time. So I decided to eat it, and do it. But it would have been a lot more fun if I hadn't taken any money for it.

[He's playing pop radio, the local college station. I haven't heard this song in so much time: INXS, "It's the One Thing." David nods, says he loves their song "Don't Change."]

You know, I went through such a bad time in my twenties. Thinking like, Oh no, I'm this genius writer, everything I do's gotta be ingenious, blah blah blah blah, and bein' so shut down and miserable for three or four years. That it's worth *any* amount of money to me, not to go there again. And I'm aware that that sounds maybe Pollyanna-ish or sound-bitish. But it's actually just the truth.

I was twenty-eight years old, and that means not taking an advance for stuff before it's done. And it's money well spent as far as I'm concerned.

Aware of your fame here?

The grad students are vaguely aware I think.

They must follow it?

I think kids in the Midwest are different than kids on the East Coast. I think *Time* and *Newsweek* are fairly inescapable. So I think they kinda know. I'm sort of so nasty when they start talking about that stuff in class that I think I've scared them into just leaving it alone.

Why?

Because it's toxic to them and it's toxic to me. That class is my uh—I'm there to learn, not to talk about my own stuff. And I'm there . . . when I'm teaching, I'm there as a reader, not a writer. And the more—it's extremely unpleasant, the more, uh, the more I'm there in a kind of writerly persona . . .

There's this weird scam in creative writing workshops that somehow the teacher's gonna teach you how—they're gonna be able to teach you how to do exactly what it is they do. Which is why these programs try to pack themselves with the best-known and most-respected writers. ("Wraters") As if how good a writer you are and how good a teacher you are have *anything* to do with each other. I don't think so. I know too many really good writers who are shitty teachers, and vice versa, to think that. I think that the teaching . . . well, the teaching has helped my own writing a lot . . . So maybe I don't think that anymore. But the writers are often interested in preserving as much of their own time as they can.

[Hums while he plays chess: not tremendously good at chess; strong, however, at humming.]

Well, *that* really didn't do a whole heck of a lot for me, did it?

Shit. All right, we've got time for one more move each and then we have to leave. I've got to brush my teeth.

I took the job for the health insurance. [Illinois State University]

[Bathroom cabinet: lots of tubes of Topol. (He's a smoker.)

Dogs: Drone is "A provisional dog, he just showed up once while we were jogging," they took him on.]

Some kind of weird, "I've made a terrible mistake with my life, I need to be selling insurance in Oshkosh" sort of feeling. [We're talking about John Barth, and other writers who've gotten in trouble. A sudden in-the-wrong-place sense. An anxiety he felt before *Infinite Jest*.] I think that happens to a lot of writers.

[Went to Arizona State University. Edward Abbey was there . . . Robert Boswell helped him more than anybody . . .]

I was so in thrall to Barth I just knew it would be sort of a grotesque thing. [Why he couldn't and didn't go to Hopkins. He patterned the longest part of his second book after Barth.]

• • •

IN CAR, MY RENTED GRAND AM
EN ROUTE TO CLASS

This is the thing—you're gonna have to sit around, you can't even be in the office, because I'm gonna have to yell at a lot of people. I have to cut it short: just because we've gotta get up at five in the morning. This is what's fucked: it's that, these poor kids, I haven't been around for two weeks. And they all are gonna have various deals to discuss. [So sensitive about all performance] I'm usually a much better teacher than this. I swear to God.

Like doing readings?

No.

You were good.

Thanks. Tower Books—that's not one I was particularly pleased with. I get so nervous beforehand, and the nervousness is so unpleasant, that that's what I dislike. And I don't think my stuff reads out loud very well. And I think I come off looking like a maniac. Mainly I'm doing what they blew up to larger type size. I give like one or two readings in colleges a year. I gave 'em ten things and they blew up five of them.

I read something ("sumpin'") different at Tower just because this unbelievably cute girl from *Spin* magazine was there, and she didn't want to hear the same thing twice, so I totally trashed the plan. (He laughs.) And I never saw her again.

[The writer Elizabeth Wurtzel was at David's KGB reading—a kind of Brezhnev-and-*Pravda*-themed bar in Lower Manhattan. She was standing right up front. We turn out to both know Elizabeth.]

I don't know how Elizabeth—Liz got like the best seat in the house, using skills I think only Elizabeth has. Ah, she's real nice. She's a good egg. Good *egg.*

When you're eighteen, you realize that—there's also a part of us that wants to be the president. And there's also a part that wants to fuck every attractive person of the gender of our choice. I mean, you know . . . Just, I think she's gotta be more—it's not an accident that she's depressed all the time. I don't know. Maybe I just project all kinds of weird stuff onto her . . .

. . .

DAVID'S CLASS
CLASS: "ADVANCED PROSE"

[Doesn't want a tape. Is comfortable with note-taking.]

Fluorescents, desks, steel wastepaper cans, boot smell, sweater smell, clock on wall, big table that David doesn't sit much behind. Fifteen students. Women sit, as at an old-line synagogue, slightly apart from men. David wearing Fryes, blue bandanna. Carrying Diet Pepsi.

Dave has noticed some surprising student errors this week.

DAVE: Before we start, let's do a moment of Grammar Rock.

They laugh. He's the ideal, the professor you hope for: lightning writer, modern references, charming and funny and firm.

The students know another thing: he's become, their bandanna-wearing teacher, during these past three weeks a suddenly celebrated man. And they want somehow to acknowledge it.

STUDENT 1: Done being famous yet?
DAVE: (Blush smile) Two more minutes.
KID FROM BACK, SUDDENLY: I knew him *well*, Horatio—a man of *Infinite Jest* . . .
DAVE: OK, you're allowed *one* reference.

Quick chatter about his media appearances. It's exciting; a piece of their private life—this room and class—has gone suddenly public.

STUDENT 2, FEMALE: I love the way the *Trib* described your office.
STUDENT 3, FEMALE: Did you wind up, like, next to Dick Vitale and Hillary Clinton?

Dave says he got real nervous on the flights, kept picturing grave etc., from tour.

STUDENT 4: Just put pepperoni and mushrooms on my Tombstone. (A take-out, grocery pizza sort of joke.)
DAVE: The words "pop quiz" is what's good about that.

They talk about his magazine photos. Dave blushes more.

DAVE: I didn't think, I didn't think—you can see my smiling maw. I thought, "Really? Is that me?"

Dave fishes out a Styrofoam cup after pawing through two wastebaskets, for someplace to put his chewing tobacco. Is also drinking a Diet Pepsi.

    Class begins with a jump from celebrity into the supernormal, the administrative.

DAVE: Office hours next week. Bring light reading material, if you have to wait in the hallway.

Begins work on student stories.

DAVE: (Offering Very Sensible advice. Lots of jobs for fiction, you have to keep track of twelve different things—characters, plot, sound, speed.) But the job of the first eight pages is not to have the reader want to throw the book at the *wall*, during the first eight pages.

He paces around the classroom. Happy, energetic. At one point, thinking, he even drops into a quick knee bend. Class laughs; they really like him.

DAVE: I know—I get real excited, and now I'm squatting.

First story: by pretty student with a Rosanna Arquette mouth. Dave on story, always using TV: "I submit, it's kinda like a Sam and Diane thing. Or *When Harry Met Sally*."

Classroom fluorescents flicker on and off, quiet flashes. Dave glances up.

Another story he likes: it's very open, but needs to be controlled. "This is just a head kinda vomiting at us . . ."

Less likable story: "This is just a campus romance story. And to the average civilian, I've gotta tell you, this is not that interesting . . ."

Now at desk. Craning up and down when discussion and story get him excited.

The student being workshopped is a punkish guy: mohawk, silver-and-yellow collar.

Dave: It's really hard to create a narrator who's alive. Take it from me.
Students: How?

Dave's advice is a kind of comedy, and makes them laugh.

Dave: To have the narrator be funny and smart, have him say funny, smart things some of the time.

He makes a flub, says quickly, "Brain fart."

He stops for a second. Holds steady. "Excuse me, I'm about to burp."

His delivery is darting and graceful: the Astaire quality of good teaching.

On the campus romance story. "The great dread of creative writing professors: 'Their eyes met over the keg . . .'"

The key to writing is learning to differentiate private interest from public entertainment. One aid is, you're supposed to get less self-interested as you age. But, "I think I am more self-absorbed at thirty-four than twenty-three. Because if it's interesting to me, I automatically imagine it's interesting to you. I could spend a half hour telling you about my trip to the store, but that might not be as interesting to you as it is to me."

Reminds the class, as it breaks. Notebooks closing, bookbags rising from floor to desktop. Ruckle noises, kids standing. The week's two lessons.

DAVE: Never—don't go there: "Their eyes met across the keg . . . " And "What's interesting to me may not be to you."

Still in good, buzzed-up mood after. Brings me a water to drink.

DAVE: Where would you be without me?

I hope it's not that same tobacco-Styrofoam cup.

• • •

ISU HALLWAY
TALKING TO COLLEAGUES AFTER CLASS

"Was it a success?" [Colleagues ask about *Infinite Jest* tour.]

No vegetables were thrown, so I consider it a success.
   I just made enough money to live off it for a couple of years, so that's good.

• • •

WE HEAD FOR CAR

I'm always going back and fucking with stuff. [Wrote two full novel drafts longhand] I did the last draft of the book on a computer, just because I needed it for the notes, I needed to be able to switch back and forth.

. . .

DINNER
MONICAL'S PIZZA
BLOOMINGTON

You can smoke in here? I can see the ashtrays. [The restaurant sound-track, right now: Huey Lewis, "Heart of Rock n' Roll." Dave: " 'I Want a New Drug' was more or less an anthem for me in the 1980s."]

I think towns under like a hundred thousand are the only places you *can* smoke anymore.

I wrote *Broom of the System* when I was very young. I mean, the first draft of that was my college thesis. There are parts of it that I think are good. But it's—I wince. Even at signings, when people bring it up to sign. I think that, "if it wasn't for that brief, It's-trendy-to-be-young thing . . ." You're probably a little too young to have benefited from it, 'cause that was really like the mid-'80s.

The paperbacks?

And they did just enough hardcovers that they could *say* . . .

Post Jay McInerney.

Yeah . . . It seems to me rather an odd thing to bring out again, that—because it was a totally different kind of fiction.

Nice to watch you blossom from what was initially a marketing thing.

Yeah. Nice.

You're the most talked-about writer in the country.

[Embarrassing to hear myself talk that way.]

There's an important distinction between—I've actually gotten a lot saner about this. Some of this stuff is nice. But I also realize this is a big, difficult book. Whether the book is really any good, nobody's gonna know for a couple of years. So a lot of this stuff, it's *nice*, I would like to get laid out of it a couple of times, which has not in fact happened.

　I didn't get laid on this tour. The thing about fame is interesting, although I would have liked to get laid on the tour and I did not.

Rock stars, sports stars do; I don't think Updike, Roth, or Barth do.

Only in *Rolling Stone* would I not worry about this. Just because I know that, the whole thing's going to be *jaunty*. But um, there's gotta be some—because it's clear that, like, people come up, they kinda *slither* up during readings or whatever. But it seems like, what I want is not to have to take any action. I don't want to have to say, "Would you like to come back to the hotel?" I want them to say, "I am coming back to the hotel. Where is your hotel?" None of 'em do that.

Happens to Aerosmith. But maybe not to Abba Eban.

Shyness and arrogance often go hand in hand, I think. It's more just, I can't stand to look like I'm actively trading on this sexually. Even though of course that's—I would be happy to do that.

Betrayal of your work self to do that?

Uhhhh, Let's see . . .

Did you think this would happen?

No, but I had this *fantasy*. I had all these fantasies about . . . It's so weird, 'cause most of the fame stuff dudn't matter to me. But I really did think, "Maybe I could get laid on this tour." Um, yeah. It would be a betrayal of the work self and you're right. In retrospect, it was lucky that I didn't. Basically, it just would have made me be lonely. Because it wouldn't have had anything to do with me, it would have just been . . . [That word, "lonely," which he'll use a lot]

Except if they're responding to your work, and the work is so personal, a kind of refined you, then trading on it is actually simply another way of meeting you . . .

Well, I agree with that too. I think this piece will be really good if it's mostly you. You talk all you want, man. You can't get me in trouble.

I think I'm the worst interviewer of all time. How do you learn to do this stuff? Because even I, I can clearly see there are certain strategies.

Not really. My strategy here is getting facts about you. Your tour: two weeks? Three weeks?

The funny thing is, of course, I saw on the schedule, "You will have this escort. Who will pick you up." And of course, when I hear escort, I think, I imagine like a *geisha*. Who will take you to the interview, then walk on your back and fuck your eyeballs out. And of course these escorts turn out to be burly *Irishmen*. You know, in their forties. Who like basically tell you the whole life story of the interviewer before you go there. So the whole thing is a little amusing.

I had two, both of them over fifty. There's a lady in Boston who I sort of wanted to adopt me. Very cool. Boston born and bred. You have to click that little thing up. [I'm having a rough time with the lighter.] Nice to meet someone else who has trouble with those.

So what's the piece about? You keep saying, "This isn't what the piece is about." What is the piece about? What does *Jann* want?

[Very aware of this, of trying to understand and shift how I will approach him. Like his feints about tour sex above; like the chess, seeing how I respond, move by move.]

What's it like to suddenly—you remember that Childe Harold line from Byron? "Woke up to find myself famous"?

Is that true? Yeah. Except the pub date was two and a half weeks ago. The book takes at least two months to read *well*. So therefore, whatever famousness is about, the *hype* is famous. You're not here because of me, you're here because of all this buzz about the book. I mean, you as an emissary of *Rolling Stone*. So I think I would be very naïve to feel any kind of Byron-like gratification—if two years from now, I've got people who like have read the thing three times, who come up and say, "This thing's really fucking good," *then* I'll swell up. I would like to get laid offa this. The shallow stuff. I would like to get laid off it. It doesn't ("dudn't") seem to be happening. Which just indicates to me that, you know, it's not really all that real.

[He has sized me up as a guy who likes "laying": shy, quick smile at finding this explanation to hide behind, further hiding it behind cigarette.

I now know he did this sort of thing as his approach, and I can see it here, his trying to guess what people wanted, what I wanted. That's who he is too: trying to read people. To be left alone, to nudge them away on the trip back through the living room, from work room to private room.]

What about money?

The stuff I said to you while we were playing chess? I got no problem making money. I went through this time in my twenties of feeling, feeling a pressure and expectation *far* in excess of anything the real world could place on you. Taking money for something up front brings that pressure back. And I don't want it. There's a real—I really enjoy a sense of *play* when I'm doin' it. And um, the nice thing about teaching is that, I feel like teaching is my livelihood. And *this* I do—and it's found money if I get any money for it.

And that's not 'cause I'm this great guy, who thinks money is the root of all evil. It's just: I'm now thirty-four. And I've discovered there are mind-sets that cause me incredible pain, and there are mind-sets that cause me less pain. And I just, um, it may be true that I could get a lot of money if I took an advance now. And I will eat my liver out, if it turns out that this was the chance to do it, and I'm now gonna miss it. But if I do it, I am buying myself a pack of trouble. That I just—and that pain, that pain, I fear that pain more than I want the money. And that's why I'm not gonna take an advance.

[Here's how I will come to think of this: he voyaged out, trying to protect himself, to become what was necessary short-term, to get his aim long-term, which was not to be affected. And it's the motor, tension, and reward in his work: the not-being-affected, not being sootily touched. It's the sensitive-person story, though to play it now you have to be willing to show a little dirty, a little porny ("I would like to get laid offa this") side too. The whole thing about trying to regulate himself, to produce a temporary self he could be comfortable and function in. Very squeezed parameters, somehow.]

Still: there's foreign sales, different markets, etc.

Foreign sales: I think I got $2,000 for *Girl* in Japanese.

It'll be very different in this case. Don't play innocent with me.

I play a certain number of games. I will not play faux innocent with you, and I'm not. The stuff that I do, um, I'm used to, um, not making a whole lot of money on. If I make a whole lot of money on the foreign sales of this, I'll be pleased. Nobody's given me that indication yet.

Film sale? Probably unfilmable . . .

Which maybe will make it rather easier to take money for it. Knowing that I will never have to see the artifact itself. Unless it's like one of these forty-eight-hour Warholian, bring-a-catheter-to-the-theater experimental things. But of course you wouldn't get any money for that, either. No, I would take that money and run for the hills. Because no, that dudn't cost me anything inside.

[A reformed person: trained himself out of most standard hungers. As it turns out, the film rights are sold about six months later.]

Agent—Bonnie—will want you to: Cooler heads will prevail.

It'll be interesting to see whether you're right or not. I'm not gonna sit here and say—you're trying to goad me into some vow, "I will never ever ever ever." And then I'll look like a *dick* if I do. But I would be pretty surprised.

[This remains chess: as if I'm trying to trick him into castling prematurely.]

I'm not trying to goad you into anything . . .

If they said, "Here's this advance, you now have the rest of the your life, we don't care if we ever get this book," I would take it. I'm not gonna take it on a deadline.

But if?

We'll see.

Five years?

We'll see.

NPR: On the show, you said you saw yourself as "A combination of being incredibly shy, and being an egomaniac, too"?

I think I said "exhibitionist, also."

But exhibitionist too?

Yeah.

Meaning?

Well, I think being shy basically means being self-absorbed to the extent that it makes it difficult to be around other people. For instance, if I'm hanging out with *you*, I can't even tell whether I like you or not, because I'm too worried about whether you like me. It's stressful and unpleasant or whatever. And I have elements of that shyness in me.

And yet at the same time, I mean it's sort of like the agoraphobic kleptomaniacs. At the same time, I think that most people—and stop me if you disagree, because I'm talking to somebody who's in the trade—somebody who's writing, has part of their motivation to sort of I think impress themselves and their consciousness on others. There's an *unbelievable* arrogance about even trying to write something—much less, you know, expecting that someone else will pay money to read it. So that you end up with this, uh . . . I think exhibitionists who *aren't* shy end up being performers. End up plying their trade in the direct presence of other people.

[He looks under the table, where I'm jiggling my leg.] You're a nervous fellow, aren't you? [I stop.] And exhibitionists who *are* shy find various other ways to do it. I would imagine that maybe film directors, it's the same way; although film directors have to deal very closely with a whole team of other people as they're making a movie, so. Partly though, I'm talkin' out of my ass, because what I'm talking about is me. And maybe five or six other writers I know real well. You know?

[He also means, I think, the story he did this year, about David Lynch.]

There's that John Updike quote: "Shyness, and a savage desire to hold another soul in thrall . . ."

But there's also, the shyness feeds into some of the stuff that you need as a fiction writer. Like: Part of the shyness for me is, it's very easy for me to play this game of, What do *you* want? What will the effect of this be on *you*? You know? It's this kind of mental chess. Which in personal intercourse? Makes things very difficult. But in *writing*, when I think a lot of what you're doing—there are very few innocent sentences in writing. You've gotta know not just how it looks and sounds to you. But you've gotta be able plausibly to project what an alien consciousness will make of it. So that there's a kind of split consciousness that I think makes it difficult to deal with people in the real world. For a writer. But that actually comes in handy.

And one of the reasons why I think when I'm working really hard, that I'm not around people much, isn't that I don't have time. It's just that, it's more like a machine that you turn on and off. And I, the idea of sitting here and being completely wrapped up in what piece will result, what your impression of me is, how I can manage that, would be so exhausting that I just don't want to do it. That's what's kind of weird—is this process of being interviewed kicks that machine. Except, now I don't have control over it, right? Now I've gotta manage it, and trust that you, that you—when writing the piece—that you are concerned about how it's gonna come off to the people who are then gonna manage it as well. So the *three* are actually kind of interestingly—there's writing, there's innocent interaction with other people, and then there's this interviewing stuff.

What I would *love* to do is a profile of one of *you* guys who's doin' a profile of me. It would be *way* too pomo and cute, to do. But it would be very interesting. It would be the way for me to get some of the control back. Because if you *wanted*—within the parameters of, you can't tell outright lies that I'll then deny to the fact checker. But if you wanted, I mean, you're gonna be able to shape this essentially how you want. And that to me is *extremely* disturbing. Because *I* want to be able to try and shape and manage the impression of me that's coming across. And it might be why writers are such shitty interviews.

Really?

Or I bet they're often incredibly upset when the thing comes out. Like Streitfeld thought I would never be his friend after the thing came out in *Details*. [The writer David Streitfeld]

What's the profit then?

I'll tell you exactly what the profit is. Little, Brown took an enormous chance doing the book. And I'm grateful, and I genuinely like Michael Pietsch, and I want the book to do well for them. I *also*— I'm not the Saint of Bloomington. [A phrase I used on phone; he's remembered it.] I want them to buy my next thing. So I want, I'm playing this delicate game of, "I don't want to be an asshole, but I also don't give myself away." There have been two or three things they asked me, that I just thought would be bad for me to do. And I said no to those—but bring me somethin' else that I'll do, that's like borderline.

Because this—you're not a bad guy. But this stuff is real bad for me, it makes me self-conscious. The more exposure I as a person get, the more it hurts me as a writer. But I said yes to this, so that I could in good conscience say no to a couple other things that are just way more toxic. And that's what I get out of it. And after this, I don't think there's gonna be much more of this.

Why do you think of it as a kind of toxic self-consciousness—

If I could get laid out of it. If one *Rolling Stone* reader . . .

I'm sure you'll get letters.

They'll take seventy pictures, and a *Details* shot'll come out. *You're a good-looking guy.* We should have 'em photograph you, and then say you're me. I'll end up getting laid, you'll end up . . .

[Courting me again]

There's just been a whole bunch, and most of 'em have just been atrocious. *I* think. Or maybe I really look like that. That's the nice thing. I can go to my friends around here, and I could go, "I don't really look like that, do I?" And they'll go, "No." Now, whether it's true or not . . . ?

But the self-consciousness is helpful to you too?

It's like everything else: It's real good up to a certain point. But there's this—here I am, the Dave who's been in *Rolling Stone.* Now I'm learning how to write short stories—"Oh no: Are *these* short stories of the level of somebody who was just featured in *Rolling Stone?*" [This is what happened in the late '80s: his panic.] *That* kind of—there's good self-consciousness. And then there's this toxic, paralyzing, raped-by-psychic-Bedouins self-consciousness.

Those things go away; like worries about where I am now, who I am now, whether my girlfriend last year was better for me, so was I maybe writing better then? Did those figures in my landscape help me orient myself better, organize my life better? It goes away.

But this is a rather stronger and more dangerous kind of self-consciousness. But you're right, my brain does work that way, and I, it's in my interest to eliminate as many possible avenues of it. And you can see, I mean, I'm not a reclusive writer, I'm not saying no to this, I'm just trying to be careful about it. And my nightmare is, I'll get to really like it. And I'll be one of these hideous: "Hey, yet another publication party, and here's *Dave* sticking his head into the picture." I'd rather be dead. I'd rather be dead. I just—because I don't want to be *seen* that way.

Why?

Because I think that's—well, would you want to be seen that way? Say how you'd feel about it, as a springboard. So that I've got a context to talk about it.

Then you're deriving your satisfaction from talking about your work, by acting like a writer, as opposed to by writing, so paradoxically you'd probably get less done.

Yes. That's real good. And there's nothing more grotesque than somebody who's going around, "I'm a writer, I'm a writer, I'm a writer." It's a very fine line. I don't mind appearing in *Rolling Stone,* but I don't want to appear in *Rolling Stone* as somebody who *wants* to be in *Rolling Stone.*

It's the whole pomo dance, that whole kind of thing. So my worry—I don't really have that much integrity. Because what I'm really worried is, *looking* like the sort of person who would appear at these parties. Now, the difference between that, and sort of *being* the person who doesn't want them is unclear to me.

But I *do* know that to the extent that like, that I derive my self and satisfaction from the work, rather than whether Mr. Lipsky's gonna come, and think what I have to say is important, is just—I'm gonna write better, I'm gonna be happier, I'm gonna be saner. You know what I mean? So like, why climb into the arena with this bull? Well. It's good for Little, Brown, I owe Little, Brown something, so.

And there's a little part of me, of course, that likes this. But that little part of me does not get to steer.

That little part can turn pretty ravenous though?

That's my big fear. If you see me like you know as a guest on a game show in the next couple of years, we will know.

[Waitress comes: Heavy tray, big Midwestern spread.] "Four slices of *sausage,* one *cheese,* two salads, dipping sauce, and six breadsticks. Also cookies. And two Diet Cokes. When you all want your cookies, just come up and yell at me. OK?"

Good heavens. Could we have a larger table, also, please? I'm just kidding.

A friend of mine and I had this joke, that various things are pomo-erotic.

That part of the brain can prove to be ravenous?

You've had experience with it?

No. But I know it can be.

You know what I'm talking about. At one point you were in grad school, one of the many hopefuls, and now you've had a couple of books published, and it awakens that part of you. And you can't kill that part of you. But you *can* reach some sort of détente with it. Where you, where it doesn't run you. And I've seen people that I think it runs, and it's just, it eats you alive. Who would want to be that way?

But many less-talented people than you get lots of attention. Which can be a little painful. Now you're getting it, and you're very good and you deserve it. This is an example of the system working.

I'm not sure I—I don't think, I don't think I've had that thought in the last few years. I mean, I've got my weird neuroses. Like I'm totally—I had this huge inferiority complex where William Vollmann's concerned. Because he and I's first books came out at the same time. And I even once read a Madison Smartt Bell essay, where he used me, and my *"slender* output," and the inferiority of it, to talk about, you know, how great Vollmann is. And so I go around, "Oh no, Vollmann's had another one out, now he's got like five to my one." I go around with that stuff. But I think, I'm trying to think of any example that . . .

Bell himself is an outpourer.

I think just: I haven't read a lot of the new stuff that's come out over the last few years. Like Steve Erickson, and *Tours of the Black Clock*— it's really fucking good. I thought Bret Ellis's first book, I thought it was very, very powerful. *American Psycho*—I thought he was really ill-served by his agent and publisher even letting him publish it, and those are the only two things of his that I read. But that's, I think this is another danger: you get lavishly rewarded for that first book, and it's gonna be very difficult for him ever to do anything else. I mean there's gonna be part of you that just wants to do that over and over and over again, so you continue to get the food pellets of praise. It's one more way that all this stuff is toxic.

Same risk for you?

Sure. Because whatever I do, the next thing will be very different from this. And if it gets *reamed,* then I'll think: "Oh no. Maybe *Infinite Jest II.*" In which case, somebody needs to come and just put a bullet in my head. To be merciful.

David Leavitt noose quote: Reviewers will use my first book as a noose to hang my second.

I think it often is. Although the nice thing about having written an essentially shitty first book is that I'm exempt from that problem. There were a lot of people who really liked *Broom of the System,* but unfortunately they're all about eleven.

[He laughs, then a little composing wince.]

Never that grinding feeling of watching someone who's not talented succeeding?

[I'm trying to give the waitress a tip, which she is in the process of failing to understand and trying to hand back.]

(To waitress) He's attempting to tip you. Here. He wants to do it. It makes him happy.

(To me) You're not supposed to tip here, you get them in trouble. Here is this—this may piss you off or strike you as disingenuous. I don't think I'm all that unusual. I don't think in terms of "more talented" or "less talented." There's a kind of stuff that I vibrate sympathetically with, and a kind of stuff that I don't. And I've seen a couple of books come out, that there was a whole lot of fuss about, I picked 'em up and read 'em. And I mean like literary, I don't mean *shit*. You know, where you can see the gears working—and I just thought, "Man, there might be somethin' here, but I just don't get it. This is just not my cup of tea."

And then I really—I think the envy stuff just so *burned* me, that it's just, idn't there anymore.

How did it burn?

All the time that I wasn't doing any publishable stuff, and I watched other people—you know, like, all of a sudden there was the new brat pack. You know, this lady Donna Tartt came? You know? And I read *Secret History*. And I thought it was, you know, it was pretty good. But feeling that, "Oh shit, now me and all these guys are displaced. And now there's just a new crop." And realizing how disposable, and that terrible . . . that terrible sense of, "I had something and now I don't and somebody else has got it instead." And then it's just—talk about . . .

[A cliffhanger; David stops.

The waitress has returned with my tip after all. David retains his thought.]

—just talk about a kind of mind-set that can get ravenous and that can tear you up. And I just—you know, I went through some of that. And I just, it's weird: I just don't wanna send any blood supply to that part of my *brain* anymore. Not because I'm this great person. But I just—then I'm really unhappy and I'm not doing any work.

Plus, the research on this thing. I'm serious, it took me out of the loop. I don't even *know* 90 percent of what's been published. I didn't even know Jayne Anne Phillips had a new book, like I told you. Until this escort in Chicago told me. I just missed like four years of this. And I'm not sorry not to be part of that world anymore. I just— there's nothing but envy, and sort of puffery, and all that stuff in it. And it's not like I'm above it. It's just that it—the amount that it hurts me, outweighs whatever good feelings it gives me.

Hemingway tapeworm quote: "Literary New York is like a bottle of tape-worms all trying to feed off each other."

Yeah: Or great white sharks fighting over a *bathtub,* you know? There's so little—the amount of celebrity and money we're talkin' about is on the scale of like true entertainment so small. And the formidable in-tellect marshaled by these egos fighting over this small section of the pie, it's just . . . yeah, it seems kind of absurd. But I'll tell ya, I was in New York when the *Esquire* thing came out. [I think he means the 1987 Literary Cosmos thing: a map, with him on the horizon as one of the "approaching comets." No, he means one of the book's few mixed reviews, from *Esquire*'s literary editor Will Blythe.] And it hit that part of me, that writer-vanity part of me. And I was right in that: It's like, I wanna go see him, how dare he? All that, like—whereas when I'm *here,* it's just more like, "Huh, what an interesting storm, going on outside my window. I'm sure glad I'm inside."

How long a part of that world?

I don't know . . . I went through Tucson. Then I went to Yaddo. I was at Yaddo twice. And I would go to New York, and give these read-ings, go to these parties. There were some of these writer-guys at Yaddo with me when I was there. And they were like five years older than me, and they were like big superstars, and I was like . . .

[Jay McInerney, Lorrie Moore, and others]

So you were at Yaddo with some literary heavyweights and you fell into that sort of casino mind-set?

[Turns off tape: He's careful.]

Sometimes at parties. It was more just, you know, you're a student, you're a writing student. You're young, you are by definition immature. And you have these ideas about why people are in the game, what they want. And most of the ideas degenerate into—devolve into—this idea of how other people are gonna regard you. So you look to these people who are well regarded, and regard them as having made it and all this kind of stuff. And I don't know if *Rolling Stone* readers are interested, it's just—most bright people, something happens in your late twenties, where you realize that this other, that *how* other people regard you does not have enough calories in it, to keep you from blowing your brains out. That you've got to find, make some other détente.

[This is his friend Mark Costello's vision of what happened to David. Mark was curious, from the beginning, to see how David would make out in the field; he lived this part—the positioning and business politics—this version of the literary life with David. David, starting out, called it the "publishing episcopacy"; a world of bishops and competing dioceses.

His friend Jon Franzen sees a different novel: a David who tried for adulthood and had trouble getting there.

Writers can be especially awful, about measuring each other and about touching fame. There's a famous New York story about a movie made of a very well-known—Pulitzer Prize, etc.—novelist's book. Halfway through the shoot, from location, the novelist's agent receives a call. An assistant answers instead. The novelist immediately says, "You know X?"—insert famous actress's name here—"I banged her." Writers eye and measure the celebrity world and don't know how to deal with the portion that falls to them; because what they're selling is not their features, physique, or their charm; it's more personal, it's their brain, their *them*, and so they get as anxious about that as a starlet would about nose or waistline. How do I husband this thing that's earning me praise and money? How do I protect and expand it? And what is it people like about me anyway?]

And I am weak enough, and easily enough plunged into these little worlds, that it's just real good for me that I'm not part of it anymore.

Easier to say that now, though? With Infinite Jest in magazines and on covers of book reviews? With your readings jammed?

I would like to think you're wrong. Here's what I was ready for: I am proud of this book. I worked really hard on it. I was pretty sure that it would fall stillborn from the presses. But that within three or four years—like *Girl* sells better now than when it first came out. I thought, hopefully it would sell well enough so that at least Little, Brown could think, "All right, we're eventually gonna get our money back," so that they would buy my next thing. In all earnestness I say to you, that was my expectation, that's what I was ready for.

When did counterindications come?

When *Vogue* and the fashion magazines . . .

[The tape side runs out.]

. . . trust the idea of people who read *Vogue* and *Elle* and *Harper's Bazaar* buying four-and-a-half-pound fairly difficult pieces of work. Y'know, when they said *Newsweek* wanted to send a photographer, I think I began to get the idea that there was—I thought maybe Little, Brown had just . . .

My first thought was fear. 'Cause I thought, "Wow, they've really kicked up the hype engine. And this means I'm gonna get *smeared*.

And shittily reviewed, at a much more public level than I would have before." So it sort of accumulated.

[Simple thing: everyone sees him differently. Bonnie Nadell, his agent, as a sensitive person she was protecting. Franzen, as a friendly rival and fellow whiz who would maybe benefit from a little simultaneous social translation. As long as he persuaded enough people of those different aspects of himself—sort of sending them out on missions—they would protect him on any grounds that needed defense. Done persistently enough, there'd be protection from everything.]

Michael Pietsch's presentation. He went to his sales force, at their conference, and said, "This is why we publish books."

I wasn't there. I know he really liked it. And I know he really read it hard, because he helped me—I mean, that book is partly him. A lot of the cuts are where he convinced me of the cuts. But also, editors and agents jack up their level of effusiveness when they talk with you, to such an extent that it becomes very difficult to read the precise shade of their enthusiasm. What's being presented for you and what they really feel.

I'm not an idiot. I mean, I knew for them to do this, this long, it really cuts their profit margin, 'cause paper's so expensive, etc., etc. That they had to really like it. And partly that feels good, and partly makes it feel, I mean, I got fairly lucky. I know this sounds very political. But I think as a house, these guys are—you can find houses where people really love books. And you can find houses where they've got a really good hype machine. But to find one that's got a combination of the two, and that also really happens to like *your* book?—it seems to me I got fairly lucky.

Sounds like it. But the indications: some months ago? Four months ago, you were saying?

November. And then things quieted down—and then, ah, same

week the *Esquire* thing comes out, came out, *Harper's Bazaar* came out. And I thought, "Oh fuck: there's just gonna be all this negative stuff about the hype. Those *idiots* for handing out those postcards."

[For six months prior to publication, Little, Brown had sent post-cards alerting reviewers and booksellers to the upcoming novel. A card with no title; then, weeks later, a phrase like "Infinite Writer" or "Infinite Pleasure." Then they announced, "David Foster Wallace's *Infinite Jest.*"]

Um, I forgot, I had to go to L.A. to do this thing about a Lynch movie. For *Premiere*. It's gonna come out next fall. It's called *Lost Highway*, it's gonna be *very* cool.

Lynch had his own trouble with getting famous. Twin Peaks, the Time cover.

He'd been through a lot before then; he'd been through *Dune*.

But when I was out there, I would go back to the hotel, and there'd be like four messages all the time, on the hotel machine, of various people wanting to talk to me.

And I'd been through—I mean, I'd been through three books. I mean, one of them—like a limited edition. You know, like a $500 advance for. And I'd been through some of this, and I realized that, unless the publishing world had changed drastically, there was some sort of . . . So I think, I think January, when I was in L.A.

What's happened since January?

[Long pause]

You know what? I think it's hard to describe, because—this is not going to satisfy you—it all happened sorta so *fast*. You know? I talked to *Newsweek* one week and *Time* the next, and there are like fifteen different people calling up, wantin' to do articles. And if they weren't incredibly obnoxious, I would talk to 'em. And then as you know, the fact checkers would call. And then I was trying to work on this Lynch piece, which was very hard and very long. And so I remember, starting at about mid-January, when I noticed I couldn't be home very much. 'Cause if I was home, just the phone rang all the time. And I remember feeling kind of excited, but bein' scared about . . . because I really thought, I was really ready for this not to be liked.

I mean—have you read it? It's reasonably hard. There are things about it that are reasonably hard. I was ready for a lot more percep- tions I think like what that lady had, that Michiko Kakutani lady. [Michiko Kakutani, lead reviewer of the daily *New York Times*.] So I was sort of . . . guardedly excited, because I felt like this could either be a lot of praise, or it could also be a whole lot more public, you know, burning, basically.

And then I didn't read it, but Michael called and said there was a review in . . . uh. Oh, I met the guy at the party. The man who's mar- ried to McGuane's daughter. Walter Kirn. And then Charis Conn called me and said, "Walter Kirn doesn't like anything, and he really liked this." And then I began to go, wow. I mean, "People seem really to like this."

You know what he said?

I didn't read it. I mean, I heard. People told me a couple of things that he said, which sounded to me really stupid. (Voice blocked by cigarette) 'Cause if I was on committees, it would so piss me off that . . .

[Walter Kirn, *New York Magazine*, 2/12: "Next year's book awards have been decided. The plaques and citations can now be put in es- crow. . . . The novel is that colossally disruptive. And that spectacu- larly good."]

Didn't go out to find it?

I went and found the *Atlantic,* because I was scared about Sven [Birkerts]. Look—it's not like I'm, I'm not some *Buddha.* It's just that, I've been through reading reviews before. They're not for me. They always fuck me up. And I'll *read* 'em. But I've gotta like finish this book of nonfiction for Michael by like the end of April. And when that's done, I'm gonna go ahead and freak out about this whole thing; I just can't do it right now.

How'd it feel, though: "As if the book is a National Book Award winner already"?

I applauded his taste and discernment. How's that for a response? What do you want me to say? How would *you* feel? I can't describe it; it's indescribable. You speculate and I'll describe.

[Slightly mean/clever smile]

I'd feel I'd known all along it was OK, and here was someone actually saying what I'd hoped to hear said.

Except you also know that—you know all along when something's really good. But there's the other part, that, "Oh no, this makes absolutely no sense to anybody else—I'm a pretentious fuckwad. People are gonna ridicule me."

So it's sort of like, um . . . here's another part. You'll like this, because this won't make me look attractive at all. If you're used to doing heavy-duty literary stuff—we're talkin' caviar for the general, that doesn't sell all that well? Being human animals with egos, we find a way to accommodate that fact of our ego, by the following equation: If it sells really well and gets a lot of attention, it must be shit. It's just generated by the hype machine.

Then of course the ultimate irony is: um, if your own thing gets a lot of attention and sells really well, then the very mechanism you've used to shore yourself up when your stuff didn't sell well, is now part of the Darkness Nexus when it does. And I'm still working that through. I've still gotta, I'm still worried that, Yeah, the book's funny, and fairly fun to read. But it's fun to read partly because I wanted to try to do something that was really *hard* and avant-garde, but that was fun enough so that it forced the reader to do the work that was required. And I think I'm worried that the fuss [his word throughout] is all about the book's entertainment value, and that people will buy it on that.

Buy it for that reason—which is good, because Little, Brown makes money. But then they'll read 150 pages and get that: "*Eeeew.* Y'know, this isn't what I thought at all." And then *not* read it. Which, I'll . . . Yeah, all right. Avant-garde, or whatever you want to call, like, experimental fiction writers, we don't write for the money. But we're not saints. We write to be read. You know what I mean? And the idea of, OK, the book making a lot of money but not getting read, is for me fairly cold comfort. Although I'm certainly not allergic to money. But you know what I mean? So, see me in a year. Y'know, if a year from now—like, if I have a bunch of conversations, like with this guy Silverblatt [Michael Silverblatt, host of NPR's *Bookworm*], or with Vince Passaro, or with like David Gates, somebody who clearly read the book closely. Um, and a bunch of people are saying it's good, then I'm probably gonna start feeling wholeheartedly good about the book. As it is, there's a kind of creeping feeling of a kind of misunderstanding.

And an amused . . . a kind of amused attempt to separate what's good, what of the fuss has to do with the book, and what of the fuss has to do with the sort of enormous engine, um, *started* by Little, Brown. But now clearly seems to be humming in and of itself. Y'know, when somebody asked somebody in New York, had they read Martin Amis's *The Information,* the person answered, "Well, not personally." Right? That—you know.

That's actually an old joke. My mom heard it about students at Stanford in the '80s. "Have you read Madame Bovary?" "Well, not personally." What does it mean to you?

This machine that has you out here, asking about my reaction to a phenomenon that consists largely of your being out here. Which of course won't get said in the essay. But, I mean, it's all very strange.

I love this song. "Magic Bus." The Who.

This is one of the few songs of theirs I like. I never liked the Who very much.

Literary heavyweights: You and them at Yaddo . . .

Yeah, and me feelin' jealous of them. And feeling like I wanted to be regarded the way they were regarded. And uh . . . what was our point?

And now you're them?

Yeah. It's weird, man. I can't help you out. It doesn't ("dudn't") feel like anything. It makes me glad I'm not twenty-five anymore. I feel a certain irony in—when I was twenty-five, I think I would've given a couple of digits off my non-use hand for this. And now: it's nice, it's nice. But I'll tell you, man, I couldn't've finished the book if I'd wanted this. You know what I mean? I really got into it. I don't think I'm the most talented person on the planet, but I work *really* hard, you know? And part of what's really hard is I work really hard at get-ting better at stuff, you know? I mean like . . .

You became a better stylist?

I think I work harder now. I think—I don't know what you were like. I think when I was twenty-two or twenty-three, I pretty much thought every sentence that came off my pen was great. And couldn't *stand* the idea that it wasn't. Because then you've disintegrated—you know, you're either great or you're terrible. And now I just, I think I'm just—yeah, I know this is gonna sound drippy and PC. I'm just,

I'm really into the *work* now. I mean it's really—and I feel good about this. Because, you know, we wanna be doing this for forty more years, you know? And so I've gotta find some way to enjoy this that doesn't involve getting *eaten* by it, so that I'm gonna be able to go do something else. Because bein' thirty-four, sitting alone in a room with a piece of paper is what's real to me. This (points at table, tape, me) is *nice*, but this is not real. Y'know what I mean?

[Long silence]

Let's be aware; we have to get up at about five. I mean I'll talk to you all you want—I just, if I get four hours of sleep tonight, I'm gonna be in real bad shape tomorrow. I learned that the hard way.

You've talked about both strands: obviously, the first strand, where you know it was really good, won out, or you wouldn't have finished the book, right?

No. The way to finish the book is to turn down the volume on the stuff that's all about how other people react. You know?

But there's a certain halfway point where you bottom out on that stuff, and then you become like a stranger brought in by the studio to wrap things up? I've always seen it as, you start a project as David Lean, or Francis Coppola, but at a certain point you get yanked and you end up as the Don Bruckheimer or the Sydney Pollack they bring in to finish the picture.

Uhh . . . Boy, I don't know, you realize—

You become the hired gun . . .

I've worked on maybe four or five things—some short, some long—that became alive to me halfway through. And this came alive to me halfway through. And I would still hear the, "This is the best thing ever written," and "This is the *worst* thing ever written." But it's sort of like, you know how in movies there will be a conversation, and then that conversation gets quieter, and a different conversation fades in . . . I don't know, there's some technical word for it. Just, the volume gets turned down. Now there's been other stuff where the volume hasn't been turned down, and I *have* finished it. Just, I was a hack: "God damn it, I'm going to finish this thing."

This thing, I got real interested in it. And I got real invested in it. And it's one reason why the big part of me that's pleased about all this fuss—other than, Perhaps I'll get *laid* in like *Akron* or something—is that I'm proud of this. In a way that for instance I'm *not* proud of *Broom of the System*. Which I think shows some talent, but was in many ways a fuck-off enterprise. It was written very quickly, rewritten sloppily, sound editorial suggestions were met with a seventeen-page letter about literary theory that was really a not-very-interesting way . . . really a way for me to avoid doing hard work.

And *this* I just, I didn't fuck off on this, you know? I mean, this is absolutely the best I could do between like 1992 and 1995. And I also think though that if everybody'd hated it, I wouldn't be thrilled, but I don't think I'd be devastated, either. It's—and that's not about being a hack, that's about that it got, it became *alive* for me.

Maybe "hired gun" was too cynical.

It doesn't sound cynical to me, but the ways that I would disagree with you I'm worried would sound occult. For me it has much more to do with, I feel like people are talking to me. I feel like this thing, this is a living thing. With whom, with which I have a relationship that needs to be tended. That I feel, not—that I feel un-lonely working on it. Which (mouth full) to be honest, I mean, there've been a few things that I've felt that way about, that ended up I don't think being all that good. Or people didn't like 'em all that much. But, um . . . I just think that it *hurts*. I think I have a really low pain threshold. I think the I'll-show-people, or, People-are-really-gonna-like-this—

thinking that way has hurt me *so* bad. That, um, that when I'm thinkin' that way, I'm not writing.

That that's this thinking in me that's gotta reach this kind of fever pitch, and then *break*. And in order for me to even start—not to get in the groove, but to get started—I've gotta find some way to turn the volume of that way down. And I think I'm more afraid—it sounds to me like you have a possibly cynical, possibly just very mature acceptance of the inevitability of that, that way of thinking. Whereas my experience has been, I think in certain ways I'm just emotionally kinda delicate, and it's just *devastating* to me to think that way. And I'm willing to do enormous work—and enormous emotional and psychological gymnastics—to avoid thinking that way.

Have you since read the seventeen-page letter about Broom?

Oh sure. It talks about how the entire book is a conversation between Wittgenstein and Derrida, and presence versus absence. I mean, Gerry [Gerry Howard, *Broom*'s editor] didn't want the book to end there. We have a cast of characters who are afraid their names don't denote, word and referent are united in absence, which means Derrida . . . you know what? It's a brilliant little theoretical document, unfortunately it resulted in a shitty and dissatisfying ending, right?

And in fact it was a very cynical argument, because there was a part of me—this was a year and a half after I wrote it, and I knew that that ending, there was good stuff about it, but it was way too clever. It was all about the *head,* you know? And Gerry kept saying to me, "Kid, you've got no idea." Like, "We wouldn't even be *having* this conversation if you hadn't created this woman named Lenore who seems halfway appealing and alive." And I couldn't hear. I just couldn't hear it. I couldn't hear it. I was in . . . Dave Land.

I had four hundred thousand pages of continental philosophy and lit theory in my head. And by God, I was going to use it to prove to him that I was smarter than he was. And so, as a result, for the rest of my life, I will walk around . . . You know, I will see that book occasionally at signings. And I will realize I was arrogant, and missed a chance to make that book better. And hopefully I won't do it again. It's why I will not run lit-crit on my own stuff. And don't even want to talk about it.

My tastes in reading lately have been way more realistic, because most experimental stuff is hellaciously unfun to read.

Because ideas are primary? And then the writing goes bad?

I'm not sure if it's poorly written: It requires an amount of work on the part of the reader that's grotesquely disproportionate to its payoff. And it seems—when I am a reader of that kind of stuff, and I'm talking like heavy-duty experimental stuff, some of which I have to read just because I do various stuff with experimental press. I feel like I am as a reader like a small child, and adults are having a conversation over my head; that this is really a book being written for other writers, theorists, and critics. And that any of that kind of stomach magic of, "God *damn,* it's fun to read. I'd rather read right now than *eat,*" has been totally lost.

So this was really one of the reasons I'm thrilled about the fuss about the book. Is: in this I wanted to do something that is real experimental and very strange, but it's also *fun.* And that was also of course really scary. Because I thought maybe that couldn't be done—or that it would come off just as a hellacious flop. But I'm sort of proud of it, because I think it was kind of a right-headed and brave thing to do. And I think, I think there's a reason why a lot of avant-garde stuff gets neglected: I think that a lot of it deserves to be. Same with a lot of poetry. That's written for other people that write poetry, and not for people that read. I don't know. That's kind of a whole rant.

I agree. Lorrie Moore works for readers, not just writers. Martin Amis . . .

But there's also, there's ways that experimental and avant-garde stuff can capture and talk about the way the world feels on our nerve endings, in a way that conventional realistic stuff can't.

I disagree. I'm a realism fan. You agree?

It imposes an order and sense and ease of interpretation on experience that's never there in real life. I'm talking about the stuff, you know, what's hard or looks structurally strange—or formally weird—I mean some of that stuff can be very cool.

But Tolstoy's books come closer to the way life feels than anybody, and those books couldn't be more conventional.

Yeah, but life now is completely different than the way it was then. Does your life *approach* anything like a linear narrative? I'm talking about the way it feels, how our nervous system feels.

[Long pause]

You mean like TV life and computer life?

Some of it has to do with TV and fiction. You watch many videos? MTV videos? Lot of flash cuts in 'em. A lot of shit that looks incongruous but ends up having kind of a dream association with each other. I don't know about you, but that's sort of—I mean, Jesus. Um, you flew here. You drove down. Probably while you're driving down you're also doing work on another piece. You're lugging your computer. You come, you talk to me. You and I have our little conversation. Then I need to go do my class and am thinking about that, then you're thinking about the phone. Then you and I go to the class. God knows what you're doing in the class. Now we're here. Now you're in a good mood 'cause you've mailed this thing off, that because of your relationship with these various other webs and commitments—

    I mean, it's more as if—Life seems to strobe on and off for me, and to barrage me with input. And that so much of my job is to impose some sort of order, or make some sort of sense of it. In a way that—maybe I'm very naïve—I imagine Leo getting up in the morning, pulling on his homemade boots, going out to chat with the serfs whom he's freed [making clear he knows something about the texture and subject], you know. Sitting down in his *silent* room, overlooking some very well-tended gardens, pulling out his quill, and . . . in deep tranquility, recollecting emotion.

And I don't know about you. I just—stuff that's like that, I enjoy reading, but it doesn't feel *true* at all. I read it as a relief from what's true. I read it as a relief from the fact that, I received five hundred thousand discrete bits of information today, of which maybe twenty-five are important. And how am I going to sort those out, you know?

And yet you made a linear narrative, easily, out of both our days, just now. Off the top of your head. I think our brain is structured to make linear narratives, to condense and focus and separate what's important.

You, if this is an argument, you will win. This is an argument you will win. [Strange: competition.] I am attempting to describe for you what I mean in response to your, "I have no idea what you're talking about."

What always strikes me is the opposite: the lack of discontinuity, *not the lack of continuity.*

Huh. Well you and I just disagree. Maybe the world just feels differently to us. This is all going back to something that isn't really clear: that avant-garde stuff is hard to read. I'm not defending it, I'm saying that stuff—this is gonna get very abstract—but there's a certain set of magical stuff that fiction can do for us. There's maybe thirteen things, of which who even knows which ones we can talk about. But one of them has to do with the sense of, the sense of *capturing*, capturing what the world feels like to us, in the sort of way that I think that a reader can tell "Another sensibility like mine *exists*." Something else feels this way to someone else. So that the reader feels less lonely. ["Lonely" again; interesting.]

There's really really shitty avant-garde, that's coy and hard for its own sake. That I don't think it's a big accident that a lot of what, if you look at the history of fiction—sort of, like, if you look at the history of painting after the development of photography—that the history of fiction represents this continuing struggle to allow fiction to continue to do that magical stuff. As the texture, as the *cognitive* texture, of our lives changes. And as, um, as the different media by which our lives are represented change. And it's the avant-garde or experimental stuff that has the chance to move the stuff along. And that's what's precious about it.

And the reason why I'm angry at how shitty most of it is, and how much it ignores the reader, is that I think it's very very very very precious. Because it's the stuff that's about what it feels like to live. Instead of being a relief from what it feels like to live.

[Deep, reverse-belch breath]

I don't know about you: My life and my self doesn't feel like any-thing like a unified developed character in a linear narrative to me. I may be mentally ill, maybe you're not. But my *guess* is, look-ing at things like MTV videos or new fashions in ads, with more and more flash cuts, or the use of computer metaphors which would only be useful metaphors if the ability to do triage and tree-diagrams resonated with people's own existence in life. That I think a *lot* of people feel—not overwhelmed by the amount of stuff they have to do. But overwhelmed by the number of choices they have, and by the number of discrete, different things that come at them. And the number of small . . . that since they're part of numerous systems, the number of small insistent tugs on them, from a number of different systems and directions. Whether that's qualitatively different than the way life was for let's say our parents or our grandparents, I'm not sure. But I sorta think so. At least in some—in terms of the way it feels on your nerve endings.

"Information sickness," as in Ted Mooney's book.

Now we're into DeLillo-ville, right? Where the bigger the system gets, the more interference there is, and all that. I'm not talking about the system, I'm talking about what it feels like to be *alive*. And how formal and structural stuff in avant-garde things I think can *vibrate*, can represent on a page, what it feels like to be alive right now. But that's only one of the things fiction's doing. I'm not saying it's the only thing. I'm working hard here to try to make sense of what it is I'm saying to you. If your life makes linear sense to you, then you're either very strange, or you might be just a neurologically healthy person—who's automatically able to decoct, organize, do triage on the amount of stuff that's coming at you all the time.

You were getting this across in the book?

I don't know. I can tell you that's part of it. I mean, the book's structured a little strange, and that's part of it. The scary thing about doing it was, structuring it that way puts a lot of demands on the reader. Is there gonna be a payoff? Is the reader gonna *feel* there's a payoff? Is the reader gonna throw the book at the wall? You know? I don't know. This stuff is tremendously—I get all excited and frustrated talkin' about it.

You can put the pieces together. But it requires a certain amount of—what's the word—prestidigitation to do it. Which I would think you would find annoying.

Like if I could articulate it, then there wouldn't be any need to make up stories about it, you know? And I always think that, until the person comes, and then I always like the person, I want to impress them, and then I sort of *try* to articulate to them. (Defeated) And I guess maybe I'm learning that I just can't anymore.

So many thoughts whirling around at any one time, that's what it would really feel like to be in here. It's a nice performance—it's nice up there on the stage. But it's not what it feels like to be in *here*. Does that make any sense to you?

More?

What writers have is a license and also the freedom to sit—to sit, clench their fists, and make themselves be excruciatingly aware of the stuff that we're mostly aware of only on a certain level. And that if the writer does his job right, what he basically does is remind the reader of how smart the reader is. Is to wake the reader up to stuff that the reader's been aware of all the time. And it's not a question of the writer having more capacity than the average person. [James Brown: "I Feel *Good*" in background, on the restaurant sound system.] It's that the writer is willing I think to cut off, cut himself off from certain stuff, and develop . . . and just, and *think* really hard. Which not everybody has the luxury to do.

But I gotta tell you, I just think to look across the room and automatically assume that somebody else is less aware than me, or that somehow their interior life is less rich, and complicated, and acutely perceived than mine, makes me not as good a writer. Because that means I'm going to be performing for a faceless audience, instead of trying to have a conversation with a person.

And if you think that's faux, then you think what you want. But I, um . . . what I've got is, what I've got is a serious fear of being a certain way. And a set I think of like, not real complicated, but *convictions* about why I'm continuing to do this. Why I'm gonna do this, why it's worthwhile. Why it's not just an exercise in basically getting my dick sucked. You know? This is the way to have Mom be proud of me, this is the way—you know what I mean? And this is a good tactic of yours, to get me a little pissed off. And then I'm gonna reveal more, I'm gonna be less guarded, but it's sort of like . . .

[He thinks—comes up with the *Harper's* essays, which I told him I loved.]

In those essays that you like in *Harper's,* there's a certain persona created, that's a little stupider and schmuckier than I am. In person, like at these readings, I feel like my job is to be exactly as much of myself as I can be. Without looking, without *making* myself naked in front of people who might be mean to me. And I don't pull an aw-shucks-regular-guy thing. It's true that I want very much—I *treasure* my regular-guyness. I've started to think it's my biggest asset as a writer. Is that I'm pretty much just like everybody else. But I don't—you know, whatever. I'm not gonna say it again. I'm not doing a faux thing with you.

And that's why I don't want to do this, week after week after week. Is if I could do a faux thing, this wouldn't be any work.

I'm sure you'll shrug it off. Once this phase is done, when you're back to writing. But the faux thing: isn't what you just said an example of the faux thing? You don't want to take the risk, the effect, of giving the full you?

I don't know whether you're a very nice man or not. No—it's very clear that you don't believe a word of what I've said. And you think that's part of the faux thing, in which case . . .

What I mean is that a lot of stuff that I thought were weaknesses of mine turned out to be strengths. [Restaurant playlist: Lady Marmalade, "Voulez-vous Coucher." I do, in fact, end up staying at Chez Wallace.] And one of them is that I am not, I'm not a particularly exceptional person. I think I'm a really good reader, and I've got a good ear. And I'm willing to work *really* really hard. But I'm more or less a regular person. And this was Streitfeld's whole thing: "Are you normal, are you normal, are you normal?" To the extent that I think of myself as different from other people, then I'm not gonna be having a conversation with the reader. And so, the normal regular stuff is real precious to me. And maybe I *am* going around, like, "I *am* normal: Look, look! I am normal." But I'm doing it for myself. And uh, I'm not—I don't have the brain cells left to play any kind of game with you or do any kind of faux thing.

. . .

NEXT MORNING
WE'RE PACKING TO FLY TO CHICAGO
AND FROM THERE TO MINNEAPOLIS
IT'S DAVID'S LAST READING: THE END OF THE TOUR
IT'S ABOUT 6 A.M. I'M A WRECK. IT FEELS LIKE I'VE CLIMBED OUT
OF A STRANGER'S TRUNK IN A PARKING LOT BY THE AIRPORT

[When I tell him I wake up without coffee but with cigarettes, he laughs.]

Brothers of the lung.

[Offers half his morning pastry]

My Pop-Tart es su Pop-Tart.

[Fortress of Solitude, trophy-case feel in guest room. All his books piled up together . . .

Call to *Rolling Stone,* while David in the shower: alcohol problem rumors] "The feeling is, 'It wouldn't surprise anybody . . .' Everybody thought the heroin thing. Gerry Howard was a little bit proud of his 'writers with problems' coterie. He sort of likes that sort of thing. He would be more than forthcoming with a little bit of massaging to give you whatever you needed. Bury it in other questions . . .

"For example, 'How was editing him; what do you think of his success; hey, what about the dope?' He's very forthcoming, perhaps to the point of making mistakes with his honesty. Tread lightly."

• • •

BLOOMINGTON-NORMAL AIRPORT
ICEBOUND: THE WHOLE AIRPORT FROZEN, LIKE A RUNNER
STUCK ON FIRST BASE, WHILE MANAGERS AND PITCHERS CON-
FER AT THE MOUND
WE'RE WAITING TO HEAR IF OUR FLIGHT'S BEEN CANCELLED
DRIVE TO CHICAGO

All I could think is that whenever the flight is late, it means there's stuff I don't have to do.

[Again: Trying to show how much he doesn't like publicity. Except if he isn't a genius, there's no good reason to read the novel. You don't open a one-thousand-page book because you've heard the author's a nice guy. You read it—once you prop the thing open at all—because you understand the author is brilliant. He's grabbed the wrong lesson: The people who seem to adore the press the way, say, Pooh loves a honey jar, look foolish; but the people who seem to hate it also risk foolishness too, because the reader knows how good press must feel, like having the prettiest girl in school drop you a smile. Like having the whole country rub against your toes and twist between your ankles.]

It's iced over.

I think there's stuff they can spray on the runway, some foamy stuff.

[A guy in a jumpsuit whose nametag says "Mark" walks by. "You guys should be more worried about the *wing*."

Everywhere we've gone, restaurants, 7-Elevens, if someone asks, "You two together?" David has said, "Yes, but not on a date." With the American Eagle desk in Bloomington, he says it again.]

"Not on a date"—you've said that with every waitress, ticket counter clerk, etc. Midwest more homophobic . . . ?

It comes off as a joke, but it also communicates that, like—I don't know, I've got a fair number of gay friends here. Who've had some terrible stuff happen to them, and have just . . .

Haven't seen any black people in town.

They all live on the west side of town, next to the Purina plant, in housing projects.

Politics?

Educated Republicans: the racism here is very quiet, very systematic.

[We're sitting in airport lounge, waiting for flight to be announced or scrubbed.]

A town with a lot of university action. Like I said, there's small towns around here—you can drive through small towns thirty miles from here, and see guys in the corner with three fingers sticking out of their hip pocket. Guys that stand there like this.

[Shows me: pinky and thumb pocketed, three fingers extended over the denim.]

I had to have this explained to me when I first came here. You know what this is? It's KKK.

Really?

Yeah. It's weird—it's like the earliest gang symbol in America. They're not skinheads, and they would think skinheads are freaks, and part of the whole problem. They're quiet, multigenerational, you know, grand wizards and poobahs and all that kind of stuff.

[Old Midwestern town, with glossary of mall stores every town has . . .]

This is an unusual town, because it's always been one of the richest towns in Illinois. Now there's a lot of State Farm here. A lot of railroad money before. Enormous tax base. Really rich. A weird kind of Mafia-ish thing. In a weird way, State Farm is to this town what Albert Finney played in *Miller's Crossing*. State Farm is the Irish gang boss. It's only I think slightly less subtle than having the mayor and the police chief sitting in his office getting yelled at by him.

Albert Finney chasing guys with a Tommy gun: "The old man's still an expert with a Thompson."

[After a moment of silence, he corrects my line.]

Yeah—it's even more over the top than that: "He's still a Mozart, he's still an artist with the Thompson . . ."

Too early to talk?

At a certain point, we have to go back and find out when our flight is.

Can you tell me a little about your background?

I grew up—I was born in Ithaca, New York, 1962. My father was in grad school at Cornell. Moved to Urbana—which is twin cities with Champaign—in 1964. Lived there. Went to elementary, junior high, and high school there. I went to Amherst College—I took a year off, so I started Amherst in 1980, started in the class of '84, got out of Amherst in '85, went to grad school that fall. And sort of did the peripatetic writer.

Published first book first year of Arizona?

How did that work? No—because I was still rewriting it part of the first semester. I think it got bought *early* spring of '86, so it came out midyear of '87. I didn't know what it meant to publish something. It got bought that first year. They were gonna kick me out . . . (Muses, smiles) Yeah. They just thought I was crazy.

[Smoking here, too: smoking everywhere in Illinois.]

I mean, in a way I made a stupid choice: They are a highly, incredibly hard-ass realist school. I was doing very abstract stuff back then, most of which was really bad. But it was just funny, 'cause it's also a really careerist place. And they had to go from almost kicking me out, to this sort of tight-smiled, "we're proud of you," you know, "that you're a U of A man." It was—I felt kinda embarrassed for them.

They tout you now?

I don't think they tout their alumni. Robert Boswell—he's a really nice guy. They invite him back a lot, throw publication parties for his books at the U of A.

They don't like me, and I think a good part of it was my fault. I think I was kind of a prick. I was just unteachable. I mean, I did what I did, and I got a lot tougher about ignoring criticism, but there was a certain amount they told me that was really kind of plausible, but I just wasn't in any kind of head to hear it. So I don't think I was *actively* unpleasant in class. But I think I had that sort of look of, you know, "If there were any justice in the world, I'd be *teaching* this class, and you'd be taking it." You know—that look that makes you want to *slap* students. I go back every once in a while because my sister lives in Tucson. I think I've seen—I gave a reading in like '89 or something.

Arizona is the only place—it's the first place I've ever lived, that I truly absolutely *loved*. Like geographically. The warmth and the—oh, have you ever been there? It's an interesting town, you can live there on practically nothing, because all the houses have carriage houses behind them that people rent out for like $150 a month. And it's a great—it's kind of, it's like a town preplanned for Bohemia, almost. And there's a whole lot, there's a really cool like leftist cultural world. Because a lot of grad students just end up teaching part-time at the U of A and living there for like ten, twenty years. And it's just really gorgeous.

Your folks are university people?

My father teaches in the philosophy department at the U of Illinois. He mostly teaches in the medical school now.

Ethics?

Yeah—he teaches both ethics and aesthetics, but he's moved more and more to ethics, because of his own writing. And then he got into bioethics. And now he's actually had to testify in a couple of these, sort of, "Was it wrong to take him off life support" stuff. I don't know, Dad's got—Dad's an Aristotelian, he's got a really complicated definition of what it is to be a live human being. Basically, I think he gets asked to testify and they never ask him again because his answers are so complicated that they don't have any effect on a jury.

But my mother teaches at a school called Parkland College, which is a two-year—like it's a community, it's a community college. Which is different from a JC.

[Food arrives.]

Put in any of my educational rants you want.

[I've got the burger deluxe: cheese slab, crunchy lettuce, block-cut fries. David stares.]

I'm not even going to *start* on the idea of eating a hamburger at 7:00 in the morning. The idea is you eat eggs, which are kind of a latent form, as your body itself is awakening. It makes a lot of sense. Because you are the food, and you're supposed to eat stuff that is nice to you.

I guess following life cycle stuff too: eggs in morning, meat at night. Birth to death.

And then you eat basically partial—and by the end you eat basically partially decomposed creatures, so . . .

Environment in house? Lots of reading?

Yeah. My parents—I have all these weird early memories. I remember my parents reading *Ulysses* out loud to each other in bed, in this really cool way, holding hands and both lovin' something really fiercely.

    And I remember me being five and Amy being three, and Dad reading *Moby-Dick* to us (Laughs)—the unexpurgated *Moby-Dick*. Before—I think halfway through Mom pulled him aside and explained to him that, um, little kids were not apt to find, you know, "Cetology" all that interesting. Um, so they were—but I think by the end, Amy was exempted. And I did it just as this kind of "Dad I love you, I'm gonna sit here and listen." My father's got a beautiful, like, reading voice, and I would like to listen to him just read the Montgomery Ward catalog or something.

Humoring him?

I was aware—it's weird, it's the same syndrome I notice in these radio interviews. That these guys' voices are so pretty, it dudn't matter what they're saying: I'll listen to their voices instead of . . . And I remember really liking to listen to Dad's voice. But I remember, I remember because there was some sort of deal about Amy, Amy got exempted from it, and was I gonna be exempted or not? And I remember kind of trying to win Dad's favor, by saying, "No, Dad, I want to hear it." When in fact of course I didn't at all.

Remember a lot of it?

I remember being hellaciously bored. And I remember picking the lint out of my navel with a pen, while Dad was doing it, and Dad saying that was the equivalent of picking your nose. I mean, I was *five.*

[We talk about slide-thing box—we find the name: View-Master.]

I was a little too old for that to have quite the hypnotic charm . . .
     You grew up where? Your father does what? And they had you late? So they had you young? [Asking me the questions back; doesn't want me, as the interviewer, to believe he has a swelled head . . .]

[My dad: Seventies advertising world, BBDO, Madison Avenue. Right Guard, Pepsi, the "Pepsi Generation" songs.]

He ran the Pepsi account? He wrote all those songs? He just kind of rode herd? "You've got a lot to live?" Those were good ones.

That thing with the puppies—

And if you turn the sound off it looks like he's being *attacked* by the puppies.

Yes! My dad pitched the ad: "Let's have a boy just being raped *by puppies."*

It's actually an effective advertising thing, because I think Pepsi really doesn't taste as good as Coke. There's a nasty, chemical component to the taste. And the fact that it competes with Coke is entirely a testament to its advertising.

Airplane hangar taste, wonderful.

Yeah—it tastes like it was made with a kid's chemistry set or something.

When read?

I was like you—I read—I've read a *huge* amount. I mean, I remember reading all the Hardy Boys books by the time I was like seven. But I also watched *hellacious* amounts of television.

My references are getting more and more dated—the shows I'm referring to, pretty soon the kids are not going to know them. Although now with cable . . .

I read a lot, but I didn't have particularly sophisticated tastes. I mean I read like Hardy Boys and Tom Swift. And Dad was really into science fiction, and I remember Dad trying to feed me Edgar Rice Burroughs, the Martian stuff. And I think I wasn't as into it as he was. I remember really liking Tolkien. But what would usually happen is Dad would read something, and if I would like it, he'd give it to me. And like let me read it. I mean, I read fairly early, but wasn't a precocious reader.

Parents and TV?

They would watch at night. It's weird, because I realize I had advantages my students didn't. Like, before dinner, um, there was just this weird hour, late in the afternoon, when, you know, dinner was more or less simmering. And there'd be music on, and they'd be reading, and we'd be reading. We'd all sit around the living room, and we'd each be reading our own thing. And every once in a while, we'd talk about what we were reading. And I for a long time, I think, thought all families were like that. And didn't realize that . . .

When did you?

When I was at school, and met—there were a lot of kids at Amherst, I met a lot of people who were fiercely smart, like great test-takers.

Who were really talented at like science or something, but you realize that they (a) didn't read, and (b) didn't like to particularly. That it wasn't something they dug a lot.

Encouraged to in the house, though?

It was probably the same for you. Overtly, no. It was just what you did. I remember I liked to more than Amy did. I remember Amy liked to draw and play with things, and partially play with the phones. And I would much prefer being by myself with a book. And that Mom and Dad were basically, "Oh cool, look: David and Amy are different." They were really '60s parents, and I don't think— there was if anything a conscious attempt to *not* give overt direction. Although of course you end up becoming yourself.

Did they want you to be a writer or no?

Oh no, I was gonna be—the big thing I was when I was little was a really serious jock. You know, I played like citywide football as a little kid, I was really big and strong as a little kid.

And then for four or five years, I was seriously gonna be a pro tennis player. And it was like my great dream. Reading was this kind of fun, weird thing that I did on the side. I mean, I had no artistic ambition.

Harper's piece, "Tennis and Trigonometry."

It's pretty good—but *Harper's* changed it a lot. It's real different than what the original is. The original was about math. He made it this really neat essay about failure. I'm really bad at saving stuff. I'm just poorly organized.

Pee-Wee—Pop Warner?

Pop Warner is slightly older—that's nationally. Here, there's a weird thing called Gray-Y, which was done through the YMCA. You could say Pee-Wee and it wouldn't be far off. But I was really good. I mean, when I was a little kid I was really good. And then I got to junior high, and there were like two other guys in the city who were better quarterbacks than I was. [Even then very competitive: knows the exact number.] And people started hitting each other a lot harder, and I discovered that I didn't really love to hit people. That was a huge disappointment. And then I discovered tennis when I was twelve, and then I got totally addicted to that.

But too late for pro?

It turned out later I think that I started too late. It also turned out, I just didn't quite have the goods. I mean, I could have been, I think, a good college player if I started earlier. And I never—one thing about me and Michael Joyce [the tennis star] this summer, and seeing these guys up close, is they're playing an entirely different game. I mean, it's like what you and I were doing last night versus serious, devoted chess players.

Did hanging around Joyce confirm your guesses about tennis?

He'd had some media coaching, clearly—he gave me level one of the thirteen levels, the thirteen levels of consciousness that would be going on. I think the best nonfiction I've ever done that I could not get published anywhere, is a long review of Tracy Austin's book that talks about—that's all about what kind of mentality would be required to go, like, "OK, I really need to get this point. So I'm gonna focus and bear down and not get distracted." And to be able to do that, and whether that's a kind of genius or a kind of stupidity. And which one. And why it results in such execrable writing.

It'd be cool to do the reverse, in a sports book: an as-told-to, but with full prose.

Couldn't do it . . . Someone else kind of did.

When you were at Brown, did you study with Hawkes?

[John Hawkes, head of the university's writing program. Sometimes there, sometimes on leave. I mention Hawkes's problem—mood elevators—and David guesses the exact name of the medication. He has the *PDR*, the *Physician's Desk Reference*, down.]

I did that weeklong visiting writer thing in November while I was cutting the thing at *Harper's* . . . taught—

PA: Flight 4432—Passengers of American Eagle Flight 4432, service to Chicago, sorry to inform you that at this time we still have not received any promising news with regard to the runway conditions here at Bloomington. Again, this is an indefinite delay. We have no anticipated departure for this aircraft at this time.

Good thing we can smoke a lot of cigarettes at this place.

How serious was the tennis?

I wudn't as good as the kids in the book, but I was good enough—there would be local tournaments, and then at a certain point there are regionals, and then there are sectionals. And I was good enough at least to get to play in sectionals. And then I would bumble through the first couple of rounds, against other schmoes like me, and then I would run into a seed. And those were kids usually who were from suburbs of Chicago, or the good suburbs of St. Louis, or Grosse Pointe, Michigan. And that was all just a joke. They would beat us 0 and 6, 1 and 6. They were playing a totally different game. And I know that I always since I started writing wanted to do a story where I sort of got to project myself into the heads of kids like that. And the kids in the Academy are even a level above them. [The kids at *Infinite Jest*'s Enfield Tennis Academy—big-hitting, nationally ranked.]

And had you started playing at three or four or five?

(Shrugs) It'd be fun to hit with Amis sometime.

I wouldn't want to do it as a piece—I'd just like to be the best writer–tennis player. I'm real hard to beat—'cause I've just played a lot of tournaments. I don't look that good, but I'm just almost impossible to beat. I know that sounds arrogant. [His second time with that word: He's more comfortable being proud about the physical, which can be measured, and which is a sideline anyway. Much more confident talking about his semigood tennis than his extraordinarily fine prose.] It's true. I'm a—I'm a somewhere between good and very good natural athlete. The ones who become really great players (a) start really young, (b) get lucky enough to be put into great coaching tracks, and (c) are phenomenally talented athletes. And tennis takes—I just didn't, don't have the foot speed and the reflexes, you know? Which you need; it's the same reason I couldn't be a major-league hitter. I don't quite have the foot speed and the reflexes.

I don't think I realized that till—um, it all got very confusing to me, 'cause I didn't go into puberty till real late. And this is part of what the tennis essay is about, and I really sort of felt betrayed by my body. And always thought that, "Well, if I coulda just developed when I was fifteen, like these guys from Peoria, I coulda been . . ." And the fact of the matter is, I couldn't.

Schacht's problem? [Ted Schacht, from the novel's Academy]

Nah—Schacht's got knee issues.

Yeah—it's weird. A lot of this stuff, I can't remember.

(To waitress) We're gonna basically just hang out here for a while.

There was a lot more stuff about these various guys and their relation to tennis. I mean, there were a number of drafts. One I cut quite a bit before I even sent it to Michael, and even I realized that, that—the tennis stuff had to be used, it couldn't be in there for its own sake, because very few people find that stuff interesting.

But no. Schacht's big thing was taking tremendously scary bowel movements and having a bad knee.

It's Orin.

Right.

Orin had your football thing too; I loved the little thing about them having to actually fly into the stadium as the Cardinals . . .

Michael really wanted that taken out, and I sorta loved it, and it was only a page and a half. I said, "Just give me this one."
A lot of the stuff that comes off as drugs in the book is intended to be more or less plausible.

2015 is when it takes place?

I had to get the dates right—I believe it's 2009, but don't quote me.
You know, I wanted it set in just enough so our kids would be in adolescence.

[Interesting and very sad: setting the novel the year after his death, somehow this is heartbreaking. His having no idea this is coming.]

I don't think it's as late as 2015.

So when you say a late puberty—sixteen, fourteen?

I'm not talking about when you have nocturnal emissions, I'm talking about when your physique changes. There's this huge deal in junior tennis between whether you're playing with the physique of a boy or a man. And like I didn't start to put on any kind of meat until I was in college. So I was basically playing with the body of a boy until I was seventeen years old.
I had withdrawn before—

I started to smoke a lot of pot when I was fifteen or sixteen, and it's just hard to train when you smoke a lot of pot. You don't have that much energy. (Laughs) So I was, like—you know, I was still going to tournaments. But I was mostly doing it, going to like hang out with the guys and party. And I was getting to the quarters instead of the semis of these tournaments. And there was just a general kind of slippage.

Second year of high school then?

Yeah: fifteen, sixteen, somethin' like that. I mean, starting really to kind of like it. And also other stuff: did a lot of Quaaludes. And by the way, there's certain stuff about this stuff that I won't talk about. *This* I don't mind talking about.

Heroin?

No. I didn't like it that much. I didn't have the constitution for it. And I'm serious—I'm not. There's no way to be a heroin addict and work that hard.

You could dispel that rumor?

Yeah—except what if they just think I'm lying?

People in New York have heard this rumor—what came down to us is that in Boston you'd gotten very involved with drugs and had some kind of breakdown.

Heroin doesn't make you break down until you stop doing it. I don't know if I had a breakdown, I got really really depressed, and had to go on a suicide ward in Boston. It had nothing to do with drugs. It had nothing to do with drugs. I had already started to lose a lot of interest in drugs sort of before then.

Worried by this rumor in publishing circles?

No, although I'd heard—Adam Begley [the *New York Observer*] had reported this rumor that I was a cocaine addict. He said Vollmann told him that, which I didn't really believe. But it just seems laughable to me, because I did I think once at a party, and I found it excruciatingly unpleasant, like drinking fifty cups of coffee or something.

It just, it seems odd to me. There are fairly well-known writers, and I don't just mean Burroughs, but writers who are big now, like with the initials D. J., who are fairly well known to have been heroin addicts who got straight. And they don't make it a secret. If I'd ever been a heroin addict, I don't think I'd have a problem saying it.

It's weird—I, like—I mean, I'm somebody who spent most of his life in libraries. I just, um, never lived that kind of dangerous life. I wouldn't even stick a needle in my arm.

How do you think that rumor got started?

Who—whom did you hear the rumor from?

Don't know.

[What do I say? From my office this early morning, while you were doing good work with shampoo, hair brush, and towel?]

It's very odd—I've got no idea how it got started. None. I think the only thing that I ever conceivably had a problem with was marijuana, and marijuana was a huge deal for me when I was about the age of Hal in the book. And then once I got to college, I mean, college was just so *hard,* it was hard to get stoned and read. And I just, it sort of melted away.

Getting-clean stuff is what you can't talk about—a program? Or what you were getting clean from?

[He looks at me, turns off tape.]

[Break]

I'm not in the program, and I wouldn't want it to come off like somebody who's in the program. And that's just how it's gotta be. [AA] And ask your friend—your friend will enlighten you about it. Talk to him. From what little I understand about it, talking to private citizens about it is very different. I believe, I don't know that much about it, but I *believe* the phrase in the eleventh tradition is "Maintain anonymity at the level of press, radio, and films." About which, it's one of the few things they're adamant about. Again, that's from . . . from what very little I understand. From what very little I understand.

Smoking out a lot in high school, less in college, then involved with drinking at Harvard?

Mmmm. I drank a lot in grad school, I drank a lot at Yaddo. But everybody did. You know? It's real weird. I don't know what—maybe it was a little different five years later, but the young writer deal, the thing was to go out and pound 'em with people and trade *bon mot*. And feel *pleased* at how successful we all were. And to do a little kinda, my dick's bigger than your dick, kinda contest of wit.

My mot *is more* bon *than yours.*

Exactly. Which is a pretty unsettling analogue to dick size, in a way.

This period—lasted from '87 to—

What, of drinking a lot?
     It's, it's, I'm not trying to be disingenuous, I honestly don't remember. And I, I, just to tell you truly, that if you structured this as some—"and then he spiraled into some terrible alcoholic thing," it would be inaccurate.
     It was more just like, I got more and more unhappy. And the more and more unhappy I would get, the more I would notice that I

would be drinking a lot more. And there wasn't any joy in the drinking. It was more like—it was literally an *anesthetic*. I mean, I just wanted to be dulled and blunt all the time. But the reasons for being unhappy I don't think had very much to do with drugs or alcohol.

So '85 out of Amherst, '87 leaving Arizona, then you go to Harvard . . .

Yeah—I started partying a lot in grad school.

Summer of '87 at Yaddo?

Yeah.

Then Harvard that fall?

No—I went back and lived in Tucson. I was finishing the book of stories. Let's see. I lived with my folks for like two months, went out to Tucson, lived there for a while.

Foundation Grant your folks gave you? That joke on the Girl with Curious Hair copyright page. [Sandwiched between the impressive "Corporation of Yaddo" and "The Giles Whiting Foundation," there's "The Jim and Sally Wallace Fund for Aimless Children."]

The "Fund for Aimless Children"—right? Yeah. Exactly.
    Yeah, they were *very* nice. They were like, you know, I was upstairs working all the time. And they would, like, not only cook the food, but they'd go to the store and get it. You know? It saved me a lot of time.

Only a two-month grant, though.

True. But I'm, as you can probably gather, not the most pleasant person in the world to live with.
    And then applied, I remember, to Harvard and Princeton, in '88, and decided to go there.

Why? Weren't you bored and done with the academic environment by then?

Yeah—I was just really stuck about writing. And um, like a lot of the reasons why I was writing, and a lot of the things that I thought were cool about writing, I'd sort of run out of gas on. And I didn't know . . . I didn't know . . . what to do. I didn't know whether I really loved to write or whether I'd just gotten kind of excited about having some early success. That story at the end of *Curious,* which not a lot of people like, was really meant to be extremely sad. And to sort of be a kind of suicide note. And I think by the time I got to the end of that story, I figured that I wasn't going to write anymore.

That my whole take—that at first I thought writing was empty and just all a game. And then I realized that my take on it was hopelessly empty, and that it *was* a game. And it was after finishing that and doing the editing on that, that I remember getting really unhappy.

And it *sounds* weird—but I think it was almost more of a like, sort of an artistic and a religious crisis, than it was anything you would call a breakdown. I just—all my reasons for being alive and the stuff that I thought was important, just truly at a gut level weren't working anymore. Does this make sense to you personally at all?

[Gentlemanly: He believes he's flattering me by treating me as a matching peer.]

It also makes sense to me in terms of what you were telling me about your history. But tell me more about it personally.

What do you mean in terms of my history?

Well, I mean you had done football for a while, and then you'd stopped because there were guys who were bigger than you. And then you'd done tennis for a while—I guess for about five years.

Yeah, except that stuff's all, you can tell by external measurements, how well you're doing with that. The writing stuff's all internal.

But it may have felt to you as if there was a sort of pattern. Where you would do something for five years, and then there'd be some reason you'd be required to stop?

Yeah—and I did heavy-duty like semantics and math logic for about five years, and then switched to writing. Yeah, you're right; I think I really perceived myself as kind of a dilettante. Um, I don't know, you're right. I hadn't realized that. I owe you sixty dollars.

So for that reason, it would make sense that there would be a five-year point where there'd be a moving-on crisis. Except there was no physical and no intellectual reason for you to stop writing.

It's weird though—but I started hating everything that I did. I mean I did, I remember I did two different novellas after "Westward," that I worked very hard on, that were just so *unbelievably* bad. They were, like, worse than stuff I'd done when I was first starting in college. Hopelessly confused. Hopelessly bending in on themselves in all kinds of . . .

And um, anyway, the reason I applied to philosophy grad school is I remembered that I had flourished in an academic environment. And I had this idea that I could, uh, that I could read philosophy and do philosophy, and write on the side, and that it would make the writing better.

'Cause see, by this time, my ego's all invested in the writing, right? It's the only thing that I've gotten, you know, food pellets from the universe for, to the extent that I wanted.

So I feel really trapped: Like, "Uh-oh, my five years is up. I've gotta move on, but I don't want to move on." And I was really stuck. And drinking was part of that. And it's true that I don't drink anymore. But it wasn't that I was stuck because I drank. I mean, it was more that—and it wasn't, it wasn't like social drinking going out of control. It was like, I really sort of felt like my life was over at twenty-seven or twenty-eight. And I didn't wanna, and that felt really bad, and I didn't wanna feel it.

And so I would do all kinds of things: I mean, I would drink real heavy, I would like fuck strangers. Oh God—or, then, for two weeks I wouldn't drink, and I'd run ten miles every morning. You know, that kind of desperate, like very *American,* "I will fix this somehow, by taking radical action."

And uh, you know, that lasted for a, that lasted for a couple of years.

Like Jennifer Beals, more or less. In Flashdance, solving Pittsburgh.

And it's weird: I think a lot of it comes out of the sports training. You know? (Schwarzenegger voice) "If there's a problem, I vill train my way out of it. I vill get up earlier, I vill vork harder." And that shit worked on me when I was a kid, but you know . . .

Everyone I know—and then people like Michael Chabon—has had second-book crises.

But my second book, it was weird, was "Westward," and it itself went pretty well, it was just a . . .

This is what's embarrassing. I know it's not that powerful for anybody, but I really felt like I'd blown, I'd blown out of the water, my whole sort of orientation to writing in that thing. Um, and had kind of written my homage and also patricidal killing thing to Barth. Who wasn't the only postmodern master I'd loved. But he was, I mean, "Lost in the Funhouse" is kind of the—what would you call it?—the trumpets, the trumpet call of postmodern metafiction.

Texture stuff in that book is really terrific also.

Now, do you really like it or are you just being nice? Not many people like that, and what I was told is you cannot really expect the reader to have read something twenty years earlier in order to get your thing. That's very pretentious but . . .

[He thinks I mean his story, not Barth's.]

Um, you talk about, I've said that three or four times somethin' came alive to me, and started kind of writing itself, and that was one of them. Although it wasn't a very happy experience.

I have other friends who hid out in academic environments afterwards, on later books, missed the discipline, the clear hours.

Well, it's pretty, it's pretty obvious, you know, what it is. What it is, is that, at a certain point you really, you have to grow up a little bit. You have to impose your own discipline—you're not in a workshop anymore.

I mean, my first two books had been written sort of under professors. Um, that's very hard. Um—and you also, I mean, your first book is play, and it's all possibility and promise. And then in the second book, it's sort of like, "All right, the first book was very lucky and you got a chance to do this. Now are you gonna do it or not?" And it's this whole—I don't know. Yeah, I think, I doubt what I went through is very different than what anybody else went through. The only difference for me is that it was very sharp, and very . . . and it was of reasonably short duration. I mean, it was like a little under two years. But it was exquisitely—it's the most horrible period I've ever gone through.

[Beeper on his watch keeps going off.]

Let's talk some more about this: this is '88—the really big difference is it was happening to you and not to somebody else.

Sure.

This two years is '88 to '90: when was the suicide watch period?

When did I go in there?

This is at McLean's?

How do you know that name?

I know people from Boston—not from there, who know you, but who—

No, there's lot of places in Boston. But McLean is . . . Actually, I did end up going to McLean, 'cause that's what the Harvard insurance was on the plan for.

Liz Wurtzel went.

God, she and I probably were on the same fucking shuttle bus from this.

Never put on antidepressants?

Um, I was early on, I was for about two months in college. It was for something else—oh no, I had terrible *insomnia.* And I didn't want to take Dalmane because I was drinking so much. So I told this long story, and they put me on something, they put me on a tricyclic. Which, I don't know how antidepressants are supposed to work, but this had the opposite effect for me. It made me feel like I was stoned and in hell. So, no, that was never an option.

They talked about shock a little bit. [Like the Kate Gompert character in *Infinite Jest*] And I decided—in a weird way, there's a whole chapter with sort of Kate Gompert lying there and the doctor talking, except it's very kind of different.

She wants it, the shock.

She wanted it. And I could see, I could see that if this got much worse, that I would be, it's sort of like somebody . . .

[The tape side runs out.]

• • •

OUR PLANE IS CALLED, OUR FLIGHT IS CANCELLED

Should we just rush the Eagle desk?

We can wait ten minutes, because there'll be a line there.

I could drive us to Chicago.

Yeah, lemme chew this for two more minutes, and then let me call Holly, and I'm gonna do what Holly tells me to do. This is the great thing, I'm not the boss. She decides, and she'll tell me what to do.

I'm not concerned about—I mean, I don't mind havin' somebody know I was on suicide watch in McLean. I'm concerned, I don't want to make this into a romantic, lurid, tormented-artist thing. What I'm telling you is, this had way more to do with—I mean this wasn't a chemical imbalance, and this wasn't because of drugs and alcohol.

This was more just, I think I had lived an incredibly American life. That, "Boy, if I could just achieve X and Y and Z, everything would be OK." And I think had really—I think I got very very lucky. I got to have a midlife crisis at like twenty-seven. Which at the time didn't seem lucky; now it seems to me fairly lucky. And I know that you don't quite believe some of my stuff about like why I'm not gonna take money for this book. But now maybe now you can understand. That period, nothing before or since has ever been that bad for me. And I am willing to make *enormous* sacrifices never to go back there.

And if giving up the chance at a lot of money for this book—it's an acceptable, that's an acceptable price, and it's not because I'm a great person. It's because I think I got really lucky, feeling like I got given certain other reasons to work and to live during this time, and I *do not* want to fuck with it. I don't. So I live—so I'm real *careful* now. And it's also why I think I cultivate normality.

[Hard to feel steady with someone saying this: Normality can't be cultivated, in the same way, as David points out in the books, that you can't try to be sincere. You either are sincere or not: It needs to be affectless.]

Um, the thing about shock is, I never had shock, and they never gave me shock. But I *realized,* I realized, I sort of got an idea of the continuum I was on. You know? And at one side was the way I usually was. And I could see—there's a fair amount of stuff in the book about depression, that is not, it's not *exactly* autobiographical, but it's lookin' I think about a quarter mile farther down on the road. I mean, I could see the filter dropping over my vision, you know, I could see the distortions.

And I think at a certain point these folks—have I ever met? Yeah, I met somebody there who'd been given shock, which scares the *shit*—you know, I'm like you, my brain's what I've got. The idea of the brain being hurt—but I could see that at a certain point, you might beg for it, the same way, like in *Alien,* they say, "Kill me, kill me." You know? Because it would be—right? There's a thing in the book—I like this thing in the book: when people jump out of a burning skyscraper, it's not that they're not afraid of falling anymore, it's that the alternative is so awful. And then you're invited to consider what could be so awful, that leaping to your death, you know, seems like an escape from it.

And I admit I have got a grim fascination with that stuff. I'm not Elizabeth Wurtzel. I'm not biochemically depressed. But I feel like I got to dip my toe in that wading pool and, um, not going back there is more important to me than *anything*. It's like worse than anything— I don't know if you've had any experience with this. It's worse than any kind of physical injury, or any kind of—it may be what in the old days was called a spiritual crisis or whatever. It's just feeling as though the entire, every axiom of your life turned out to be false, and there was actually nothing, and *you* were nothing, and it was all a delusion. And that you were better than everyone else because you saw that it was a delusion, and yet you were worse because you couldn't function. And it was *just,* it was just horrible. And trying to be at Harvard, and to read about "freedom of the will" with John Rawls while thinking this way was just extremely unpleasant.

Anyway, that's that story. And I don't mind—it's not a privacy issue. I'd be concerned: I don't want to come off like I'm romanticizing it or something. [Somehow this is the saddest.]

Not at all how it sounds. It clarifies to me why you don't want to fuck with your rhythm.

[Typical shift: Slurp-spits an ice cube into his glass; he's chewing tobacco.]

Just between you and me, so I feel like I'm talking. Is that, do you have any experience with anything like this?

• • •

LATER

I think part of it, I just had never *lived,* everybody I knew was in that world. I had no idea, I had no idea that 90 percent of what I was getting out of books I really loved was this sense of a conversation around loneliness.

[We're standing at the entrance to Bloomington airport, smoking next to electric doors, talking about school and writing.]

I thought it was all, I really thought I was a head. That I was nothing but a head. And I think this period in my late twenties, when my head hurt so bad, that I had to find some other part of my body, you know, to like live in. And that I even started to suspect—and it's not like I had any kind of experience. Or I've come to any conclusions. It's more like I just threw a lot of stuff out.

And the great irony about this—maybe you can understand this. I, I, I'm not being disingenuous, the stuff about the fuss about the book [the soft glaze he keeps using for it: "the fuss about the book"], and people thinking the book is great, is *nice*. But the thing I really like is that it's not more important to me. You know? Like, like I really loved workin' on this book. I worked as hard, harder on it, than *anything*. You know? And I decided this is a little experiment. I was gonna do it for the sake of the book. Fuck it. If I couldn't even sell it, fuck it. You know? That I really sort of—you know at the end of *Thief,* when James Caan tears up the picture of his life?

Michael Mann. I didn't see it.

Really? That's not a bad movie. Well, the end is kind of stupid.

It means to me like, this is sort of what happened to me. You know, it was probably very much the same for you. You know, you're in Brown, who's gonna make it, who's not? And then you get, like, you start being able to make a living. So you get all that affirmation from the exterior, that when you're a young person you think will make everything *all right*. And I realize that sounds reductive and pop psych or whatever. But to realize—like you say, when it happens to *you,* when you yourself realize, "Holy shit, this *doesn't* make everything all right." Um, for me, it fucked with my sort of "metaphysics of living" in an incredibly deep way.

And I think that the ultimate way you and I get lucky is if you have some success early in life, you get to find out *early* it doesn't mean anything. Which means you get to start *early* the work of figuring out what *does* mean something. And the biggest thing that I like about what's going on, to be totally honest—and see, you're being very good, 'cause now I'm starting to like you, and so I'm saying this stuff, and it may sound crazy. I really like that this doesn't, that this isn't that big a deal to me. That it like—it's *nice*.

But what I really remember is the times when working on that book was really hard. And I just gutted it out, you know? And I finished something. And I did it for the book, not trying to imagine whether David Lipsky would like it, or Michael Pietsch would like it. And that I feel like I've built some muscles inside me that I can now use for the rest of my life. And I feel like, "All right, like I'm a writer now." Whether I'm a successful writer or not, I don't know. But like, like this is who I am, this is what I do. And I know now how to live in such a way that I'm doing it for the work itself. Which I'm aware can kinda come off sounding very pretentious. And it's also, it's what everybody says: "Ah, that other stuff doesn't matter."

What I'm trying to say to you is, I went through a period so bad, that that stuff *had* to stop mattering to me, or I think I would've blown my brains out. I came reasonably close. Or I could have at least tried in such a way that I would have damaged myself trying horribly.

[Break]

• • •

ONLY SOLUTION: WE'RE DUE IN MINNEAPOLIS TONIGHT
THE FLIGHTS FROM BLOOMINGTON ARE ALL BEING HELD, SO
WE'RE GOING TO GO BACK IN MY RENTED GRAND AM, OVER THE
SLICK ROADS, OFF TO CHICAGO/O'HARE

[We're finishing two more cigarettes in the automatic airport door now. Flexing our fingers, smoking—it's cold in the outdoor breeze.]

I suspect—I'm not saying I've been successful at it. But I think that if avant-garde stuff can do its job, it is tremendously difficult and not that accessible, and seduces the reader into making extraordinary efforts that he wouldn't normally make. And that that's the kind of magic that really great art can do.

But the best thing is to show what TV can't, to use the ways books are better than TV.

Except of course the hard thing is to do both at the same time. Because a book has to teach a reader how to read it. So the structure stuff starts right at the beginning.

   We sit around and bitch about how TV has ruined the audience for reading—when really all it's done is given us the really precious gift of making our job harder. You know what I mean? And it seems to me like the harder it is to make a reader feel like it's worthwhile to read your stuff, the better a chance you've got of making real art. Because it's only real art that does that.

But as it gets more complex, reader will feel they've wandered into a class-room where they missed the first few weeks of the course.

You teach the reader that he's way smarter than he thought he was. I think one of the insidious lessons about TV is the meta-lesson that you're dumb. This is all you can do. This is easy, and you're the sort of person who really just wants to sit in a chair and have it easy. When in fact there are parts of us, in a way, that are a lot more ambitious than that. And what we need, I think—and I'm not saying I'm the person to do it. But I think what we need is seriously engaged art, that can teach again that we're smart. And that there's stuff that TV and movies—although they're great at certain things—cannot give us. But that have to create the motivations for us to want to do the extra work, you know, to get these other kinds of art. And I think you can see it in the visual arts, I think you can see it in music . . .

Easier though, I'd think. Makes them realize it's more fun faster.

Which is tricky, because you want to seduce the reader, but you don't want to pander or manipulate them. I mean, a good book teaches the reader how to read it.

[Later: hoped to shift attention from himself. Note in front of his ISU office: "D. F. Wallace is out of town on weird personal authorized emergencyish leave from 2/17/96 to 3/3/96 and from 3/5/96 to 3/10/96."]

The old tricks have been exploded, and I think the language needs to find new ways to pull the reader. And my personal belief is a lot of it has to do with voice, and a feeling of intimacy between the writer and the reader. That sorta, given the atomization and loneliness of contemporary life—that's our opening, and that's our gift. That's a very personal deal, and here are seventeen ways to do it.

[Later]

There's a thing in Lester Bangs's *Psychotic Reactions and Carburetor Dung,* about certain music giving you an erection of the heart. And that term really resonates for me. "The Balloon" gave me an erection of the heart. ["The Balloon," a Donald Barthelme short story.]

For me a fair amount of aesthetic experience is—is erotic. And I think a certain amount of it has to do with this weird kind of intimacy with the person who made it.

No other medium gives that to you?

Yeah—although you feel a kind of weird intimacy with actors in drama, although it's a bit different. *That's* more I think an enabling of the fantasy that you are them, or getting you to desire them as a body or something. It's interesting: I've never read really good essays about the different kinds of seduction in different kinds of art.

Achievement?

I have a more nebulous idea of achievement. I guess getting a really good review in *The New York Times* when I was twenty-five was what, what'd you say?—two and a quarter—would be when you were twenty-five. What's interesting is that five years ago, I would have, I think I would have sneered at you and said, "Uh. How bourgeois." When in fact, what I think I've realized now is that we're basically exactly the same, we've all got our jungle gyms, you know? And because of the world you grew up in, it's success. And the world I grew up in, my parents didn't care that much about money, but they cared a whole lot about sort of professional prestige within their communities. If you write philosophy books, you're basically worrying a whole lot about what other philosophers think, and that's just about it.

My mom is a painter: a different code from the world she was in . . .

Did you admire her?

I did. And I still do admire her. The pain of it was hard to be a part of. You know, it was in my house, do you know what I mean? So it was hard to . . .

Sure. I bet she must have hurt real bad over it too.

[Strange, warm, small-town counselor sound]

She's witty, and she reads Emerson and Nietzsche and all that, so I think she found something funny in it. But it was also really hard. To watch. I mean, you know . . .

(Soft voice) Yeah. No, I know what you mean. It'll be interesting— I'll bet, I mean, I don't know you, but I'll bet there'll come a time when you realize you're always gonna have about as much success as you need, and that's fine. Where you'll just feel like you can draw a free breath about it. And maybe not for all time—it's just, that's sort of, that's the best thing about what's going on right now. Is I feel like, "You know what? This doesn't run me." And it's flattering to have *Rolling Stone* send you out here. But it doesn't, it doesn't mean to me what it would have meant to me ten years ago. And I realize that that's precious.

Why?

Because if it means that much to me, then I'm real fragile and real breakable. 'Cause what if you *don't* come? Or what if you don't like me? Or what if the next thing gets a bad review, you know what I mean? 'Cause then I'm like—what am I like? Well, then I'm like something made of glass, that has to be treated just a certain way or he breaks. Right? And I don't mean, I mean, I'm not a guru, it's not like I'm exempt from this stuff. I just remember real well how much it used to mean.

What would it have meant ten years ago?

I think it probably would have just hastened things. Because it would have been absolutely great, I would have tried *incredibly* hard to impress you, in about a thousand different ways. Would have put on a whole lot of faux stuff, you would have left, I would have waited on tenterhooks for the article, the article would have come out. And if it wasn't savage, I would have had exactly an hour of a kind of *greasy thrill* about it. And then there would have been a feeling of utter emptiness. Which is the feeling of, "Now I'm back to being made of glass, what's the next thing I'm going to find that's gonna handle me just right?" You know what I mean?

   And it's not like that I'm not like that at all, anymore. But I'm just like, I know that when all this is over—I know that the biggest part of me is looking forward to all this *bein'* over, so I can get back to work. And that that's the most important thing. And that that's good because I can live that way. I can't—if I depend on this, then I'm gonna be miserable except for once every five years? You know what I mean?

[Screwing up his face]

That's well said.

But it's not just well said—I mean, it's really truth, I mean I'm really telling you the truth.

It'd be like being a sort of veteran courtesan who didn't need to get paid exactly anymore . . .

Yeah; that's a good example. It's being a really good whore but knowing that the clocks tickin', and that various things are headin' south.

I'm worried about you calling Holly. [Holly, his publicist at Little, Brown, is set to issue a decision about our getting to Minneapolis.]

["Welcome to Bloomington-Normal," an airport sign says. "We're sold on Bloomington-Normal—Armstrong Realty."
    We're standing in the opening and shutting automatic door, talking about graduate school.]

Fights—the professors'd say, Don't use pop references (a) because they're banal and stupid, and (b) because they date your piece. And it's just sort of like, I mean I think, I don't know about you, what kind of stuff you do. Me and a lot of the other young writers I know, we use these references sort of the way the romantic poets use lakes and *trees.* I mean, they're just part of the mental furniture. That you carry around.

Shakespeare used Greek myths the same way.

Although I'm also aware—the culture has a whole weird, complicated relation to its pop self, or something like that. Because I know that, like, when I make that *Gilligan* reference in class, everybody laughs. And there's a jagged edge to it. Because everybody's a little uncomfortable with how familiar it is. I mean, so there's this whole, there's this very neurotic relation to it. But a lot of that stuff I don't much think about in the writing. A lot of that stuff to me is just kind of like . . . describing a landscape or something.

[I tell David I'm very interested in the married relationships question—how people maintain emotional and physical interest.]

Is that why you're not married at thirty? Is that kind of a chilling . . . ?

Why aren't you married at thirty-four?

You first.

Um—I think it's hard to fill that role . . . to cast it and to fill it when you know it's for thirty or forty years . . . someone who, whatever mental landscape you're in, they're going to be in it too, you need someone who'll fit any landscape you can imagine.

I'm not that systematic about it. I've come close a few times, and each of those times that I came close involved, you know, a three- or four-year thing. And then when it didn't work out—if a few of them don't work out, then you've been sort of *at large* for nine or twelve years, and you haven't gotten married. I think the larger thing is probably that I am . . . that I tend to be interested in women that I turn out not to get along very well with. And the ones that I get along very well with, I'm not interested in in a kind of romantic way. So that I've got a lot of really good women friends. But I tend to have a really hard time with girlfriends, because the ones I'm attracted to are a lot of fun you know for, in the standard ways, for like a couple of weeks. But in terms of the daily, let's-go-shopping stuff, that we tend not to get along really well.

Why not?

I don't know. And I have friends who say that this is something that would be worth looking into with someone that you pay. But a lot of it too is that—yeah, I don't think of it, I can't put it as well as you did about the mental landscapes, I just know I'm hard to be around. Because kind of when I want to be by myself, like to work, I really want to be myself. And I will just go away. And women don't like that. Unless they themselves are writers, and then in which case I don't want to watch *them* go away.

Is that—not our taxi.

That's not for us. You were incorrect . . .

[Car glazed over with ice. Like Batmobile. All contours smoothed. David gets the scraper out of the trunk, goes to work: windshield, chunks of spray, back window.]

This is an adventure. Don't lose the scraper. This is my good-luck scraper. A good Midwestern boy develops a relationship with his scraper.

[We're driving. Out from the tangle of the airport. David has brought a Savarin coffee can for his chewing tobacco.
　　Savarin can falls over on hard turn.]

You don't want to do that after the spittoon is full.

[We're on I-55—slushy and crowded—driving to Chicago.]

Why did movie idea, in Infinite Jest, attract you? I have a hard time turning off a TV.

I would have a real hard time talking about it in any way that you would be able to get a paragraph—Jesus, what's *wrong* with people today?

[Road conditions, swervers jumping into our lane.]
    What the fuck is with him?

Did you get movie idea first, or come to you later?

How is it when you work?

[We talk about Philip Roth . . .]

Roth writes for two years, but mostly to get voice. Throws away all for eighteen months, writes book in last six.

I think that's sort of what happened to me. Except it was more like three years of doing other stuff that stank, that then sorta set me up to do this. This was a weird thing because this started on page one, and ended on the last page. I was working on it in order. It sort of . . .

Written in the order it has now, more or less?

Yeah—the changes are from Michael's cuts, I had to move things around. It's quite a bit shorter than it was.

Twice as long before?

No. It wasn't that much longer. It was about five hundred pages longer. Of which four hundred unambiguously needed to go, and the other hundred was painful.

That's like losing a whole novel.

It's not really a novel; it's not supposed to *be* a novel.
    The definition of novel is . . . I never thought of this as a novel, I thought of it as a long story.

The whole time you were working on it?

No actually—the original title was *A Failed Entertainment*. The idea is that the book is structured as an entertainment that doesn't work. Because what entertainment ultimately leads to, I think, is the movie *Infinite Jest*. I mean, that's the star it's steering by. Entertainment's chief job is to make you so riveted by it that you can't tear your eyes away, so the advertisers can advertise. And the tension of the book is try to make it at once extremely entertaining—and also sort of warped, and to sort of shake the reader awake about some of the things that are sinister in entertainment.

Like what?

Oh, Jesus.

[Long pause: Clicking of turn signal, swabbing of wipers]

Y'like candy?

Yeah. Of course.

What if you ate it all the time? What would be wrong with that?

Bad for teeth and very fat very quick.

Real pleasurable, but it dudn't have any calories in it. There's somethin' really vital about food that candy's missing, although to make up for what it's missing, the pleasure of masticating and swallowing goes way up. There seems to me to be some analogy to what—I'm talking about very seductive commercial entertainment. There's nothing sinister, the thing that's sinister about it is that the pleasure that it gives you to make up for what it's missing is a kind of . . . addictive, self-consuming pleasure. And what saves us is that most entertainment isn't very good. (Laughs)

Addictive how? Like Die Hard—the best action, probably.

The first *Die Hard?* I think it's a great film.

Brilliant, right? Sharp script, smarter than most art movies.

But also very formulaic, and rather cynically reusing a lot of formulas.

Terrence Rafferty's line: "a formula action picture, but the extra-strength formula . . ." That film is about as good as an action film can get . . . consequences keep mounting up as they don't usually in that sort of movie.

Uh-huh.

That kind of movie then? Or MTV? Or TV?

I guess entertainment would describe a continuum—I guess what I'm talkin' about is entertainment versus art, where the main job of entertainment is to separate you from your cash somehow. I mean that's really what it is . . . And I'm not, there's nothin' per se wrong with that. And the compensation for that is it delivers value for the cash. It gives you a certain kind of pleasure that I would argue is fairly *passive*. There's not a whole lot of thought involved, the thought is often fantasy, like "I am this guy, I'm having this adventure." And it's a way to take a vacation from myself for a while. And that's fine—I think sort of the same way *candy* is fine.

[Of course, one interesting thing is he buys Pop-Tarts and stuff to eat; lots of candy.]

The problem for me is in entertainment, it's, at least in the book— God, if the book comes off as some kind of indictment of entertainment, then it fails. It's sort of about our relationship to it. The book isn't supposed to be about *drugs,* getting off drugs. Except as the fact that drugs are kind of a metaphor for the sort of addictive continuum that I think has to do with how we as a culture relate to things that are alive.

[David talking, and the wipers going, and the other cars sort of leaving wakes ahead of us, as visuals for serious thoughts about entertainment. His point about five hundred thousand bits of information.]

So I think it's got something to do with, that we're just—we're absolutely dying to give ourselves away to something. To run, to escape, somehow. And there's some kinds of escape—in a sort of Flannery O'Connorish way—that end up, in a twist, making you confront yourself even more. And then there are *other* kinds that say, "Give me seven dollars, and in return I will make you forget your name is David Wallace, that you have a pimple on your cheek, and that your gas bill is due."

And that that's fine, in low doses. But that there's something about the machinery of our relationship to it that makes low doses—we don't *stop* at low doses.

You were talking about passion, with regard to Hal and others giving themselves away to a discipline, as opposed to entertainment.

[Hal is the lead character in the tennis academy sections. Meanwhile, I want to pull over to the shoulder and knock ice off the noisy loud rubbery wipers.]

I'm not saying there's something sinister or horrible or wrong with entertainment. I'm saying it's—I'm saying it's a continuum. And if the book's about anything, it's about the question of why am I watching so much shit? It's not about the shit; it's about me. Why am I doing it? And what is so American about what I'm doing?

The only thing that I knew for sure, I wanted to do something that wasn't just high comedy, I wanted to do something that was very, very much about America. And the things that ended up for me being most distinctively *American* right now, around the millennium, had to do with both entertainment and about some kind of weird, addictive, um . . . wanting to give yourself away to something. That I ended up thinking was kind of a distorted religious impulse. And a lot of the AA stuff in the book was mostly an excuse, was to try to have—it's very hard to talk about people's relationship with any kind of God, in any book later than like Dostoyevsky. I mean the culture, it's all wrong for it now. You know? No, no. Plausibly realistic characters don't sit around talking about this stuff. You know?

So . . . I don't know. But the minute I start *talking* about it, it just, it sounds number one: very vague. Two: really reductive. And the whole thing to me was so complicated, that you know it took sixteen hundred pages of sort of weird oblique stuff to even start to talk about it. And so I feel *stupid,* talking about it.

Why?

Extemporaneously. I feel stupid talking about it this way. Because it's like, because I don't have a diagnosis. I don't have a system of prescriptions. I don't have four things that I think are wrong. I don't have four different . . . opinions about it. It seems to me that it's more of a feeling, a sort of texture of *feeling.*

You know, why are *we*—and by "we" I mean people like you and me: mostly white, upper middle class or upper class, *obscenely* well educated, doing really interesting jobs, sitting in really expensive chairs, watching the *best,* you know, watching the most sophisticated electronic equipment money can buy—why do we feel empty and unhappy?

[But that's in *Hamlet,* too, just w/o the channel surfing.] You know? And you put the question that way, as a rhetorical question, and it's Yeah yeah yeah yeah. But what the book's tryin' to do, is put questions like that in a way so that it's hooked into your gut a little bit, and you *feel* some stuff about it. And you feel like, "Hey, this is *me* a little bit." And, and . . .

Not being reductive or simple at all.

[Break. Oddly, the writer who does approach, finds a way to talk about religion, is Stephen King, who he thinks is underrated. He gets toward it in *The Stand*.]

This isn't for the tape, this is just for you—because he's got this part about that. [In *The Stand*] You've gotta look real closely to see what's cool about King, because most of it's I think very cynical shit.

He tries to sound how people really speak, although he's got two or three tricks. He's just got a real limited range; he can do the same character and brain voice over and over and over again—which would be fine if he didn't write two books a year.

[We talk more about Stephen King . . . whose work he knows astonishingly well.]

Moving away from cars-possessed-by-the-devil to *Stand by Me,* which is a coming-of-age story that has a sweetness about it. The kid in *Firestarter,* just that girl is real interesting. He's got an almost Salingerian feel for children . . .

Oh—the reason why I think you oughta do a book about TV, is this problem is not gonna go away. I don't know about you, but in ten or fifteen years, we're gonna have virtual reality pornography. Now, if I don't develop some machinery for being able to turn off pure unalloyed pleasure, and allow myself to go out and, you know, grocery shop and pay the rent? I don't know about you, but I'm gonna have to leave the *planet. Virtual. Reality. Pornography.* I'm talking, you know what I mean? The technology's gonna get better and better at doing what it does, which is seduce us into being incredibly dependent on it, so that advertisers can be more confident that we will watch their advertisements. And as a technology system, it's amoral.

It doesn't . . . it doesn't have a responsibility to care about us one whit more than it does: It's got a job to do. The moral job is ours. You know, Why am I watching five hours a day of this? I mean, why am I getting 75 percent of my calories from candy? I mean, that's something that a little tiny child would do, and that would be all right. But we're postpubescent, right? Somewhere along the line, we're supposed to have grown up.

But if the most intelligent, promising, and educated people go into designing the candy, then it's impossible to turn down.

Then we're talking about Turkish delight and C. S. Lewis. If I can put it into a couple of sentences that you can quote: see, it's more like, Yeah, this is the problem. Is that, is that entertainment lies on the addictive continuum. And we're saved right now, because it's just not all that good.

But if you notice that like—I'll watch five or six, I'll zone out in front of the TV for five or six hours, and then I feel depressed and empty. And I wonder why. Whereas if I eat candy for five or six hours, and then I feel sick, I *know* why.

Reason I feel bad is guilt. My parents operated a very clear and effective NPR/PBS/New Yorker propaganda course: that TV is bad, it's a waste of time, you don't want to be somebody else's audience. And home is the most convenient place to be an audience.

It's not bad or a waste of your time. Any more than, you know, masturbation is bad or a waste of your time. It's a pleasurable way to spend ten minutes. But if you're doing it twenty times a *day*—or if your primary sexual relationship is with your own hand—then there's something wrong. I mean, it's a matter of degree.

Yeah—whereas at least if you wank off, at least some action has been performed. That you can point to it and say: yes, I have been effective.

All right—you could make me look like a real *dick* if you wanted to print this and extend the analogy. But there is a similarity. Yes, you're performing muscular movements with your hand as you're jerking off. But what you're doing is running a movie in your head, and having a fantasy relationship with somebody who isn't real, in order to stimulate a purely neurological response.

I think one of the reasons that I feel empty after watching a lot of TV, and one of the things that makes TV seductive, is that it gives the illusion of relationships with people. It's a way to have people in the room talking and being entertaining, but it doesn't require anything of me. I mean, I can see them, they can't see me. And, and, they're there for me, and I can, I can receive from the TV, I can receive entertainment and stimulation. Without having to give anything back but the most tangential kind of attention. And *that* is very seductive.

The problem is it's also very empty. Because one of the differences about having a *real* person there is that number one, I've gotta do some *work*. Like, he pays attention to me, I gotta pay attention to him. You know: I watch him, he watches me. The stress level goes up. But there's also, there's something nourishing about it, because I think like as creatures, we've all got to figure out how to be together in the same room.

And so TV is like candy in that it's more pleasurable and easier than the real food. But it also doesn't have any of the nourishment of real food. And the thing, what the book is supposed to be about is, What has happened to *us*, that I'm now willing—and I do this *too*—that I'm willing to derive enormous amounts of my sense of community and awareness of other people, from television? But I'm not willing to undergo the stress and awkwardness and potential *shit* of dealing with real people.

And that as the Internet grows, and as our ability to be linked up, like—I mean, you and I coulda done this through *e-mail*, and I never woulda had to meet you, and that woulda been easier for me. Right? Like, at a certain point, we're gonna have to build some machinery, inside our *guts*, to help us deal with this. Because the technology is just gonna get better and better and better and better. And it's gonna get easier and easier, and more and more convenient, and more and more pleasurable, to be alone with images on a screen, given to us by people who do not love us but want our money. Which is all right. In low doses, right? But if that's the basic main staple of your diet, you're gonna die. In a meaningful way, you're going to die. (Passionate)

But you developed some defenses?

No. This is the great thing about it, is that probably each generation has different things that force the generation to grow up. Maybe for our grandparents it was World War Two. You know? For us, it's gonna be that at, at a certain point, that we're either gonna have to put away childish things and discipline ourself about how much time do I spend being passively entertained? And how much time do I spend doing stuff that actually isn't all that much fun minute by minute, but that builds certain muscles in me as a grown-up and a human being? And if we *don't* do that, then (a) as individuals, we're gonna die, and (b) the culture's gonna grind to a halt. Because we're gonna get so interested in entertainment that we're not gonna want to do the work that generates the income that buys the products that pays for the advertising that disseminates the entertainment. [He loves the A-B, 1-2 construction.] It just seems to me like it's gonna be this very cool thing. Where the country could very well shut down and die, and it won't be anybody else doin' it to us, we will have done it to ourselves. (Laughs)

Actually come to that point?

No, again, we're talking about a continuum, and I'm talking about the end point. I'm talking about the logical extension.

I'm talking about ingenious problems where advertisers begin suddenly to realize that they have to make the shows less entertaining because absenteeism from work and the GNP is declining, and it's hurting their revenues. And that these corporations are going to perhaps run into very sort of ingenious double binds.

Maybe it's why daytime TV is so sloppy; they want to encourage you to be in your office.

No. Right now we have the *least* interesting double bind: the shows get less interesting so that the commercials seem more interesting by comparison. Or the shows seem more like commercials, so that the commercials seem less like *intrusions* than seamless parts of the shows. Those are all fairly easy to see, and they're not very interesting double binds.

The real interesting double binds are going to be when cable comes, and the initial, the initial—the immediate advertising-revenue motivation is lost. And it's more done, now done through Pay-Per-View or subscription.

Like the Web, the "Interlace" in the book—in fifteen years?

Yep. And the big thing, if you're doin' movies or packaging any sort of thing, is to get in on the Interlace grid. That Interlace will be this enormous gatekeeper. It will be like sort of the one publishing house from hell. They decide what you get and what you don't.

Because this idea that the Internet's gonna become incredibly democratic? I mean, if you've spent any time on the Web, you know that it's not gonna be, because that's completely overwhelming. There are four trillion bits coming at you, 99 percent of them are shit, and it's too much work to do triage to decide.

So it's very clearly, very soon there's gonna be an economic niche opening up for gatekeepers. You know? Or, what do you call them, Wells, or various nexes. Not just of interest but of quality. And then things get real interesting. And we will beg for those things to be there. Because otherwise we're gonna spend 95 percent of our time body-surfing through shit that every joker in his basement—who's not a pro, like you were talking about last night. I tell you, there's no single more interesting time to be alive on the planet Earth than in the next twenty years. It's gonna be— you're gonna get to watch all of human history played out again real quickly. [Odd—a passive TV metaphor here, ending this passionate speech: we'll be watching.]

Why? What meant, exactly?

If you go back to Hobbes, and why we ended up begging, why people in a state of nature end up begging for a ruler who has the power of life and death over them? We absolutely have to give our power away. The Internet is going to be exactly the same way. Unless there are walls and sites and gatekeepers that say, "All right, you want fairly good fiction on the Web? Let us pick it for you." Because it's gonna take you four days to find something any good, through all the shit that's gonna come, right?

We're going to beg for it. We are literally gonna pay for it. But once we do that, then all these democratic hoo-hah dreams of the Internet will of course have gone down the pipes. And we're back again to three or four Hollywood studios, or four or five publishing houses, being the . . . right? And all of us who *grouse,* all the anarchists who grouse about power being localized in these media elites, are gonna realize that the actual system dictates that. The same way—I'm absolutely convinced—that the despot in Hobbes is a logical extension of what the State of Nature is.

[Later, airplane: Dave reading in-flight catalog about a dog dish setup that doesn't stress the canine spine.]

The posture dogs have been eating off of for fifty million years hasn't been doing them a stitch of good.

[Talks slangily, like Huck Finn grown up and Ph.D.-ed, Huck with doctorate.]

• • •

IN THE GRAND AM
STILL ON I-55, ROAD TO O'HARE

[To tape] *Dave's saying he notices on days when he brushes his teeth with his left hand as opposed to his right hand that he thinks more interestingly.*

[Mouthful of tobacco, "No Seatbelt" tinging from dashboard] Best of luck putting that into any kind of context that'll be interesting. "As we drove up to Chicago, Dave began a system of loose associations, some of which follow here."

[Break]   .

[Trying to track O'Hare signs into actual O'Hare, with mixed results.]

This is what's known as the David Wallace driving maneuver, over-reliance on signs.

[Break]

[I ask if he thinks his being handsome helps him.]

You'd have to come and put me down if I even *start* thinking that way.

To begin thinking what way? About how books are sold, or about the qualities of your book?

Or about *toothsomeness* or whether—I mean there's a, there is a part of me that, you know, that wrestles with every one of these questions. Do you want to do a *Rolling Stone* interview, do you want to do X, do you want to do Y—that worries that what I'm doing right now is being a whore. And you know cashing in somehow, or getting some little celebrity for myself. That will, from some bizarre set of misunderstandings, sell more copies of the book. Fine, and you can quote that. I'd prefer you do it, if you did it, in a context where I didn't sound just like a total dweeb.

No, in fact I'd probably cut off the whore part. It's too much.

Yeah, you don't need—I mean, if I'm all that worried about being a whore, then why am I doing this? It sounds very easy to say, but it's just—it's sort of . . . When you say that, I'm not playing dumb, it's more like I'm, I'm sort of letting just one paw—one front paw of the tiger out of the cage to try to understand a little bit what it's about.

[Break]

I mean, there's a part of me that's still not real mature, that's afraid that, like, I would rather *not* be read and complain about it, and not feel like I had that pressure on me, you know? You know? My consciousness was really formed in this kind of avant-garde, neglected, if-you-get-a-lot-of-attention, therefore-you're-a-whore-and-an-idiot. And it's, I mean I've already said, it requires a certain amount of—I want to be able to reconfigure my map in a way that isn't just *conveniently* reversing all that stuff.

[Wipers making weird rubbing noise because ice is caught underneath the blades; a frozen, Midwestern-style problem.]

But doesn't end up with me, you know . . . I mean like, this has been fairly fun and hasn't hurt. And it's gotten me thinking about certain stuff. It's not like I'm doing it—it's not like I've done *twenty-five* of these, you know? Or that I'm going on like, you know, *Love Connection*. So and I don't want to go around wincin' about it.

[Break]

Is fiction going the way of poetry or no?

I think *avant-garde* fiction has *already* gone the way of poetry. And it's become involuted and forgotten the reader. Put it this way, there are a few really good poets who suffered because of the desiccation and involution of poetry, but for the most part I think American poetry has gotten what it's deserved. And, uh, it'll come awake again when poets start speaking to people who have to pay the rent, and fuck the same woman for thirty years. That's off the record: that's really nasty.

Do you worry that fiction could end up becoming the kind of pleasant hobbyist's backwater that reading poetry has become?

If it does, it won't be the audience's fault. And it won't be TV's fault.

[Hiss of another Diet Pepsi can being cracked: little carbon dioxide sigh]

I disagree with you. I think it could easily be the audience's and TV's fault.

I have this—here's this thing where it's going to sound sappy to you. I have this *unbelievably* like five-year-old's belief that art is just absolutely magic.

And that good art can do things that *nothing* else in the *solar system* can do. And that the good stuff will survive, and get read, and that in the great winnowing process, the shit will sink and the good stuff will rise.

[His watch beeps: I keep wondering if it's mine.]

But who's going to be trained to read acutely? I mean the skills you need to read, not for a computer, but for fiction, you'll lose the training.

But realize the limitations of space, time, and historical situation.

You're talking about nobody will be trained to read the way *we* read. Which means that if people are reading in more short bursts or whatever, that art will find a way to form conversations with readers in the brain voice or vernacular that they've got. And for a while, when they, you know, what's—is it Nietzsche's term or Heidegger's term? "The old gods have fled and the new gods have not come"? It will be a bleak time. But I mean—Jesus, if the thing made the jump from oral, you know, jongleur ballad, to printed text, then I think it can—

"O'Hare River Road," that's what we want. So you want to at some point to drift *left*. We're *clearly* not going to make the noon, are we?

No. It's 12:04 . . .

Shit. The next is one fifteen. We're going to have to go to the desk and change. She said that one fifteen was empty.

[Break]

What were you afraid of in the reception of the book?

I was afraid people would think it was sloppy, poorly—that it would seem like a *mess*. Instead of an intentional, very careful mess. That it would seem . . . But the fact that she would think that this was just every thought I seemed to have for three years put down on the page, just made my *bowels* turn to ice. [Re: Michiko Kakutani]

Because that was of course the great dark terror when I was writing it. Is that that's how it would come off. So seeing that she really really liked Updike was a tremendous shot in the arm. [Updike's *In the Beauty of the Lilies*]

Why?

Because Updike, I think, has *never* had an unpublished thought.

And that he's got an ability to put it in very lapidary prose. But that Updike presents one with a compressed Internet problem, is there's 80 percent absolute *dreck,* and 20 percent priceless stuff. And you just have to wade through so much purple gorgeous empty writing to get to anything that's got any kind of heartbeat in it. Plus, I think he's mentally ill.

You really do, don't you?

Yeah. I think he's a *nasty* person. And I'll tell you, if you think *I* hate him? Talk to—bring up his name to [to J. Franzen].

[Break]

. . .

12:45, WE'VE MADE IT
PARKED AT O'HARE AIRPORT
WE RUN—WE HAVE 20 MINUTES—
TO UNITED AIRLINES TICKET COUNTER, TO JETWAY, TO FLIGHT

Boy, are we gonna feel silly if this crashes.

[I mention that the woman at the United Airlines desk only had eyes for him. That Dave, on the road for three weeks, is pumping out celebrity glow, the look people give, the trim, radiant impression of being watchable.]

Yeah, it's the sweat pouring down—she was watching the sweat pour down my face. It drives 'em wild.

[In Bloomington, when we were talking with the ticket agent, and the flight was cancelled, he put his head down on the counter. And groaned. Also, the wintergreen smell from his chewing tobacco in the front seat. The ice on the car, the tobacco can spilling over.]

Just another of my series of, one long series of SNAFUs on the reading tour.

[In the car, he told me a funny story about reading at Iowa State. Also, the Richard Powers story: going to the writer for help when he was being asked to cut four hundred pages, very interesting. He wanted to raise the money and buy the rights back to the book.]

[As we walk down jetway: Dave still wondering if we should board.]

I always fear that when I really impose my will on something, the universe is gonna punish me.

• • •

ON PLANE NOW
PAGING THROUGH THE LIBRARY IN THE SEAT-BACK POCKET
THE GIFT CATALOGS, THE "SAFETY GUIDE TO THE BOEING 757"

[He's fascinated: he's *really* reading it. Everyone I know has always treated it as a hotel's Gideon Bible: drawer ballast, nothing you'd open.]

Does that affect your feeling of safety as you sort of are riding on—it looks like it requires two mild muscle spasms to remove the *door.* Bonk, bonk; bonk. Well. There's got to be some occlusive seal on it or something, right?

Also, it looks as if the jet is perhaps in flight, and he'd just gotten tired of being on the plane.

Exactly. He's sort of like, "You know, since we're on the grass, since we've landed on the grass, perhaps we'd like a *stroll.*" "Let's considerately wait by the soon-to-explode wing, and help people as they slide off of it."

[I remember what that guy Mark said at the Bloomington airport.]

Of course, the problem is the wings are full of fuel.

Yeah, not good to be over the wing. [Still fascinated by the Safety Guide.] This is what I like, is like: "How interesting. An oxygen mask has dropped down." Look, her eyes are totally unafraid. "I think I'll put it on. Why—no, I'll put one on my child." It's just this . . .

[Closes it, looks at cover. Clouds and sky.]

This was my major complaint about the cover of the book.

[Voice comes over Boeing PA: "Flight crew, take your positions, prepare for departure."]

Is that it looks—on American Airlines flights? The cloud system, it's almost *identical.*

[On safety booklet for 757]

Oh, that's funny. What did you want instead?

Oh, I had a number of—there's a great photo of Fritz Lang directing *Metropolis.* Do you know this one? Where he's standing there, and there are about a thousand shaven-headed men in kind of rows and phalanxes, and he's standing there with a megaphone? It wouldn't have been . . . Michael said it was too busy and too like conceptual, it required too much *brain work* on the part of the audience. . . .

Because you were making a metaphor on the cover?

No, I just thought it was *cool—*

They used the Brit version of my cover after they saw it. It's a cover I like.

Auhhh! (Dry shocked exhale of disappointment)

You didn't like that cover? I think it's good-looking.

No, it's *real* good-looking. It's just, why do *you* get to have any influence on, I—

[Break]

[I go to bathroom to make notes. He began that phrase by saying, "This I always find funny. That they don't seem at all worried. You know, just opening up the thing." It was the door illustration on the jet safety guide.]

[Looks at wing: we're juddering down the runway.] See the wing, see how it ripples and shudders slightly? Then you start thinking about, you know, like the *metallurgical* composition of the wing—and how well they've calculated the stresses.

[His fears of flying]

I wasn't all that good at physics in high school. And we're gonna— basically our lives are about to depend upon physics. What is it: the under exceeds over, there's lift?

CAPTAIN, ON PA: Good afternoon ladies and gentlemen, I'd like to welcome you aboard. This is United Airlines Flight 1453.

[Why he prefers crazy women; and feels he's ended up with lots of crazy ones . . .]

Psychotics, say what you want about them, tend to make the first move.

That's a great, great line. [To tape] *It's about the women he's dated. Because he's shy.*

[Break]

It's just much easier having dogs. You don't get laid; but you also don't get the feeling you're hurting their feelings all the time.

[I laugh.]

You don't, though, right?

He began by saying, "The thing is, it's just much easier having dogs."

I emphasize it's a platonic relationship with the dogs.

[Break]

[Told the counterwoman at UA, again: "Not on a date." "We're traveling together—not on a date."]

[The pilot came back to check the ice on the wing, and then when he explained what he was doing, he looked at us very squarely and said, "Do you know who I really like, gentlemen? Me."

   He seemed to think we were wondering why he'd take the trouble. A little disquieting.]

That's what he said? "You know who I really like?" Were we talking about who we liked?

[Pause]

Is this one of these deals where we have a sudden intuition, and bolt off the plane on the tarmac?

I think it's too late. I figure we just have to accept.

Hey. Look, read the packet: We're two arm motions away from liberty. Except then, of course, one would get out of a crash, but there's all this whole *Appointment in Samarra*–type madness. That story makes my stomach hurt. Or it's a *Twilight Zone* episode.

[Has brought Heinlein to read on flight]

You made some remark at the New York reading that Ethan Hawke took umbrage with.

No no no no no. It'd just come off—

Well, what it makes you look is glamorous . . .

No it doesn't. No, what it does—all right, I'll tell you. But if you use this, though, you've gotta tell the truth. Which, the truth is, what happened is, I got really nervous, and had one of these *brain farts*. One of those nanosecond inspirations. Another thing that's out of your mouth and then you're reaching for it. There was this whole long thing about "unsuccessful actors, the kind who would in previous decades have been in infomercials." It's all in the videophone thing. And then I'd inserted, "And Richard Linklater films." Thinking that he would not find this hostile. (Shakes head at his decision) Yeah, I have a movie star at my reading, and I'm inserting false stuff in some weird, hostile ass-kiss, and uh . . .

You put that in the videophone section?

Yeah. But it was just—I just *inserted* it, reading it out loud. I mean, I didn't write it in. It was like, "Oh, I'll put this in, and it'll be funny."

But according to Charis, he was *really* pissed off. And then I felt like, "God, this poor guy. He can't even go in the back, he didn't want to be acknowledged, he just wanted to listen to a reading." And I, because I'm nervous, feel like I've gotta pull some condescending shit on him, and I just felt like an *asshole*. Felt like a *true* asshole. And if you would, I'd appreciate your having me acknowledge that I felt like a *serious* asshole.

I missed that part of the reading, because at that point I was in the corner of the bookstore.

Believe me, it's a loss I think you can weather.

[Break]

. . . I got my own white robe in each hotel, and decided I had arrived.

In which, in San Francisco? The Whitney?

No, I just—I don't know why I said "Whitney." Hang on, I can even check it.

They deserve a plug, for putting a bathrobe in their bathroom. It seemed to me an incredibly touching and considerate thing. [Unfolding publicity call sheet, reading.] "See *Salon*. Laura Miller." The *Prescott*.

[Break]

In Seattle, they also had—

Alexis, the Alexis Hotel.

[He explains: a place with animal heads on the wall and stuff, the Alexis.]

[Break]

Ah, you're fine. $120 by the night. [He's checking how much tonight's hotel will cost, to see if it would break me.]

[Break]

[Pulls out Kodiak chew]

Now I can enjoy full nicotine satisfaction, and you cannot.

This is his prepping to chew the Kodiak stuff, talking about how "The rules on the airplane, whatever the nightmare of the food is, actually discourage people from chewing tobacco. Because those few people who know how to chew tobacco would be chewing tobacco all the time."

[Smiles; he gets a kick out of my repeating things he says into the tape machine.]

Those people who know how to chew tobacco would be chewing tobacco all the time.

[Break]

Two separate drafts of this book were written—were typed, David says—with one finger. 'Cause he can't type very well. Two drafts of this book were typed with one finger.

But a really *fast* finger.

"But a really fast finger."

[Break]

He asks for an additional foam cup—says he's allergic to plastic—because he wants to spit tobacco into it, and knows that if he uses the see-through plastic it could gross people out.

[The Hyde Street Gift Catalog]

Boy, there's some interesting stuff in here.

[Hyde Street Gift Catalogs on plane: he says he's been reading them back and forth on each trip leg, getting to know the stock.

He's looking at an extension, a gardening tool, that would allow you to remove wasps' nests from trees and eaves.]

Oh, I *like* this—I like this guy's expression as he's putting it in there. It looks like he's working for the National Security Agency or something. "This'll resolve that situation." Oh wait, there's another one, where a man's using the stomach exerciser: it looks just like he's having a bowel movement. Where is this?

[Public address system: "You'll notice we've turned the Seat Belt sign back on . . ."]

Look at the expression on his face. He looks like sort of an autistic person having an orgasm. Yeah, hours of fun with that thing.

[PA: "Please make sure that your seat belt is securely fastened. We'd like to say thanks for flying with us today. It's been a pleasure having you on board, hope to see you again soon in the near future."

Our pilot, like everyone, doing his job, which also requires a little promotional work, a little future-sales stuff . . .]

[Break: We're landing.]

They told you you're number fifteen on the bestseller list.

Oh, yeah. (Nervous, faking unconcern)

What did you make of that? Exciting, isn't it?

I *guess* . . . (Slightly nonconvinced sound in voice) I don't really know what it means. I don't think very many people buy hard-covers, so I don't think it probably *takes* a whole lot to get on that list.

But there are also a lot of books that aren't on that list.

This is true. I'm trying to work out my system of like—how to accept this without thinking of the karma about it.

Martin Amis's The Information—you were talking about it at dinner—never made that list.

So what *does* make that list? Stuff like, um, *Primary Colors?* Or, um, *Men Are from Venus, Women Are from Mars?*

That's been on for about two years. More.
    [To tape] *David said that this is why, when they started, he and his publicist reached an accord, which is "There's information that it's better for me not to have."*

I don't want it rubbed off. And if I were *stronger,* I could hear it and then just . . .

Did you ever think you'd have a bestselling book, though?

No. Nope. And there's a part of me that's just immensely . . . pleased, and surprised. It's not, I don't mean to walk around pullin' this long face about it.

[Break]

How many printings? It's in fourth?

It's in its sixth printing now? They do all these little printings, and now all the stores are out of stock. And so, the stores are pissed because they're afraid that people won't buy it after a week's wait or somethin', so they're trying to do all kinds of . . .

How small are the printings?

(His voice lifts, a little, when he feels he's saying something—wistfully, dreamily, upping the volume to jam the mixed feeling—that's charged, that isn't entirely sincere or true.) I don't know: Like ten thousand or fifteen thousand each?

(Normal) I think the book is so expensive and the postage is so much, that they're really afraid of having too many.

[But he does know the number and size of the printings; can't help knowing.]

I mean, he [Michael Pietsch] has fifteen books he's working on, he line-edited this *twice*. We're having conferences when he's, like, lying in bed sick with the *flu*. I mean he really—I know it sounds like horseshit, but he really did the old-time. . . . Like—and I know this wasn't, he must have had to put a lot of himself on the line, to even get them to *take* this. Given that it was so long. I mean, I think he's a little bit of a hero, and it would be nice if he got some of the good attention out of it.

[Break]

Book is sort of heavy . . .

My friend said when it hit his porch, it made a sound like a *car bomb* going off.

[Break]

[We talk about his friend Jon Franzen's cover story "Perchance to Dream"—which will become well known as "the *Harper's* essay." A piece about how hard it is for novels to get noticed in the classroom with movies and TV.]

This is going to be in *Harper's*. And DeLillo had this one great quote in the piece. Where DeLillo says, uh . . .

PA: (New voice) Ladies and gentlemen, we've just landed at the Minneapolis-St. Paul International Airport. Local time here is approximately 2:28. And you're still on the Central Time Zone. (Camping it up) We're gonna be taxiing for a few more minutes. . . .

(Laughs) So she talks this way normally?

PA: (Engines cycling down, that big, deep, vacuum-cleaner sound) Just a reminder: The airport here in the Twin Cities is a smoke-free environment. Smoking only is permitted outdoors.

(Corrects her) "Permitted *only* outdoors." It's not the only thing that's permitted outdoors.

[Irritated as a grammarian and as a smoker]

Funny.

DeLillo said, "That if serious reading disappears in this country, it will mean that whatever—it will mean that whatever we mean by the term *identity* has ceased to exist."

That's a great line . . . did Franzen press him on it, or . . . ?

I think so. All I know is, um—all I know is the stuff that's actually in Jon's essay. I think Jon had lunch with him like a couple of times.

So you read the essay? [Coming out in *Harper's*]

Uh-huh.

And you liked it?

Yeah. It's sort of—

[Break]

[We talk about Bloomington-grounding snowstorm: Dave, paying attention to everything, had apparently charted its approach.]

I didn't wanna tell you when you showed up, that storm was coming out of the Dakotas for two days.

• • •

WE'RE MET BY THE ESCORT, DRIVE THROUGH THE CITY, AND CHECK IN TO THE HOTEL WHITNEY

[Long drive, local sights, the hotel a big former cotton gin by the Mississippi River. Huge spiral staircase in lobby.]

CHECK-IN GIRL (TO ME): And you have a room with twins.
DAVE: Yes, Anita and Consuela.

[Break]

. . .

LUNCH IN MINNEAPOLIS

[Dave has been traveling in ten states' worth of different cars for nearly a month: His own vehicle is a decade old. It's like speed-dating, getting to see what's available, if he were only unattached. So he keeps hearing one message in his head—a consumerist one, which surprises him.]

"Get a new car, get a new car"—but I would never get a new car until I figured out what to do with this one. It's like a marriage, almost.

[The waitress sweeps by.]

Just a fairly low-rent tea? I've learned the hard way.

[There's a "V" on the menu, marking the vegetarian dishes. Dave asks the waitress—]

Do you count chickens? Chickens are very stupid.

[We do some TV talk. He loves *Seinfeld,* thinks *Friends* is "a little gooey." He says it was scary, after being broke so long in late '80s and early '90s, to buy the Bloomington place. His first house. We do some dog talk. Jeeves was his first dog: "I got him because he was so ugly, no one else wanted him—now he's like a cover-girl dog." When the magazine photographers come, Jeeves keeps pushing into frame, and tried to eat the *Newsweek* guy's lens cap.

Nervous about NPR show tomorrow, and about his last reading tonight, at the Hungry Mind.]

The jungle gym of my own psyche. But I'm the one that has to teeter on it.

• • •

ON WAY TO READING AT THE HUNGRY MIND,
A FAMOUS, PROUD INDEPENDENT BOOKSTORE

ESCORT: I don't know if it's a good time or not, or whether you
    guys wanna see it, but I could take you to the square where
    Mary Tyler Moore throws her cap in the air. Lots of clients have
    wanted to.

[David passes.
    The reading organizer wants three sections, plus Q and A.]

If I do two sections, it's gonna be twenty minutes. If I do three, it's
gonna be *forty.*

ESCORT: [They know the reading math inside out.] Well, you could
    do twenty, then could do one Q and one A.

My main objective is to avoid Q and A. Which tend to be excruciating.

Have you done them before?

Oh, yeah. At least here I'm being told beforehand. You know, in Iowa
there was a Q and A on the *radio,* that I had not been told about.

Huh. You dislike them?

Yeah. Just stuff like "Where do you get your ideas?" Which is actually a—I get them from a Time-Life subscription series, which costs
$17.95 a month. And the pressure to say something witty and inter-
esting in response, when in fact my mind . . . It's like a flashbulb
goes off in your mind? Sort of? It's just . . . *light.*

[We laugh. We're all finding him the tiniest bit funnier; he has the preperformance focus and weight, he's the guy who's heading on-stage, and we're part of his reading entourage. It makes him automatically glossy and interesting. Almost everything is charming, for no good reason.

We'll be meeting two of David's friends—one, Betsy, was in graduate school with him at Arizona; the other, Julie, is an editor at *City Pages,* the Minneapolis *Village Voice.* "My friends," David says, "are a resolutely unglamorous lot." We stop, door opens, freezing St. Paul weather, Julie crowds in. David talks with her about the *City Pages* reporter. They did an interview before we left for the reading.]

Do you like readings?

I like it once I forget myself. So that right now it's terrible, and the first ten minutes will be one of those awful like I-can-feel-my-heartbeat, and everyone else can *hear* it. And then after a while I just forget it. One reason I don't mind going long is that when it gets to twenty minutes, just as I'm starting to halfway enjoy it, um, it's over.

I read about this store in articles about independent booksellers a bunch a times.

[I'm talking like Dave now: Infectious . . .

David is gone; the bookstore, Hungry Mind, was sold and shuttered; that world is closed too, of the thousand-page novel, the escorted reading tour; the Whitney Hotel is gone, Dalton's, it's a period that's gone. There's just his work, which needed all those things to launch.]

It's got its own newsletter that I think is fairly well thought of. (A "rather" sound to David's voice.)

ESCORT: Yep. The *Hungry Mind Review.* I think they're *very* well thought of.

Now, has this reading been publicized pretty well in town?

ESCORT: Yeah, they do—the gal ["Gal"—so Minneapolis] that runs this, Laura Baratto, does a great job of publicizing it. Everybody knows about her, so that if it's the Hungry Mind, everybody knows. Y'know: press release. It's got such a great reputation I think that everybody comes. This newsletter is so good.

They're gonna do this man Michael Chabon. I know he's about two weeks behind me.

For Wonder Boys.

[David is talking to Julie, about how escorts had been hired.]

The mind reels. I think *geisha*, in full hairpins. But the person in the first city was a six-foot-five Irish *man.*

JULIE: Oh no kidding, where was that?

That was in—I'm sorry, that would be the second city. That was in Boston. A big Celt.

[Break]

[David's having a cigarette. Our escort has moved to celebrity talk. Famous people I've driven. She notices David's cigarette.]

ESCORT: I wouldn't give you a *lecture* about smoking. I just, it's just gonna be . . .

[Shirley MacLaine came through Minneapolis on reading tour. Ron Wood.]

Escort: He signed *everything*. People's coats, their arms, legs. Peter O'Toole . . .

Peter O' Toole came for a book tour?

Is he still alive?

Escort: He did a trilogy, I'm not sure what's happened to the trilogy. He was on book tour, and he was *wonderful*. He was absolutely wonderful.

I would *think* so.

Escort: He looked like he had been ridden hard and put away wet. But, boy, was he, he was *great*. We went under a bridge coming over here, he wanted to go see Saint Paul . . .

. . . and screaming bobby soxers. (To me) Are you prepared to give me a butt?

Oh yeah. Of course.

[We've arrived, and step outside the car.
    David is talking about readings for *Broom of the System* and *Signifying Rappers,* a book he did about hip-hop music.]

And I'd never before gotten an advance for a book in the form of a gift certificate for *Sears.*

[We stand outside the Hungry Mind; it's so snowy, white, and lamp-lit that it feels like the soundstage for a movie. Open on a university bookstore in the Northwest, starring someone spunky. So pretty I wouldn't accept it in a movie.
    I creep forward, look through window for Dave—who isn't will-

ing to, but wants the data—doing reconnaissance work. How big and impatient is the crowd?]

There's no empty seats anywhere except for right up front.

Anybody look *dangerous?*

Mm-mm. No.

ESCORT: Minnesotans are nice. Friendly. Don't worry.

[She's mistaken his stage nervousness for actual lack of confidence, which slightly irritates him; for the remainder of the trip, she'll keep reassuring David the reading went well. She'll say, "I've heard a lot of readings. Believe me, you were fine." She doesn't realize he has a kind of perfect confidence. She'll do this when she isn't spending her behind-wheel time reminiscing about Peter O'Toole or how charming John Updike was, which bugs David.]

It looks like a sit-down version of the Nordstrom's catalog inside . . . All that heavy, puffy clothing, boots and mittens.

Yeah. [He power-ups my joke.] It's better than that. They sorta look like they're waitin' on the moon. This is great: I'll sweep in exactly at eight . . .

[Break]

[We're inside a kind of reader's green room at the Hungry Mind, talking with the woman who oversees the readings. David asks for a drink, to foil dry mouth. Then asks, even better:]

Do you have any artificial spit?

[Everyone laughs.]

No, it's called Zero-Lube. It's an actual pharmaceutical product.

Really? Artificial saliva?

Yeah, but it's *way* better. Mark Leyner used to write catalog copy for the Zero-Lube company. It's way better than water, because it *lubricates*. You don't get that *clicky* sound.

READING LADY: I'll remember that.

I'm becoming a grizzled veteran at this. Next tour I bring a case.

READING LADY: What would you like to drink?

Water. No ice.

READING LADY: Oh. OK.

Because then I will crunch the ice *in* the microphone.

[We head back outside for another cigarette.]

[Staring at audience] *Didn't Hal's dad make a movie like this?* [From *Infinite Jest*]

Called *The Joke*, yeah. What we need is an enormous screen projecting this back out.

[Shakes his head, smiles.]

You've gotta understand, this is about as sexy as the tour gets.

[Our shoes and boots make a sound on the snow like hands rubbing or scrunching over balloons.]

READING LADY: Is this going to be in the article?

You bet. But not your asking.

Are we going in? Oh wait— [I've lost my scarf; it's a shadowy puddle on the snow.]

[Inside, David goes off to do "Job one," which means "Finding the loo." The Reading Lady says, "Go through the back." Curious, excited, student-y heads turn as he crosses to the bathroom. The Reading Lady escorts him as far as the washroom door.]

I can take it from here.

[Break]

[Here someone picks up a book of mine from the reading table, opens it, drops it back down.]

[Break]

[Dave, before the reading, looks up, chews a nail, verifies there won't be a Q and A, asks something about the crowd, tests to make sure his water is "not sparkling."]

(To himself, looking over the room) This is the swan song, this is the finale. [It's his last event for *Infinite Jest.*]

READING LADY: How do you want me to introduce you?

The ones, the gang, the ones around here for the performance? Please tell them, a good stiff monotone—I can provide that.

READING LADY: They're not looking for Al Franken. Who's great. He was out here, he *killed* last week.

Do you want us just to come in from the back, or . . . ?

READING LADY: It depends. Some people don't mind making an entrance. And some people are very uncomfortable with that.

That sounds like me.

READING LADY: Whatever you're most comfortable with.

You don't want me to do that, because that would involve my not being here.

[Everyone does a *Yikes* laugh.]

ESCORT: (Helpfully) He means, going back to the hotel.

What do I do while you're introducing me?

READING LADY: You would just have to sort of stand.

And I kind of look at the floor? It's not going to be one of these hideous, ten-minute long . . .

READING LADY: Oh, no, no. Everything I do is short.

[And he starts to read. He's careful. As he begins, he sounds too breathy to himself on the speakers.]

Does this sound all right? Am I like fellating the microphone? Am I the appropriate distance?

[He reads; he's a finger licker; wets a fingertip while turning the pages.
    As a performance, the whole thing is astonishing: the drive to Chicago, the plane to Minneapolis, the hotel, the car from the hotel—all this transportation expertise marshaled, just so he could

arrive in this room and share some sentences he'd worked up in this basic, private, lovely way.

And then, when the reading is over, and David's about to leave, the reading woman looks at him and pulls a fast one.]

READING LADY: I'm sure if you have any questions, David wouldn't mind answering them.

FIRST QUESTION: How do you get your ideas?

. . .

AFTER READING
HUNGRY MIND BOOKSTORE
THE SIGNING LINE
A LONG, EXCITED LINE

[It's not an easy process. People want to talk. They're thrilled when they get to the table: blushing, excited. David draws a smiley face next to each signature. One woman looks at hers with a frown. She's not sure what it is; she believes he's drawn a computer.]

It's a smiley face. If you want, I could put Wite-Out over it. It's your book.

[Someone pulls out a copy of *Broom of the System*.]

Oh no. This old thing.

[After the signature, he does a birthday-candle blow over the ink, to dry it.]

Little, Brown taught me that.

[Some readers attempt a second of Match-Wits-with-David at the signing point, dropping an insight, trying to compress something of who they personally are and what they feel about him and the book into a few seconds. It's strange, and it's why writing celebrities are different from tennis or movie celebrities. Writing is communication, which people do on and off all day; writing is the professionalized version of what they're up to all the time. Fans at tennis matches sometimes show up in the stands wearing wristbands and tennis shirts—and for these few seconds at the signing, they're stepping onto the court with David.

That desire, in those blushing seconds, to make a mark, to be as attractive a mental human package as the evening's attraction.

One flustered, excited, embarrassed reader in the queue reaches the front and David. A tall guy: goatee, vest, jeans, a huge, white-man's Afro.]

Guy: Are you glowing? Unbelievable. The *City Pages*. That's our local newspaper. Alternate news. Goddamn beautiful, man. Where to next? You cover some *incredible* material.

[Dave signs.] Thanks. I've been to like ten cities.

Guy: No, I meant, uh, bookwise. You know? What's playing on your heart song?

If you talk about it, then you don't do it.

Guy: True. Very True. But is there something, that you've *zeroed in* on, for the next project? Or are you contemplating—

[This is painful. Shy, flustered; the guy trying to be expansive, intimate, cool, making human contact. He doesn't realize you *can't*, the moment's not designed for that.]

Yeah. I mean, I finished that like almost two years ago, so. This is—

there's this lag, we're always on to other stuff by the time this stuff comes out.

GUY: Ever write poetry?

No. (Clipped, nervous)

GUY: Thank you very much.

Thank you. [A woman plunks down *Infinite Jest*.] Hello. (Glares at me) *Yes?*

Oh, no no . . .

• • •

IN CAR
WITH BETSY AND JULIE

[About working with photographers] I was hoping that someone would call me "babe," you know? And someone would say something like, "Work with me, people!"

[The *City Pages* guy said he told someone about the book, that he could do a greater service to fiction, if he left off writing entirely and just copied out versions of *Infinite Jest* longhand, which he could then pass out to his friends. What a strange thing for David to hear. He has an odd expression telling us the story.

It's very icy in the car. We're smoking out the sides, windows cracked, cold air leaking in. David calls it "our hypothermia smoking tour of the Midwest."]

• • •

NEXT MORNING
WE GO TO RADIO INTERVIEW, MINNEAPOLIS NPR
IN THE ESCORT'S CAR

[Prebreakfast broadcasts are a luxury for him; he doesn't own a TV]
This morning, a simultaneous broadcast of *Falcon Crest, Magnum PI,* and *Charlie's Angels*: an orgy of crap.

[The escort, who doesn't seem to approve of what David's wearing—jeans and turtleneck, his long hair up in a bun—is cooing over John Updike. He wore tweed, a tie, etc.

This morning's taping to be locally broadcast in five states as part of *All Things Considered*.]

My ambition is to not embarrass myself—which, if you know me, is a pretty serious ambition.

ESCORT: Believe me, you'll be fine. If you loosen up.

The great thing about not owning a TV, is that, when you *do* have access to one, you can kind of plunge in. An orgy of spectation. Last night I watched the Golf Channel. Arnold Palmer, Jack Nicklaus. Old footage, rigid haircuts.

[We smoke outside. David's hair is still wet from the shower; it steams in the cold air.]

• • •

IN NPR STUDIO
NPR GUY: TALL, CHRIS ISAAK SIDEBURNS, BLACK CONVERSE
HIGH-TOPS. LONG SPIDERY FINGERS. LOOKS LIKE HE MIGHT
HAVE PLAYED COLLEGE BASEBALL.

NPR Guy: We're gonna record digitally. I hope that's OK.
Dave: So only yes and no answers?

[A small, brilliant joke. I write it down.]

[David sees me writing. Turns to me.]

If you do a really mean job, I have twenty years to get you back.

[They end up doing a lot of on-air talk about how drugs get named.]

I'm a hard-core aspirin man from way back. Bayer under the tongue,
which is the way my parents taught me.

[Dave talks about using acupressure for headaches: clamp down on
meat between thumb and forefinger. As usual, he does a table-turn,
as the interviewer continues to ask about drug names. He smiles.]

You're revealing a lot about yourself. You're very interested in phar-
macology. I can get you a *PDR* guide.

[The drugs, actually, sound like characters in Tolkien: Talwin, Sel-
dane, Paxil, Haldol. The names of orcs and elves.]

As we leave, NPR Guy: You're not in town on the twenty-first, are
    you? We're having a snowman burning. It's a Minneapolis tradi-
    tion. The firemen really like fire.

. . .

BACK IN ESCORT'S CAR
EN ROUTE TO THE WHITNEY

The problem with these radio guys is they have such beautiful voices, you just want to listen to the voices, and not what they're askin' you.

[Escort, a little hurt, mentions writers who've been rude to her. David commiserates, apologizes on their behalf.]

It's hard when you're traveling. I want to be rude and snappish to people who can't hurt me. What I do is go home and be rude to my dogs.

[At the hotel, he immediately flips on the TV. *Starsky and Hutch*. I step into his nice neat hotel bathroom. When I return, TBS or whatever is promo-ing *Charlie's Angels*, coming up next.]

Again? We'd all rush home after football practice for this.

[The episode is "The Sammy Davis Jr. Kidnap Caper," with Sammy Davis in a double role: himself and a street hustler. The first scene, he's arguing with his accountant. "Didn't I ask you never to talk about taxes during *meal time?*" Sammy asks on the screen.]

[We leave the Whitney via its grand spiral staircase. Dave stops midway. I say it's like Tara, from *Gone with the Wind*. And again he ups my joke.]

I always want to have a big, Vivien Leigh gown.

• • •

WE DITCH ESCORT
HEAD TO MALL OF AMERICA
THEN TO MOVIES: ONE OF DAVID'S KIND, "WITH THINGS THAT
BLOW UP"

A dumb boy movie. A piece of camp art, like the tornado movie.

[We're on a balcony at Mall of America, looking down at Camp Snoopy.]

Humidity is a few points higher in here too. They must mess with the air.

[To tape] *David is talking about the amusement park complex—Camp Snoopy—in Mall of America. The humidity is higher, and the air smells like chlorine.*

[Break]

[What's funny is how much of David's world, of extraneous information, the week is: his five hundred thousand bits of extra information hammering at you. Burning snowmen, mall roller coasters, airline gift catalogs, drug names, TV dialogue.
    We're looking down at a sort of enclosed grotto. We keep hearing screams from people taking the Camp Snoopy water flume.
    Across the way: a restaurant. Hulk Hogan's Pastamania.]

When I think pasta, I think Hulk Hogan.

[And then, because he's here—although generally he has a specific mall fear: "one I can't get in and out of in thirty seconds"—David figures he ought make some use of the place.]

I actually need to get sneakers, too. This is what happens to me in malls. I want a Vikings T-shirt and also a bathrobe and sneakers. The Vikings shirt's gotta be *just* cheesy enough.

[Dave is now staring down at Legoland.]

There must be a way to make cheap furniture, where you could use Lego.

• • •

TO MOVIE AT MALL OF AMERICA
BROKEN ARROW
JOHN TRAVOLTA, CHRISTIAN SLATER

[In our theater seats, way up front, slammed against screen: David a commenting and empathizing audience. His saying "Oh, boy" when a guy gets thrown out of the train. "Oh jeez" when Christian Slater is going to jump into a railcar. And "Oh boy, oh wow, oh jeez" and then "oh wow" at the end, after Travolta and Slater go hand to hand and Travolta gets speared by a nuclear missile. He winces away from the screen—because he has a slightly soft face, when he winces his cheek kind of folds in. It's got a lot of lines in it. And then he says, "That was a cool shot at the end when Travolta gets impaled by the thing." Remember, he likes movies where things blow up.
    I've seen the movie already, so I watch Wallace watch. In the end, as the thrill plot kicks in—Christian Slater helicoptering after the train containing John Travolta, Samantha Mathis, and the active

nuclear device—he stops making gags. Before that, he's doing *Mystery Science Theater 3000*.]

. . .

THEN, HIS FRIEND JULIE'S HOUSE
STUDENTISH DIGS: ST. PAUL

[Potato chips in bowls, pop (Dave's word for soda), sofa. The TV-watching side of Wallace has clearly been activated: It's a monster. After the morning's orgy, and the lunchtime break, and the movie, at his friend's house we watch an HBO film a classmate of Wallace's is starring in—*The Late Shift*, about Letterman versus Leno, the titanic struggle for hosting rights on *The Tonight Show*.

And then, as all of us stretch and begin wiggling and yawning away from the TV, Wallace, that trouper, wants to watch more and more.

He knows the *Late Shift*'s lead actor, John Michael Higgins, from Amherst. Where Dave disliked him.]

JULIE: Why?

He was just very cool and popular and I wasn't, was the basic offense. To be honest.

[David is determined. So we watch *another* movie, a 1963 Bible epic called *Sodom and Gomorrah*. Which is 154 minutes long.]

. . .

NEXT MORNING
PREPARING TO LEAVE

[His first morning since starting the book without a specific, *Infinite Jest* job ahead of him. He seems a touch stunned and lightened. Book finished, published, tour complete.

David is cleaning up for the chambermaid. Very generous. Didn't order himself breakfast.]

[To tape] *He doesn't want to do any more room service because he doesn't want to be more beholden to Little, Brown to do more press stuff. Turns to me: "Press stuff like* this, *well, actually."*

[And on the airplane, he buckles in, then instantly goes down. A heavy sleep. He's gotten his book out. Softly pouty, butterfly mouth slightly open. Handsome. A little silver in his hair, falling over the ears. A pink smear of sun behind his profile.]

. . .

BACK IN CHICAGO
O'HARE
FRIDAY NIGHT

[Through baggage claim, to slushy roadway and wind outside.]

[After we land, talking about contracts. Doesn't want contract for a novel, even at five years.] If it was five years, it would just be *pain*. And I'd be being paid to undergo pain, which I don't want to do. No one can look after me long term—I've learned—except me. I've learned no one can look after me long term better than I can. The only way we really learn things is the hard way.

• • •

IN CAR WHICH IS FROSTED OVER AS WE ARRIVE
IT'S SPENT THREE DAYS IN THE COLD

[The car has grown an ice layer, bumper icicles, and a gray frost beard on the windshield in our absence. It's a kind of superaging Rip van Winkle we abandoned to the lot. Hardly looks to be the same car.

Door makes cracking sound as opened: everything left inside the car is frozen. Our Diet Pepsi stock is frozen; my Snapple has snapped its glass bottle, what spilled out is frozen on the rug, a slushy brown square. The pack of cigarettes is cold, like a kind of delicacy pulled from the fridge. It's freezing in the car; it takes a moment to poke the key through the ice shield over the lock. Glazed. The whole car is encased in a slick ice. It's been waiting there faithfully for us.]

[Break]

It took him a second to ID R.E.M.'s new album.

This doesn't sound like them—cool.

"Strange Currencies" is very sad and sweet.

[Break]

[I take his Savarin can—his spittoon—to use as an ashtray, an idea he rejects.]

Cigarettes, cigarette butts, give you that incredible *reek* when you learn to spit.

Dave adds, "Learning to spit is part of the aesthetics of this."

(Smiles) Someone repeating my things into the tape is an incredible ego boost. I should hire someone to do it.

[Break]

[I talk about the appearance of detail in his work, the introduction of it, how it started in the *Harper's* pieces. He says his teacher, MacArthur-winner Brad Leithauser, said the same thing.]

He said the same thing about not having enough sensory or emotional detail in your sentences?

No, I remember—I remember the first draft of *Broom of the System*, that was my thesis. He was in—he was part of the thesis defense, and he talked about how the physical stuff seems very schematic. And he actually brought up—I hadn't read *Pnin* yet. [Nabokov novel right before *Lolita*.] And he brought up a scene from *Pnin* to talk about what it was he was saying that was missing from mine.

Did he use that snow scene?

The what?

The snow scene when the guy's walking through the library?

No, I forget—he may even have brought up the glass bowl scene, I can't even remember.

[We'd made a bet to check the detail at the Hungry Mind in St. Paul; but we forgot. He guessed the thing got broken, the sadder ending, I didn't.]

We didn't check the glass bowl. At this point you'll have to take my word for it.

I prefer to take your word on the glass bowl. You seem to—your memory for stuff you've read I *trust*. It's fairly impressive.

[The "fairly"—I like the exactitude. Not "entirely": "fairly."]

Oh, thanks a lot. I do a lot of rereading too, so . . .

No, I believe in Harold Bloom's theory of *misprision*. So it may be that my misreading it was actually—

[I hold off on running "Strange Currencies" for him until we get clear of the O'Hare debris field, the horrible choked jam of an airport, with people driving crazy distracted nervous on the way in, or crazy distracted slow on the way out, talking with someone they've retrieved and love. On the road, we can enjoy it with some cigarettes and some speed.]

You were talking before about your Alanis Morissette obsession?

(Smiles) The Alanis Morissette obsession followed the Melanie Griffith obsession—a six-year obsession. It was preceded by something that I will tell you that I got teased a lot for, which was a terrible *Margaret Thatcher* obsession. All through college: posters of Margaret Thatcher, and ruminations on Margaret Thatcher.

Sexual?

Unspecifically . . . sexual. *Sensuous* perhaps.

You have to help me remember to bring that up . . .

It more involved—like having *tea* with Margaret Thatcher. Having her really enjoy something I said, *lean* forward and cover my hand with hers. [I laugh.] Very . . .

[We're shouting over R.E.M.; it's easy to forget I'm working; it seems more like I'm just driving with a friend. Which is what he wants; he's a natural, socially. You feel you want to work with him, or for him; you feel enlisted.]

I mean, I didn't really go through puberty till I was like *nineteen,* so things were fairly *fuzzy.*

By puberty, you mean, your body getting bigger, 'cause you obviously de-veloped gonads and crap like that, right?

My voice didn't change till I was nineteen. I think I had a wet dream when I was like seventeen. I told everybody about it.

Yeah, I didn't have a wet dream until I was twenty-two. I tried to swear off masturbating once for about three months. Other than that, I wasn't going to have one.

(He corrects me) People have wet dreams, even if they're masturbat-ing. Otherwise no one would ever have one.

Well—

No no no no, but what about your—Mr. Lipsky has said, he finally *stopped* masturbating in order to have a wet dream. The implications of which will escape *no one.*

Hmm. It won't surprise anyone who knows me.

[Break]

[Now we're driving on I-294. It's late, empty. He's holding the tape. It's very quiet in the car.]

Your tour's over. How do you feel?

I was in a really good mood yesterday. And now today I feel bleak, 'cause I'm aware I have to go home and sort of . . . *feel* all this, instead of just sleepwalk through it.

What do you mean by sleepwalk through it?

Well, when you're meeting a whole lot of new people and having to do things, you're in—I'm in a constant low-level state of anxiety. Which produces adrenaline, and kind of shuts down—there's a difference between short-term, people-based anxiety. And sort of deep, existential, you know, fear, that you feel kind of all the way down to your butthole. And that, I, that's . . . that's what I'll have when I'm alone.

What does that entail, exactly?

I don't know. I mean possibly over stuff like this comin' out and the *New York Times Magazine* thing coming out. And—I think the big one is, I've just, I've just . . . I was talking with Betsy about this at lunch. Is if I, if I fuck up on this, it's gonna be, that it just goes into my expectation bank. And I'll think that the next thing that I do has to get this amount of fuss. Or you know, has to have this many people like it.

And but if I do that, it's gonna take *way* longer to do anything. And it's gonna be really painful, and I'm gonna have to wrestle with burly psychic self-consciousness figures in a way that I—that I sorta hope I'm done with.

What do you mean: "that you hope you're done with . . ." Had you wrestled with them in the past?

Oh yeah. That was—that was a horrible thing in the late twenties. Just, you know: Is this, sitting down and having to go, Is this publishable? What will—you know—how will it look typeset? What will people say?

Which is just—I mean I know it sounds very vapid. And I guess maybe a lot of people learn how to just shut it off right away. But I um . . . It got especially bad after the second book. Even as bad—I mean the second book didn't do well. It didn't *sell* well. But I still felt like it was really good. And instead of being pleased about that it was really good, it just upped my *expectations* of myself. In a way that was not . . . It wasn't, you know, an affirming, "By *gar*, we're going to do *better* next time." It was more like, just a *paralyzing*, lower-lip-trembling way. I now have to—let me just shut this off so I can shake this tobacco out.

[Break]

[On what he calls the "spasms of this"] It's almost impossible not to have these kind of spasms, you just try to have them be as ephemeral as possible.

You said—how did you feel when the plane touched down? You know, I mean, this tour—was it fun? Was any part of it fun? I mean, was it a kick to be going around? Honestly. I mean, every writer, you're sitting around your house, you're writing, and you're hoping you'll have the most possible readers. You're hoping the house will get excited about it and you. You're hoping, you're hoping that there will be people like me coming—or else—I mean, you have to be hoping that.

Yeah. But it's weird. One of the things I don't like about myself is, I have a very low capacity for *enjoyment.* Of an actual thing that's going on. 'Cause I manage to turn almost anything into something scary. My hope is that when you and I bid each other a fond farewell, and this phase is truly over, that besides just quivering . . .

For instance, that first reading at KGB. Having it be so crowded that I couldn't get *in.* Or having a lot of flashbulbs going off. That was *neat.* And it was scary at the time, and I'm not just sayin' that. Given that I—that I'd given two different readings in New York where not enough people came to hold the reading. . . . It was some kind of, it was some kind of neat vindication.

How did you feel . . . ? Were you proud? Pleased? Did you feel like you'd done it?

[It's often slightly hard to hear him talk, because he always—we always—crack a window, to avoid the smoke, which I actually don't mind swilling in. Our hypothermia-and-road-noise tour.]

No. The problem is, at the time I was just terrified because there were all these people looking at me. Because I'd like to be the sort of person who can enjoy things *at the time,* instead of having to go back in my head and enjoy them then.

. . . Don't you think the people who actually can't enjoy that kind of thing are the ones that actually get stuff done? Because the people who can just get fat off of sort of temporary achievement are the ones who don't keep going farther.

You're describing something that they use the phrase "resting on your laurels" for. And I think there's got to be some sort of continuum. [One of his words.] I think there's an ability to savor and be satisfied with something that doesn't just result in, um, stasis.

I guess you could squat on your laurels, right?

Squat your laurels . . . [Repeats my joke, and then improves it] Or sort of sitting in the vicinity of your laurels and looking fondly *at* them.

But also be ready to keep moving, right? Not . . .

Yeah. There's got to be a way to use the laurels to make the work *better.* Instead of, if . . . And I'm scared that I won't. I'm scared that I'll fuck up, and plunge into a compressed version of what I went through before.

Has anybody dealt with that well . . . ? Certainly no one our age . . .

Our age . . . I mean your man Updike I think is a fairly good example of someone who could just—just is really into the *work.* And doing the work. And there's fuss or there's not fuss, but he just does it. But no, I haven't seen anyone our age that's handled this attention particularly well. That's one reason we keep this—this part of it, whether it's enjoyable or not, to *set* fairly strict limits.

Do you have a nightmare image of the worst case?

Well, the worst case of it . . . The worst-case nightmare of this is that—is that though I don't feel it yet, I truly, truly enjoy it. And I'm startin' to turn into somebody who flies to New York every weekend for publication parties, shoves my snout in front of other people's photographs, and becomes this grotesque, capering figure. I think my *terror* of that is sufficient to keep me from doing it. But that would be worst-case.

Have you felt the tug at all?

No.

It must have been nice to walk into a room where you were so obviously the center of attention: and you were the center of attention in the literary world, which is the one you belong to. I mean, there have been now five or six weeks, where aside from Primary Colors, the book being talked about—and that's not even a serious book, you know what I mean— aside from that book, the book people talk about is yours. Which is never an experience you've had before.

[The whole world of NPR fiction interviews, readings, escorts, sidewalks outside bookstores; the sub-rosa underground railroad of book publication, with its indoor library lighting and bad complexions, and its lower-budget imitation of big press junkets for things like movies and TV series. A secret society, with its own rituals and observances, now mostly changed or gone.]

It's true. "Nice" I think is a good word for it. It doesn't feel . . . I don't know, "nice" is a good word for it. It's not *incredibly* nice, or life-changing. Or terrible. But it is—you *know* this though. But maybe your readers don't, there's such a lag between the time that you're really into the book, and the time when the book comes out, that I'm now—I mean, my big worry is am I going to get this manuscript delivered to Little, Brown in time? They're pressing to get it out quickly I think so that they can—

[Sound of wind like breeze hitting a sheet of sail: sudden ripple, the car waggles.]

Capitalize.

Yeah. Capitalize on this. How am I going to deal with that? And what if I discover a couple of things really don't work, and I need to take the summer to redo them? I mean, this is not alien to you.

[Trying to get me on his side again, reminding me of our shared craftsman-ness. Chess, but the effort is not so much to win as to get all the pieces on the same side, our men to be the same color.]

No . . . Is it like taking a new friend you've once had a kind of crush on? And then introducing them after you've ceased to . . . like them as hotly? To other people . . .

It might be. I don't know about "not like so much."

You don't feel so close.

I don't feel—yeah, you don't feel like it's part of you.

But you did feel it was part of you when you were working on it?

Yeah.

What do you mean?

It was just very *hard.* I've never done something where I've just had to hold so many discrete pieces of information in my head at any one *time.*

    You ever see *Johnny Mnemonic?* (He laughs, to be quoting a Keanu Reeves movie) There was almost this . . . I mean, he gets this sort of *data overload,* and his ears bleed. And it was just—it made things very hard with *girlfriends,* it made things hard with *friends.*

Why?

Because there just wasn't very much of me that was *left over.* Not because of, "oh, all-consuming artistic thing"—it was just like, that, I was thinking about it *all* the time, I was working on it *all* the time.

Were you dating in that period or no?

Yeah.

And do you think the relationships were hurt by this?

Yep.

Did you ever feel like just saying, "Look, I'm not at my best. Please bear with me, stick around, for a year or two and this will be over"?

Uh, no, I never, it never occurred to me to say that . . .

It never occurred to you to say that?

Yeah, although it's also—uh-oh . . .

[Toll booth coming up.]

I've got a bunch of change actually in my bag. . . . The next one is fifteen cents.

[We clink over the money; we'll lose the cover on the gas tank at Exxon.]

No, but I've also got a pretty good idea. I mean, you're probably the same way, this is what I do: And I know, six months from now, it's going to be like this on something else.

Yeah.

You know, my big worry is, Am I gonna have a hard time digging myself into that situation? (Laughs) You know?

Yeah. And in fact you hope to be digging yourself into that situation, don't you?

Exactly. But it's also—I'm also almost thirty-five. And I'd like to get married and have kids. I haven't even *started* to work that shit out yet. It sounds like you're doing better than me.

Well . . . what kind of hours do you work, when you're working?

I usually—I usually go in shifts of three or four hours with either naps or like you know fairly diverting do-something-with-other-people things in the middle. So like I'll get up at eleven or noon, work till two or three.

[The tape side runs out.]

[We've pulled into a Denny's. Both order hamburgers now: it's a late enough hour for the day's meat portion.

We settle at a table in the smoking section. It looks like smog in a valley, interrupted by the peaks of truckers' caps, heads nodding over plates and coffee.]

Dave, re publicity: interviewers' approach to a lot of things seemed based on reviews and not on the book.

I want to *suggest* that.

[To tape] *There's a lot of smoke in this restaurant, a lot of smoke in all the restaurants we've been to in the Midwest. I'm surprised there's a smoking section at every Denny's. David adds, after we sit down, that "there's even a chain-smoking section in the Denny's."*

(Looking round) High proportion of people wearing *caps,* too. High proportion of people wearing caps.

Quote was—that there are even chain-smoking sections in some Denny's.
    So, I was surprised that they put it there also . . . I wonder if there may be interior clues in the book. They checked that crap with you, didn't they?

[We're talking about how *Time* decided the book was set in 2014.]

They actually didn't, but I did pretty well. I mean, the only reason why I know what the date is, is because I had to go, you know, I had to go find a perpetual calendar. And make sure that the days of the week and the dates that they are matched up.

. . . we know it started in the first term of President Gentle's administration, so . . .

I think you guys would be—it's either 2008 or 2009, when we get home I've got the perpetual calendar there. And I could see which one. It's another thing about the remoteness, is like: you asked me this three years ago, and I would have talked your ear off about it. And in a weird way, I sort of *forget*.

But recreational chemicals again. Wild Turkey, you smoked, uh—There's that dope-smoking guy in the opening.

(Annoyed) Why is this of particular interest? We talked about this at the *airport*, before the flight.

We did, I thought I'd get you on it again. Just because, I called some people in New York while we were in Minneapolis, and everyone had heard that thing about you . . .

I guess—I don't know whether you believe me or not. It's just not *true*. For one—because for one thing, it's not true for any reason other than that my constitution is very weak. And I would've, you know, it would've fucked me up, for a long time. I just couldn't—I mean, I *know* people who have been serious cocaine and heroin users. For over a decade. And they have *hearty* constitutions that I just don't have.

So which rec chemicals have you tried?

I did some acid in high school. I did a lot of it for about six months and then—I never felt like I was the same again after that. It messed with me. I would encourage those of your readers not yet at puberty to stay away from stuff until you're at least—say, until your first wet dream. Not to do stuff. I don't think children were meant to . . . Did a fair amount of psilocybin in college but I would do it over vacations. I didn't do anything when the semester was going on. [Funny. A very sensible, homework-filing drug user.] Smoked a reasonable amount of dope, particularly in college and grad school. And . . . uh . . . and drank a *lot*.

When did you stop smoking dope? No coke . . . or?

I think I did coke twice. And I think people who are wired to like—I mean, I think drugs and alcohol for me were a shut-the-system-down thing, instead of a rev-the-system-up thing. For instance, I'm not a huge coffee drinker now. Um, and cocaine for me felt like, there was none of the euphoria. There was none of the feeling of being inspired. It was rather like having consumed twenty cups of coffee, that horrible tooth-grinding stomach . . . that um, hot-stomach feeling.

The reason that it's hard for me to shake, is the sense that there's some other thing about the drug thing. That you haven't gone into. I mean, I can understand your reasons. But there's so much about drugs and addiction in the book, about addiction in the book. That there has to be something stronger . . . a little bit stronger than what you're talking about.

The thing about it is that, is that . . . I mean, this is something that gets *frustrating* to me. The drug stuff in the book is supposed to be basically a metaphor. Now, I did make it my business, I mean, I got very assertive research and finagle-wise. I mean, I *hung out*. There were twelve halfway houses in Boston, three of which I spent *hundreds* of hours at. Because it turned out you could just sit in the living room, and nobody is as gregarious as somebody who has recently stopped using drugs. And that—and that I got—I mean I got a lot, I did what you're doing now. Except over a *much* longer period of time and much more subtly. Um . . . and I think that I'm fairly good at creating certain impressions. I was *not* and *never was* a heroin addict.

OK. But about addictions in general: You split up your experience, I obviously can't say this with great authority. But between Orin and Hal, you gave him your chewing tobacco, for example. And you say that Hal is "genetically hard-wired for addiction to chemical substances." And that would lead me to wonder.

[Hal, the character closest to him . . .]

Well, I think it's fairly clear that I am too. The only thing I'm dithering about is what substances I was with. And one reason I think why—I mean, I remember smoking, and I'll tell you this—I smoked black tar heroin. You know what that is? That you put on a cigarette? At a party once. And I *really, really* liked it. And this was—this was the period in the late twenties. And the weird thing is, is that I *did* it at the time that I was starting to go to some of these meetings, and really became convinced that this was some sort of, that it was some sort of neuro-logical condition they were talking about. And *knew* that if I went and acquired more of it, that I was just—that I was just *gone.*

So the rumor I heard in the late '80s that you had gone to Harvard, something had happened, and you had gotten involved with drugs while you were a student, that was untrue.

It's *factually* false. It is true that I was drinking *a lot* when I was there.

When did you stop smoking pot?

I stopped smoking pot—I think I stopped smoking pot right about the time I got out of grad school. You know, it wasn't any kind of big decision. I just, it wasn't shutting the system down anymore. It was just making the system, it was just making the system more unpleasant to be part of. My own system.

WAITER: Has anybody helped you all yet?

Not one bit.

[Break]

To avoid this being turned into a locus of indictment, not by you but by somebody else who reads this, I would say that—I mean, I think there's nothing trivial or unimportant in the book. And that one reason for that is that Michael—I mean, I was really able to take some help from Michael on it.

Who do you suggest I talk to about the book? Your agent? Michael? Who else?

I'll tell you, there was a guy . . . One of the guys who really helped me about this is an editor—did you see that magazine that Betsy said "Do you want to borrow" that's at my house? His name is Steve Moore at Dalkey Archive Press. D-A-L-K-E-Y, it's in, that's actually in Normal. He's sort of the guy who got me my job, told me about it. He's an editor of this review and he read it in manuscript, read the thing early. And actually—I don't know if he recommended cuts, he had me move a certain amount of stuff around. This was I think in the next-to-last draft—moved some stuff closer up to the front. It was real weird, it was a toss-off suggestion, but it was very helpful because it helped me structure the thing differently. But *he* was somebody who read the thing in manuscript. Umm . . .

I will talk to him. Anyone else? How can I reach Mark Costello, do you think? Actually, the odds are I'm gonna want to talk to your parents. [Dave shakes his head.] *You don't want me talking to your parents?*

They're real, they're real private people, and would have a hard time with it. I hereby request you don't. They also—

You don't have to go any further.

OK. Just to tell you, they also wouldn't be that *helpful.* They didn't read the thing until—like—

Now, I would ask them about what you were like as a kid . . .

I'll tell you, I can—I can give you—I can give you Mark, and Bonnie would be able to tell more about that. (Thinking) Costello, Costello. . .

Give it to me over the phone. We don't have to use Denny's time for it.

Turn it off for a second. [Break] It was real cerebral—

Do you think you've gotten less cerebral since? [David nods.] I think you have too.

But I think a lot—maybe at least for somebody who comes out of a more theoretical avant-garde tradition, I think the aging process is a thawing process. I think you can see that.

Some people never thaw that way, though.

Manuel Puig, Márquez, Cortázar, all of them thawed.

WAITER: You all OK so far?

. . . Even Nabokov didn't deal so well with it. His first remark, after Lolita, was: "Of course, this should all have happened thirty years ago." With attention, he became crazy.

Really?

The last twenty years . . . Read his collected letters. After '59, his letters have this seigneurial sound . . . A perils-of-celebrity story. I don't want to tell you what to read, but . . .

That's just the name of it: *The Collected Letters?*

In the beginning, they're very charming. He's this young writer. And then later on all the charm gets squeezed out of them.

"Seigneurial" means what?

. . . like a kind of baronial tone, inviting you to walk outside and tour the grounds . . . 'Cause now he can begin throwing his weight around . . .

He had *enormous* weight before that, though.

Yes, but in a very small readers' group. If you check it he began acting very, very differently.

WAITER: If y'all can do me a favor, and kinda just make a little bit more room. Your food's ready. I'll bring that out for you. All right, thanks.

[Another groaning table of food: three glasses, one less see-through for David's tobacco, big Midwestern ceramic platters of iceberg salad and thick-cut fries and gravy and beef and slightly char-lined buns and icy-looking tomatoes. He seriously likes to eat.]

[Break]

So I was pushing you on the rec drugs angle.

Right.

And drinking was a harder thing for you?

I was sort of a *joyless* drinker. I mean, I think I just used it for anesthesia. I also remember, I mean really buyin' into—I don't know how much you yourself escaped this. And I realize the references to you will be cut. But it's fairly hard to get a book taken, you know, when you're in grad school. And to get a whole lot of, you know—to get your juvenile dreams fulfilled real fast.

I think I had this idea of: you know, went to Yaddo a couple times. And I saw that there's this whole image of the *writer* as somebody who lives hard and drinks hard. You know, is found in amusing postures in gutters and stuff. And this whole . . . And I think when you're a *kid,* you know, and you don't have really kind of any *idea* of how to be what you want to be, you fall for these sort of cultural models. And the big thing about it is, I don't have the stomach or the nervous system for it. I get really, really drunk. Then I'd be sick for two days. Like sick in *bed,* like a bad flu. Just kind of *debilitated.*

What were the years on this? When you were drinking heavy . . . ? Were you a falling-down drinker? A waking-up-in-the-curb drinker? Can we have some more napkins by the way? I hate to trouble you . . .

No, that's the whole thing. A lot of my reticence about this is it just won't be very good *copy.* Because I wudn't that way at all.

[I begin talking like him too; saying "dudn't" and "real" and things like that. His tug, on the objects around him, is that strong.]

It was a—had six shots of Wild Turkey, two cans of Pabst Blue Ribbon. And then get *violently* ill, and be throwing up. Throw up for most of the rest of the night. And then throw up for most of the rest of the next day. And lie in bed and not get any work done.

I'm gonna stop pushing in a second. This book contains all of your emotional experience with geography: Boston, Tucson, New England . . . everything else in your life is in there.

But no. In fact, the *schema* of various things are, but—

I don't mean it's autobiographical—which for me by the way isn't a negative term . . .

I would expect—don't fall for this, because you yourself know it. I mean, I don't know if *The Art Fair* was an autobiographical—but from the fact that your mom, who's an artist, was in some sense in there or whatever, don't fall for the fact that this is some sort of *coded* story, of kind of my own experience.

I don't think it was code. I think the things that interested you and grabbed you over the past thirty-four years are in that book. And since one of the dominant themes is addiction, I would assume that that was one of the things that interested you or appealed to you or to which you had some natural affiliation.

But I'm also aware . . . that some addictions are *sexier* than others. And that there's going to be an idea, you know, this whole heroin-addict thing. I think my *primary* addiction in my entire life has been to television. And that the fact that I don't have a television, but now enjoy sitting in the second row of movies where things blow up—this is not an accident. But I am aware that that makes, that that's of far less interest, you know, to readers. Than the idea of like heroin, or of some grand, you know, something that confirms this mythos of the *writer* as some sort of titanic figure with a license to, you know . . .

You know I don't believe that myth.

I know you don't believe that. But I also know that among the things swirling around here is you want the very best article you can have. And you can write whatever you want, but the fact of the matter is, I'm not being disingenuous. I wasn't—I wasn't an interesting or Falstaffian or larger-than-life type of addictive figure.

What I *am* is—and it's the same thing—Betsy a couple days ago was doing this, like, "How did you do all this work on corporate culture and the corporate mentality and how corporations work?" And you're probably sorta the same way. One of the things about being a writer is you're able to give the impression—both in the lines and between the lines—that you know an *enormous* amount. That you *know* and have lived intimately all this stuff. Because you want it to have that kind of effect on the nerve endings. And it's like—it's something that I'm fairly good at. Is I think I can seem, I think I can *seem* like I know a whole lot about stuff that in fact pretty much everything that I know is right there. It's a very tactical research-type thing.

It was funny watching you yesterday, because after we watched the movie, it seemed like that part of your brain awakened. Because then we went and watched television at your friend's house. And then even when the first TV movie was over, you wanted to watch more *television. And then went back to your room, and watched still* more *television.*

And it's not—you know, it's not that that's damaging or fatal or anything. But it's—I mean, I think—the thing about the addictive mind-set and the addictive continuum, I think some of that stuff is really me, 'cause I *see* it.

I see that, for instance, my nicotine use has *taken off* on this tour. I mean, I'm somebody who normally chews tobacco five or six times a day, and uses it for work. I'm now smokin' and then chewin'. Chewin' and then smokin'. Wantin' you to buy a Diet Pepsi so I'll know I've got something to spit in, I mean, I can *see* it. It's the way I as an organism react to stress.

But I don't think I'm all that different. I'll bet you've got three or four things, you know, that you're like that with. And one of the things I noticed in the halfway house is the difference between me and like a twenty-year-old prostitute who is dying of AIDS, who'd been doing heroin since she was eleven, is, is a matter of accidents. Choices of substances. Activities to get addicted to. *And* having other resources, you know? I mean, I really love books and I really love writing, and a lot of these folks never got to find anything else they loved.

Before we go into that, you do *keep going back and forth on whether or not your drinking was something you couldn't control, or something that got out of control at a certain point.*

[Nods to machine: wants to sound out his answer first] OK. [Break]

With your drinking . . .

I would say yeah. Because, basically because I wasn't gettin' any work done. And it wasn't helping me work. And it also—I was *sick* all the time. And so if by "out of control" you mean wanting to stop . . . or realizing that once I started, I would always get to the point where I would get sick—and not being able to help that? Yes. If you mean, was I somebody walking, I was not somebody walking around with like a *flask*. It was not like *The Lost Weekend*. It was not the—*nor* was it like any of the romantic writer-as-alcoholic-type thing.

It was just unpleasant?

It was unpleasant and wasteful. And I began to see more and more that I was doing it, that I wasn't doing it the way grown-ups do. There's this guy named Schacht in the book who's sort of—he's kind of *sketchy*, because I didn't understand his mentality very well.

But he's supposed to be sort of the way a normal grown-up is. I mean, he uses stuff occasionally, to make a fundamentally OK life even better. You know? And that's like, for instance, how my parents are. My dad will have one gin and tonic before dinner. And he likes it. It makes him feel mildly good, loosens him up, helps him relax.

I don't know about you, I was never like that. You know? I would drink . . . I don't know that I ever had just *one* shot of Wild Turkey. Or one beer. I would have, like, twelve. You know? And then I would always feel shitty, and always pound my head and wonder why I did it. And then like a week later, I'd do it again.

Now, how long did that last? That period?

Probably about a year and a half, or two years. Here's where it got scary to me. And I don't mind telling you about this.

The scary thing to me was that . . . I mean I was going through a lot of confusions about sort of writing, and art, and all this kind of stuff at the time. And I thought quitting drinking would help.

It made things *worse*. I was *more* unhappy, *more* scared, *more* paralyzed when I quit drinking. And *that* scared me. And I think the period that I really consider a kind of *dark*—

WAITER: You guys still doing all right . . . ?

The period that I think you know about, where I went in on suicide watch, was *months* after I had stopped drinking.

And what had caused that . . .

(Testy) We have already gotten to it earlier. You asked me about that at the airport.

We got there halfway and we weren't quite finished. That's the cool part and the problem with having done this on a trip, in a fractured way. You mentioned being addicted to TV, that appeals to me, because I've had to go through that sort of my whole life. TV addiction. I've had to go through that for as long as I've been alive . . .

I sort of think, anybody our age *has*, whether they recognize it or not.

I wonder if people who have the ability to finish a long book, to see a task through till it's finished, have a particular weakness. . . . The problem with TV watching is, it's never finished. So you have the capacity to do something intensively for a long period of time, and perhaps a little bit past what's useful, and it gets applied . . .

Yeah, you're right. I've actually got friends—Betsy, for example. I was *shocked* that she has a TV, she *never* had one the whole time. It was one reason why in grad school we had very little to talk about. Most of my matrix of experience has to do with television, she would *not* understand references.

Huh. How much TV did you watch when you were a kid for example . . . ?

I had to be limited. I was limited to two hours a day on weekdays, and four hours a day on weekends. And I could only watch one *rough* program. My parents determined the definition of *rough* up until I was like seven or eight. And I can remember once doing something really terrible, like I think hurting my sister badly, or uh making a terrible mess. And having Saturday morning cartoons denied me. And feeling almost like I was going to *die,* the sense of deprivation. This was in—this was in Champaign, so I would have been like four or five.

What cartoons were you watching?

What were the big cartoons back then? (Voice gets momentarily expansive, self-searching, Garrison Keillor and spooky. A reminiscence sound) I remember *Space Ghost. Jonny Quest* was really big. But there were also really cheesy shitty ones back then too. It's *odd,* I remember cartoons once we moved to Urbana and there were things like *Scooby-Doo,* or the *Super Friends* where Ted Knight was the voiceover. But I was older then, I was like eight or nine then. There was some period when I was a very little kid that I had a very *intense* relationship with cartoons. Kind of like what Julie was talking about, like little kids with cars and trucks. But I don't remember the specific cartoons very much. I remember the show *Wild Wild West.*

Oh—I adored that show.

And I remember being *really* upset during the Vietnam War, because they would keep intruding on that show, to give updates on the war. And the violence and battle and the war of course didn't make any *sense.* It wasn't *exciting,* it was just mostly jerky cameras and, you know, bad, bad *film*—like bad film quality. And people in kind of ugly *khaki,* and I never understood it.

[I ask David what else he liked as a kid: it's the big, fish-out-of-water family shows—*Beverly Hillbillies, The Munsters*—actioners like *Mission Impossible* and *Batman.*]

How did your parents enforce the two-hour thing?

Well, they were home. Mom didn't start work until I was almost in sixth grade.

So they would say: "That's enough. That's enough, David, it's been two hours, you have to stop"?

No, it would be like, I would get home, and they'd help me *plan out* how I wanted to spend my two hours. I mean, it was a very intense thing.

Debate the choice with you? Like . . .

I got one rough program a week. And I remember they had, I remember *Wild Wild West* was a young prog—was a—I'm sorry, was a *rough* program. And that I always spent my rough program on that. They *didn't* count *Batman* as rough, which I remember at the time seemed like this *incredible* mistake on their part. But looking back on it, it was very cartoonish.

Campy. What about like the bionic shows . . . ? I mean, you mentioned Charlie's Angels, it's the same era . . .

Bionic Man came out when I was ten or eleven. So that—I was quite a bit older. I mean, I remember watching those. I remember even at the time, I could tell Lee Majors was a *pathetic* actor. And I remember wondering why, if he was running sixty miles an hour, his hair didn't move.

Ha! That's a good question, actually.

Which in a way is significant. 'Cause I think it means that my total, entranced, uncritical absorption into this fantasy world of TV was starting to be over. Like I remember noticing in *Scooby-Doo* that Thelma always lost her glasses at some point. And it was always the amusement camp operator going around in a costume, and feeling pissed off, that like it couldn't be any more sophisticated.

But what you're describing doesn't sound addictive at all. It seemed like your parents had it under control. As you got older, did you start watching more television?

Look, I'm not talking about one of these . . . this—I mean, this in a way is what the book's about. It's not about, "He watched television until his *bladder* let go," or something like that—it's more just, it's a *reliance* on something.

What I'm talking about is, my mom would joke that it was dangerous for me as an adult to have my own television. I could start watching TV at nine on a Friday night. With people waiting for me. Wouldn't stop still two or three on Saturday morning.

Yeah. I'm with you.

I'd say I was going to make plans for after work in the morning, I'd turn on TV just while I was getting dressed, and end up watching TV till about ten or eleven at night again. So I had to get rid of cable.

Yeah. Yeah.

But when did that happen to you?

In college we never had it—we never had a TV in the room. Mark, who was my roommate all through college, didn't like TV. And I *knew*—and I was a *complete* just total banzai weenie studier in college. But I remember there—um, I mean I was really just *scared* of people in college. I remember, for instance, I would *brave* sitting in the TV Pit. There was like a central TV room—to watch *Hill*

Street Blues, in college, 'cause that was a really important show to me. In grad school, when I lived in an apartment, and could have my own TV, um, I remember I began watching a hell of a lot more. Although I made a decision that I would never *write* when it was on. You know: that I would never sit there and clip stuff off while watching TV. Which is—have you had a similar—?

Yeah, I wouldn't do it. I mean, I've done spell-checks with TV on, but I know I can't do that. I remember trying to write some book when I was in high school during that McEnroe–Borg tiebreaker at Wimbledon. Was it like '81 or somethin' like that?

[His speech fully infiltrating mine.]

The first one was 1980. That one Borg won. And then McEnroe ended up winning the U.S. Open.

We're talking about in 1980 . . .

So you would have been fourteen.

I remember that, and I remember trying to do that and being very happy I could do both things at once. But it proved not to be the case.
    During high school, when you went to your friends' houses, would you watch more than you watched at home?

When I went to my friends' houses we would do bones. That's what I went to friends' houses *for.*

I preferred my dad's house over Mom, one reason, because no restrictions on TV at all. But there was no place where you had free—

You know, and realize, this is, you know, it's not . . . I would just be concerned. I'm not saying, you know, "TV's evil" or, you know: "Look out. The youth of America is . . ."

It's just more like it, it's got to do with this—here's this *easy, passive,* I-can-feel-like-other-people-are-in-the-room, but I don't really have to do anything. (Laughs) That it's just, that it's real *easy.* And I think I've, my whole life, had a real penchant for avoiding the hard and doin' the easy. And then part of, you know, part of why we're here is to kinda learn how to not do that so much. That it's ultimately less painful not to do that. Which I know sounds like a piety. But . . .

No. It'd be a good end quote. Don't edit yourself. I think that's a great remark. What's the most TV you ever watched?

In a sitting? I remember watching the entire Jerry Lewis telethon one time. But that was sort of, just to see whether I could do it.

How old were you then?

Fifteen, sixteen years old.

Could you?

Yeah. I watched the entire thing.

How did you manage that, if you had this restriction on your TV?

Not when I was fifteen, sixteen. That was when I was a very small child. At some point, particularly—both Amy and I, once we got into school and began getting grades, and my parents figured out finally that we could get our homework done, function, be on athletic teams, *and* still watch what seemed to them to be just absolutely *mind-crushing* amounts of TV. They really relaxed about it all. I had the restriction until I think I was about eight or nine.

Your folks wanted you, prescribed that you be on athletic teams . . . ?

No. I just meant . . . I mean, Amy played softball and I played ten-nis. And I think Mom and Dad's *nightmare* was that—'cause you got to remember, this was when, this might be a crucial four-year difference. I think TV really started to become a pervasive part of the culture in like the mid-'60s. And *that's* when I was—that's when I was growing up. My parents didn't have any experience with it, you know?

All the PBS/NPR parents even now try to restrict their kids. For all the good reasons.

Yeah.

If your parents had had some idea of what you should be doing, it would be like Avril and James. [The parents in the novel]

No, truly, my parents are very unathletic. My father had wrestled in high school, early in college, but had stopped. And I discovered tennis on my own, taking public park lessons. I'd been a *huge* fan of football when I was a little kid; even at twelve, though I had lost a lot of size advantage on other kids, and was looking for another sport.

No, it was more just that they could see—that my parents are *intelligent,* and they realized that it wasn't, that they were projecting certain fears about TV onto their kids, and that we were giving the lie to them. I mean, my parents never leaned on us about grades or athletic teams, and both Amy and I were pretty functional as little kids.

OK. So aside from the telethon . . . what's the most you ever watched at a sitting? Even now I'll go on these kind of benders when I decide to schedule them. I'll go on a bender now where I'll decide I'm going to start watching, I'll start with The X-Files on Friday night, and then decide to go on until, I'll realize . . .

But it's also sort of—I mean, it'll be on for a while. Then you get restless and maybe you'll make a phone call while it's on or maybe you'll— [I'm shaking my head] No?

Not me.

See . . . maybe we're a little different.

No. If I get into that phase and someone calls, I'll get off as quickly as I possibly can . . .

Now if I get that deeply *immersed* in something, what'll happen to me now is that I'll fall asleep. You know? Because I'll get so relaxed. I think the most that I've ever sat and just stared at and watched would have been, you know, late in high school, and we're probably talkin' about eight hours.

Ha. And you haven't watched that much TV since?

You mean all in a sitting? I can remember a couple of times having the *flu,* you know. And like being at my girlfriend's house with the TV on, and just lyin' there with the set on. And just kind of drifting in and out of consciousness, you know. But that's—you seem to me to be meaning something different, by watching. Maybe in the posture of the Bose-through-that-speaker commercial. Where the guy's just kind of sitting in the chair like this . . . ? [Demonstrates: Hunkered in chair]

(Laughs) *You've never done that.*

I also, here's the—like the thing that's killed it recently for me, is the channel-surfing thing. Is because, I always have this terrible fear that there's something even *better* on, somewhere else. And so I will spend all this time kind of skating up and down the channel system. And not be able to get all that immersed in any one thing.

But the problem is, there always is something better. So you can always find something else to watch.

Yeah, but there's this terrible *anxiety*, this gnawing anxiety about it. That was the great thing about last night, I just decided, I'm gonna watch *Sodom and Gomorrah*. This is gonna be cool.

No, but when you can trapeze to something else . . . swing on to the next bar . . . there's always a next bar coming . . .

That's true.

I mean I could go home now *and watch ten hours of television.*

Fill me in on something . . . [Shuts off machine]

[Break]

. . . and read for a couple hours, and it's much harder if there's a girl there. Because they want to interact. No, I'll tell ya, I mean, in a certain way, I'm a little bit—but I *am* with reading I think kind of like what you are with TV. I mean there's lots of times where I've read for three, four days in a row, pausing only to eat and sleep.

[Break]

So when you said TV addict, you were just being colorful. Or you see a potential for it, even though you've never exercised it fully.

I think, I think what you're betraying here is you and I have a some-what different understanding of "addict." I think for you, the ad-dict is the gibbering, life-that-completely-grinds-to-a-halt thing. And for me—and the thing that the book is about, is—it's really about a continuum, involving a fundamental orientation. Lookin' for *easy* pleasurable stuff outside me to make things all right. And I'm not saying there's anything wrong with it. But I'm saying it's a continuum, and that we *slide*.

[Eventually, the first thing I got home, I pulled out the dictionary and looked up the word "continuum." To see exactly what it and he meant.]

And it's much more— This is one reason I was afraid the book was just not going to make *any* sense, 'cause I wasn't sure anybody else saw it this way. I mean, I began to see *significant* relationships between—a significant similarity between my relationship to television, and some of these people in the halfway house's relation to, say, heroin.

Or, you know, if you ever go to like—I went to this one thing called SLAA? Oh, Sex and Love Addicts Anonymous? Where guys would, like, would go to prostitutes, you know? And get thousands of dollars in debt on their credit card. 'Cause they just couldn't *stop*. That it seemed to me that the *only* differences, that the differences were relatively unimportant. That there's more just this sort of desperate *hunger*, enormous hole to be filled. And a real inclination to look outside, for like *consumer products* mostly of varying kinds, to fill it. And that's what seemed really like, movingly American about it to me.

In the book, when you had Murat? . . .

Marathe.

. . . talking to Steeply. He said, Your country . . . if you make it available to, a sad thing about Americans is if you make it available, they'll take the entertainment that leads to death. That's why Infinite Jest is a good movie.

Because any person you give that choice to would take that choice . . . other cultures are as fixated with television as ours . . . sometimes farther, they can't see the distinction between what's real and what's not . . .

[Yet his radical desire to give people something they *can't* stop reading: his editor at *Harper's* described his work as the literary equivalent of cocaine. So addiction is also a metaphor for how much you want readers to love a book. To be hooked. It's an *artist's* great ambition. Forget the other stuff in your life: family, work, outdoors . . . focus only on me. The level of approval and applause, that a writer looks for: I dropped everything for you.]

Naipaul does this too . . .

For me the thing . . . And again, now, this is just my opinion, and I couldn't—I can't win an argument with you. But I think there is kind of a difference, and it has something to do with what's sad. And there's this *desperation* to give ourselves away to something. To be—what do you call it? There's a German word for it, it means a sort of Wagnerian falling into, that I think our culture really encourages. And I think other cultures—particularly more repressive cultures—could simply ban it. Find mechanisms to deny its supply. That sufficient demand would not automatically result in its availability. That a number of factors would make it— makes it more of a problem here. But in another way, I mean the movie's not just a *MacGuffin,* it's kind of a metaphorical device . . . it's kind of showing you what the end of this continuum might be.

[This is his chalk talk, his sales pitch for the book's material. He's good and effective.]

. . . I remember writing in the margins, that all cultures would make that same choice about watching the movie.

Steeply, Steeply has the same argument. And it's a terrible argument because Marathe is basically a fascist. You're talking about a culture that teaches people how to make moral choices, that teeters very easily into a culture . . . into a totalitarian, authoritarian culture.

But a culture that *doesn't*, and that prides itself on *not*—the way sort of ours does, or has recently . . . I think we're just beginning to see, that on either side of the continuum there are terrible prices to pay.

You give no answer to this question then . . .

I don't think there's an answer. You mean, are there laws that should be passed? Or is there public education we can do—my personal suspicion is that for the really deep important questions, there aren't any answers because the answers are *individual,* you know? I mean, there's no culture . . . I mean, the culture's *us,* you know? The country's *us.*

So no answer: either that kind of freedom or that kind of guidance.

I think it's—I mean I think the whole thing is an enormous game of Little Red Riding Hood, and you're trying to find what's just right. And you, you know—what is it?—you can't find the middle till you hit both walls? You know? The thing that really scares me about this country—and again, I'd want you to stress, I'm a private citizen, I am not a pundit. Is I think we're *really* setting ourselves up for repression and fascism. I think our hunger, our hunger to have somebody else tell us what to do—or for some sort of *certainty,* or something to steer by—is getting *so* bad, um, that I think it's, there's even a, Hayek's *Road to Serfdom,* I mean, makes a similar argument economically. But I think, you know, in Pat Buchanan, in Rush Limbaugh, there are *rumbles* on the Western horizon, you know. And that it's going to be, that the next few decades are going to be really scary. Particularly if things get economically shaky, and people for instance—people who've never been hungry before, might be hungry or might be cold.

Cliff Robertson. Three Days of the Condor.

[He laughs.]

[Break]

There's always been that pull, but I assume . . . I mean you went to a good college, you knew about Louis Hartz and the liberal box. [I nod. I have no idea.] There's always been some great . . . Louis Hartz is this political scientist who talks a lot about this difference between American politics, say, and Europeans. And that we don't tend to get *extremism* with the kind of political influence here that there is in Europe. And that one reason is that there has been this peculiar kind of liberal centrism. That we're very *nervous* about extremes.

I don't know about you, and I don't know what your friends are like. But this seems to me to be a sadder, more hungry generation. And the thing that *I* get scared of is, when *we're* in power, when we're the forty-five-year-olds and fifty-year-olds. And there's really nobody—no older—that no people older than us with memories of the Depression, or memories of war, that had significant sacrifices. And there's gonna be no check on our, um, *appetites*. And also our hunger to give stuff away. And I'm aware—I'm again, I'm speaking as a private citizen, I do not know any other generation. I'm talking about kind of a feeling I have, that's somehow way down in my stomach . . .

You think this generation is more prone to—

I think this generation has it worse or better than any other. Because I think we're going to have to make it up. I think we're going to have to *make up* a lot of our own morality, and a lot of our own values. I mean, the old ones—the '60s and early '70s did a marvelous job of just showing how ridiculous and hypocritical, you know, the old authoritarian Father's-always-right, don't-question-authority stuff was. But nobody's ever really come along and given us anything to replace it with. Reagan gave us a kind—I mean, the Reagan spasm I think was *very* much a story about a desperate desire to get back to that. But Reagan sold the *past*. Reagan enabled a fantasy that the last forty years hadn't taken place.

And we're the first generation—maybe people starting about my age, it started in '62. We *grew up* sorta in the *rubble* of kind of the old system. And we *know* we don't want to go back to that. But the sort of—this confusion of permissions, or this idea that pleasure and comfort are the, are really the ultimate goal and meaning of life. I think we're starting to see a generation *die* . . . on the toxicity of that idea.

Dying in what ways? I mean, literally dying?

I'm talking about the number of people that—I'm not just talking about drug addicts dying in the street. [Watch beeps again. I keep thinking it's my watch in the bag.] I'm talking about the number of privileged, highly intelligent, motivated career-track people that I know, from my high school or college, who are, if you look into their eyes, empty and miserable. You know? And who don't believe in *politics,* and don't believe in religion. And believe that civic movements or political activism are either a farce or some way to get power for the people who are in control of it. Or who just . . . who don't *believe* in anything. Who know fantastic reasons not to believe in stuff, and are *terrific* ironists and pokers of holes. And there's nothing wrong with that, it's just, it *doesn't* seem to me that there's just a whole lot else.

And if you look for instance—some of the stuff's in an essay about TV that was in that, I mean, and I'm kind of quoting it. But I really believe, that I think if there were *one,* like, archangel of this mentality, it's Letterman. You know? Who's the *master* of the dead-pan, ironic echo of old truisms, that expose their vacuity. And *his* hip sophistication at seeing *through* them, and his hip invitation to *us* to *join* him in his superiority over them. And that it's—Letterman for me is this *fascinating* trans . . . I mean, he is an archetype, it seems to me, of this era. I don't see anybody or anything past him, except for extremists, you know? Rush Limbaugh, who uses a Letterman-like irony to ridicule liberal positions. But the device, the mind-set, is still there. I don't know what's going to come after it, but I think something's gonna have to. I mean, something's gonna have to.

What do you think it will be?

My guess is that what it will be is, it's going to be the function of some people who are heroes. Who *evince* a real type of *passion* that's going to look very banal and very retrograde and very . . . You know, for instance, people who will get on television, and earnestly say, "It's extraordinarily important, that we, the most undertaxed nation on earth, be willing to pay higher taxes, so that we don't allow the lower strata of our society to starve to death and freeze to death." That it's *vitally* important that we do that. Not for them, but for *us*.

[But it's funny, there's a real detachment, almost aesthetic. Not that it's good for the freezing, but for us. I don't mention this.]

You know? That our *survival* depends on an ability to look past ourselves and our own self-interest. And these people are going to look—in the climate, in the *particular* climate of our generation and MTV and Letterman, they're going to look *absurd*. They're going to look like, What do you call it? Pollyannas. Or, um, you know, suffragettes on soapboxes. They're gonna come off bombastic and pretentious and self-righteous and smug and, um . . .

But in a weird way, I think they're . . . At some point, at some point I think, this generation's gonna reach a level of *pain,* or a level of *exhaustion* with the standard, you know. . . . There's the drug therapy, there's the sex therapy, there's the success therapy. You know, if I could just achieve *X* by age X, then something magical . . . Y'know? That we're gonna find out, as all generations do, that it's not like that.

That at a certain point, we're gonna look for something. And the question for me is, what?—is what comes after it? Some Ralph Reed, knuckle-draggin', fundamentalist, you know? Easy atavistic bullshit that's repressive and, that's repressive and *truly* self-righteous and *truly* intolerant? Or is there going to be some kind of like, you know, something like what the founding fathers and the Federalists did. You know? Are we going to like look inside our hearts and decide that, things have been fucked up, and we're going to make some rules that are good for everybody?

. . . I want to argue two things with you that I've noticed about you since I've been with you since Tuesday. That when I mentioned my feelings for Pat Buchanan, because of those same things?

When you mentioned . . . ?

When I mentioned my affection for Pat Buchanan because he was at least talking about people who are in that, that you kind of smiled at me. Second thing is that, when I mentioned Pauline—that was why Pauline Kael was jazzed up by the end of Scrooged. When Bill Murray comes out and makes a speech that's actually heartfelt, after having been a facetious prick for so long. She wrote a passionate thing about it. And yet you found that movie painfully bad. I think you may feel the conflict about wanting something that's truthful, and then also being able to see through it. Those two poles are really really really powerfully in you in a way that you're not aware of—

[I'm doing his "really really *really*" thing too.]

I'm aware of it to the extent that I make no pretense that I'm not *firmly* a member of my generation. And I do not claim I am exempt from any of the stuff that I seem to be indicting the generation about. What I'm talking about is, This is our job. This is our bed to lie in, you know? This is our—and I agree with you, there are reasons why I think—the end of *Scrooged* has been set up by so much elbow-nudging, broad, Bill Murray mugging for the camera, that I think the movie, in a cowardly way, undercuts any attempt to make a statement at the end.

Because Pauline Kael found that brave and passionate in just the way that you're asking for. For the same reasons. The essay she wrote on that . movie was just what you're talking about. . . . Because he had been the exemplar of that thing we were talking about on the airplane: that was the question from when he first showed up—was his thing "hip mock sincerity" or "mock hip sincerity"?

The thing about Pauline Kael: she's not read as much as she used to be. But Pauline Kael is one of those voices that I'm talking about. And Pauline Kael has this great thesis about, what's terribly pernicious about a lot of movies, is that they make the bad guys wholly unlike you. They turn them into cartoons. That you can feel superior to. Instead of making you realize that there's part of the villain in all of us. You know? And she would be—she would be a good model for the kind of thing that like, I mean, I think if, if like your age or people a little bit younger, if there were like ten Pauline Kaels? Who could go along and, you know?

When you were talking before, I remembered this quote: "We live in the twilight of the old morality: there's just enough to make us feel guilty, but not enough to hold us in." What do you make of it?

Whose quote is that?

What do you make of the quote though?

Who said it?

Updike, in a story from 1962. So it may be that people feel that same thing in any generation.

The thing that makes me uncomfortable about it, is the phrase "all morality," my guess is—

Sorry. I meant to say "old morality."

Yeah, my guess is—[So we've ended up doing Wallace Shawn and Andre Gregory in *My Dinner with Andre*.]

[The tape side runs out.]

• • •

AT DENNY'S
OFF I-55 SOUTH
WILLOWBROOK, ILLINOIS
BETWEEN O'HARE AND BLOOMINGTON

[David observes that once I'm at my desk] you'll be able to construct anything you want.

What I love in this sort of piece is getting the quote, I love people's dialogue rhythms.

But you know that writing down something that somebody says out loud is not a matter of transcribing. Because written stuff said out loud on the page doesn't look said out loud. It just looks crazy.

. . . Janet Malcolm thing, the postscript to Journalist and the Murderer *. . . about Jeffrey MacDonald's quotes.*

Something else you've read I haven't read, what?

The Janet Malcolm thing, you were quoting from it before. About Jeff MacDonald, that killer—

Jeffrey MacDonald? That's about that writer and Jeffrey MacDonald. Yeah, I read it a long time ago.

[Checks tape] *We should make sure this thing is spinning, that we haven't stopped.*

Got it. I am your able lieutenant.

We don't have to do it for about forty more minutes.

Um um um um um. This business of—this business about marketing yourself, there's nothing wrong with that. Unless we're allowed to think that that's—that that's *it*. That that's the *point*, that that's the goal, you know? And that's the reason we're *here*—because that's so empty. And you as a writer know that it's—if you as a writer think that your job is to get as *many* people to like your stuff and think well of you as possible . . . And I *could*, we could both, name writers that it's pretty obvious that's their motivation? It *kills* the work. Each time. That that's maybe 50 percent of it, but it misses all the magic. And it misses, it doesn't let you be *afraid*. Or it doesn't, like, let you like make yourself be, be vulnerable. Or . . . nah, see, I'm *not* . . . Anyway, anyway.

[Thumps table]

We were talking about movies. Let's go over some directors: Woody Allen.

Never much liked Woody Allen.

Why not?

Dunno. I think part of it is that, when I was at Amherst—I mean I'd never really heard of him. But I remember seein' *Everything You Ever Wanted to Know About Sex,* and bein' real excited, 'cause I thought it was going to be real sexy. And then not. So, on the East Coast, he was so trendy. And I'd heard so much about him before I ever saw him? I also think—I don't think his humor's all that subtle, it seems like a *shtick* to me. But I know, like I've got really smart friends from New York, who just think he's an absolute genius. It's sort of . . .

OK, the blowing-up-stuff directors. Walter Hill you don't much dig. Richard Donner?

Don't know that much about Richard Donner.

Lethal Weapon, Superman. OK, Spielberg?

I think Spielberg's first few things were *magic*. And he's got a real feel for how . . . for how to make film work on your nerve endings. You know, the chase sequences, even in a terrible movie like *Jurassic Park,* that scene with the truck chasing them down the tree?

I love it.

His ability to milk, um—to put you on this sort of emotional roller coaster. He for me is a prime example of Hollywood killing what it loves. By just dumping money on it, you know? And making him too important. He and *Cameron* I think are the two most vivid examples. Cameron would be making *so* much better movies if they gave him a seven-, eight-million-dollar budget on each one. And said, you know, "Do your best." Y'know? Don't indulge your love for really cool special effects. Make a story that like—that hangs together and treats the audience like grown-ups and means something.

We were talking . . . reason the scene works in Jurassic Park . . . same reason good fiction works . . . Based on details . . . Tree is dripping wet, we know it's been raining all night. But then that truck is stuck in a tree, we know it's going to fall. The consequences of the details.

But it also makes sense, in a whole lot of ways. It has to do with the *exhaustion* of, "They've been through *so much*," you know? And more of this—so there's this exhausted, "Oh, this!" That lets you get a little bit of a laugh, that charges up your battery for the next time the next branch cracks. And then it ends with that marvelous: "Well, we're back in the car." It allows you to laugh—like Spielberg knows exactly how much adrenaline to inject in your bloodstream, and when to let it ebb and when to . . . But the danger of that is, what that is, *really*, is manipulation. I mean, he's a *master* manipulator. And a couple of times, when I think he was younger, and more naïvely idealistic—like *Close Encounters of the Third Kind*, even though it had a very silly reductive government-is-evil-and-they'll-spray-you, and only the aliens are good. But even that stuff, there was this innocent . . . That, *Jaws, E.T.* There was this marvelous, "God, we're all kids again," back in that movie. But then starting with, I don't know, stuff like *Hook*, or—

Always.

Or—well, there was something about *Always* that made me *cry*. That whole bit about "Now I can tell you everything." That whole business about his coming back and loving this woman and her not being able to see him. I've always, that kind of shit's always gotten me. The first—*A Guy Named Joe*, the first version of that, knocked my socks off too. But there was also this—or the thing in *Schindler's List* where when he—the one thing that movie absolutely depended on was a coherent picture of the moral metamorphosis of Schindler. And we don't get it. We see a couple kind of moments, shocking moments. But we see him change from this coarse figure to this good weeping person, and there's no coherent story of how that change took place.

Maybe grace is invisible.

Maybe grace is invisible, but one of the things that's magical about art is that art can set up contexts where we can understand and identify somehow with how one can put oneself in the position of being influenced by grace. And that movie, that was a riveting movie in a lot of ways. And like a lot of the camp stuff was hair-raising. But that movie had the heart of a whore and was a cheat. And that ending, of having all those survivors go back? It was very moving, very cool. But what a cynical, you know, like-me-because-I'm-about-something-noble, instead of delivering on the art stuff. I mean—did Kael ever review that?

No, she talked about it in her interview. That's what she said too.

Did she say that? Well, that makes me feel relieved. Because I think I was the only—I was so worried about hating a movie like that, 'cause right away you worry that people are going to think you're anti-Semitic.

That's one of the few films I cried in, was that movie . . . Did you read comics as a kid—

Braveheart I really liked. 'Cause that's my fucking *ancestor.* William Wallace was like the first famous . . . um . . . he was like the *grandson.* The father in Argyle had actually emigrated from Wales. Those two brothers. And Wallace means "from Wales" in Scotch-Gaelic. Anyway, so I would go—I think I saw that four times. Just to hear guys in kilts going, "Wal-lace, Wal-lace!" (Laughs)
    Even though it was not, it was probably not the most sophisticated. But the analogy is, I think probably, if you're Jewish, and you've got all that ethnic history like in your consciousness, Spielberg dudn't have to *do* much. To push your buttons. And *that* thing . . . I mean *Braveheart,* I *wept,* as he cried "Freedom." Which I'm *sure* from the outside looks so cheesy.

I liked that scene, actually. I liked it ending that way.

He was perfect, though: he was never weak, he was never cowardly, he was never . . . There was no, there was *nothing* in there—I couldn't *recognize* myself in him at all, you know?

He was entirely other. In a way Schindler was too . . . what about comic books as a kid?

Not particularly.

Because it's funny. Spielberg's framing devices come from D.C. Comics, faces pushed to the center, I hated those frames as a kid, but it works in movies.

Yeah, I don't know what it was, I never liked—what I really liked, were these *kid cycle* books. The Hardy Boys. Tom Swift. Franklin W. Dixon. Frank O'Hara was a big—there was another Frank O'Hara, who wrote a lot of short stories, like "My Oedipus Complex," and all that. No, Franklin W. Dixon, who it's *fairly* proven was toward the end of his career a committee that was also Carolyn Keene and the Nancy Drew books. And I *also* read all the fucking Nancy Drew.

Did you?

Yeah. I don't know what it was, I loved that kind of soap-opera-like serial thing.

[Like his long book; a whole world]

OK. What movies have you really liked in the last two, three years?

The biggest, most important movie experience of my life, was in the spring of 1986. When I was in grad school and saw David Lynch's *Blue Velvet*. Where, it's weird, I can talk about it, 'cause I just finished this essay that's all about this. But—

[He turns off the tape.]

[Break]

You were in graduate school?

OK. There were this—there were like five or six of us. Who were sort of experimentalists, avant-gardists at the U of A. And the U of A was hard-core, Updike *New Yorker* realism. And they thought—they basically thought we were *assholes*. And the painful matter of fact is that we were. We were pretentious and cold and cerebral. But we also really didn't believe that the answer was to go back to writing nineteenth century. I mean someone has to live in a brownstone and have a cat, you know? I'm talking about coming out of my experience.

And I remember goin' to see *Blue Velvet*. And I saw it with three women. One of whom walked out, and the other two of whom walked out just raging about it. And I didn't have the balls to say anything. 'Cause I . . . I . . . it absolutely made me *shake*. And I went back and saw it again the next day.

And there was somethin' about . . . it was my first hint that being a surrealist, or being a weird writer, didn't exempt you from certain responsibilities. But in fact it upped them. And the magic of *Blue Velvet* was that it so *clearly*—I mean I've got this whole theory that you don't want to hear about. That Lynch is really an *expressionist* in the way that like *Cabinet of Dr. Caligari* is expressionist. Or that he's very much about *manifesting* his inner states on the film, and it's actually a very sick thing that drives him to make films.

But the magic of that was . . . For instance, some of the stuff I know: that final scene, when Jeffrey is in that apartment and the Yellow Man is standing there and he's dead, but he's just standing there? It comes out of a dream that Lynch had. He's *admitted* it. It's completely dreamlike. But it's also absolutely *right*. And it just— and it so completely opens out, and it's just one of those little off things in every frame, that instead of seeming gratuitous or stupid or pretentious, actually makes those frames mean a whole lot. It was my *first* realization that there was a way to get at what these realist guys were saying, that was via the route of the surreal and expressionist. But that it was tremendously scary. Because, for instance for me, *Wild at Heart* dudn't work at all. That all these things are red herrings, and they go *nowhere* and the characters are interchangeable. But the difference between that and like *Blue Velvet* is a hair's breadth, in so many scenes.

[Silverware sounds, beeping sounds, working restaurant: talk and hum]

That's what's interesting about his mechanism. That he could make a film so soon after it that was that bad . . . I also wonder if all the attention he got after making the TV series and Blue Velvet, I mean he was on the cover of Time. I mean, it must have been strange and hurt. I mean, I think that may have something to do with the failures of those movies.

I think that's—that had a lot to do with the problems of the second season of *Twin Peaks,* and a lot of the problems of *Twin Peaks: Fire Walk with Me.* The thing is, Lynch had already been through the experience of *Dune* in the early '80s. Which I think was his real trial by fire. And where he could have—it could have either broken him or he—

He turned down a lot of money and a lot of shit to take De Laurentiis's offer. Look, here's this tiny budget but *you* get control. I think he's kind of a *hero.* But anyway, that movie was huge for me.

I happen to like Dune. Kenneth McMillan.

Happen to like what?

Dune.

Dune is all right. But *Dune*—I mean, you probably know this, *Dune* was cut 50 percent, not by Lynch, right beforehand. It's incoherent.

I mean that lady who starts out and narrates it, we never see her again. Um, the little girl, that horrible actress who plays his little sister, whose mouth movements don't match her. . . . But there were great little touches. Kenneth McMillan was *incredible*. What were other—oh, just the mechanisms of the water retention, the worms. Have you noticed that the worms in that, with that sort of triangular snout opening up, it's *identical* to the worms in *Eraserhead*? That little worm in the cabinet that he's so obsessed with and plays with? It's very, very, very, *very* strange.

[Just keeps tossing on the modifiers, loping them on]

He disliked the film so much that when it's shown on TV, he's taken off the director's credit . . . The way the guild works, credit goes to Alan Smithee, who's apparently directing a lot of films . . .

I didn't know that. I didn't know that.

. . . that's the director on that movie . . . On TV, directed by someone Smithee.

It's interesting too, 'cause thinking of '86, right about that same time, *Brazil* came out. Which was another thing that used *dreams* in a really powerful, sort of coherent way. And I think one of my—I mean, I'd always used sort of dreamy stuff. But I had never as a young writer realized that you still had an obligation to make a kind of narrative. That really the goals of realism and the goals of surrealism are exactly the same. And they're indescribable. But they're two completely different highways that have the same destination. And I'd never snapped to that before.

David Lynch, *Blue Velvet* coming along when it did, I think saved me from droppin' out of school. And saved me maybe even from quittin' as a writer. 'Cause I'd always—if I could have made a movie, right at that time? *That* would have been it. I mean, I vibrated on every frequency.

Including the fact that it was absolutely horrifying. That that's not a movie about a kid discovering horror in a town. It's about a kid discovering that he—that there are parts of himself that are just like Frank Booth. [Not afraid of cliché; the *only* way to deliver this, at this late date, would be to be ironic.] And it's a weird movie, 'cause the *climax* comes at the end of act two, when Frank turns around in the car, and looks at Jeffrey and says, "You're like me." But it's the one—except for the voyeurism scene—it's the one shot that's out of Jeffrey's eyes. And it's all *very*—

I thought that was a stagey moment, though, a tiny bit, because that was the point of the movie.

Yeah. But so many critics missed that that was the point of the movie. So many of the critics missed that it was a coming-of-age movie. And thought it was a, you know, "Gee-whiz kid discovers corruption underneath." You know? You have the surface of the super-saturant colors, and waving firemen, and then underneath—they utterly missed it. I mean I had to *read* all that stuff for this essay, it was like very few critics *got* what was going on—

Pauline didn't.

Yeah, but her review is like a page and a half. And *she's* more interested in the fact of how disingenuous it is. Her big line is there's very little art between you and Lynch's psyche in this. You know, that it's really like watching somebody's id get projected onto the screen.

So what kind of stuff were you writing before that movie came out?

Let's see, I can remember exactly. *Tch tcho tcho tcho thch tcho.* I had written—I was taking Old English, and I'd written a story about a village in England, that was all in Old English. And I'd written a long novella that actually ended up coming out in a magazine, about a WASP who passes himself off as Jewish. Even with his wife—and is exposed when his wife gets terminal cancer. But both things were basically vehicles for me to show off in various technical ways. Like to do really good, a kind of really good kitschy Jewish voice and dialogue. And it was more like that's what I want to do, now how can I structure a story so that I can?

I mean, it was all—and I was *so* arrogant. I would have this defense, that when the professors would say they didn't like the stuff, I would think it was that they didn't understand the grand conceptual schemes I'd laid on it. But I was not willing to realize that I'd laid the grand conceptual schemes on a substructure that was essentially, "How will this enable me to show off in way X?" "How will this enable me to show off in way Y?" And it's something that I see in, for example, Leyner. Who I think is *very* gifted. But he's somebody whose vibe I always get: The point of this is that Mark Leyner is smart and funny. The point of this is that Mark Leyner is smart and funny. And it's fine. And he earns every cent he gets.

But it's like, you're loppin' off 30 percent—the intangible thing in art that can make the stuff, you know, worth not watching TV for.

Is it worth not watching TV for?

Good—I think the good stuff is. But also, I mean art requires you to *work*. And we're not equipped to work all the time. And there's times when, for instance for me, commercial fiction or television is perfectly appropriate. Given the resources I've got and what I want to spend. The problem is, when I'm trying to derive all my spiritual and emotional and artistic calories from that stuff, it's like living on a diet of candy. And I know I'm repeating that over and over. I can find very few analogies that work well.

It's in the book . . .

It's in the book but it's about little kids—whether the parents are going to keep little kids from eating candy. Yeah. And I also—it's another thing that I have. Is, you've watched me eat a lot of sugar on this tour? I'm hypoglycemic. If I eat sugar, I get a headache and feel shitty, and I shouldn't do it. But once I eat a little bit, I get a craving for more and more and more and more and more. [I nod: another one.] Yeah, interesting.

Something you learned from Blue Velvet and from Brazil is that the details matter, even in something that's not realistic.

Yeah. That whatever the project of surrealism is works *way* better if 99.9 percent of it is absolutely real. And that you can't just—you know. And that's something . . . I wouldn't even be able to put it that clearly if I didn't *teach*. Where I see my students, you know—"not enough of this is *real*, you know?" "But it's *supposed* to be surreal." "Yeah, but you don't *get* it." Surrealism doesn't work. I mean, most of the word surrealism is *realism*, you know? It's *extra*-realism, it's something on top of realism. It's that one thing in a Lynch frame that's off. That if everything else weren't picture-perfect and totally structured, wouldn't hit. Wouldn't punch the viewer in the stomach the way that it does.

Why don't you have a TV?

'Cause I'll watch it all the time. Having to go over to friends' houses to watch TV *works*. It's very much like taking an Anabuse or something. I mean, it just lowers the amount that I can watch.

So you'll just call friends, "Clear out, here I come." Or will you watch it with them?

I'll make plans. I'll say, you know, "Are you guys going to watch some TV?" If it's something I want to watch, I'll come over.

Otherwise, you would watch it all the time?

Yeah, I don't even know if I would *watch* it. It would be like what it is with you, it would be on all the time—it would be my version of a fireplace. It would be a source of warmth and light in the corner, that I would occasionally get sucked into.

[Break]

[Dave, as check is gliding toward us: "Is Jann paying for this?" Serial question. Also again, to waitress, "We're traveling platonically," or "We're not together, etc. etc., not that way." I mean, a standard gag of his.]

David thinks that Kevin Spacey and Anthony Hopkins are in an arm-wrestle for best psycho of the last four or five years. Where does Christopher Walken fit into that?

Which Christopher Walken?

King of New York. Comfort of Strangers.

Yeah, that seemed like, didn't see that. I thought he was *great* in *True Romance.* Just in that little, "the Pantomime." "Men have seventeen, women's got twenty-one."

[He does a not-bad Walken. Gifted mimic.]

Ha.

"My father was the heavyweight champ-ion of Sicilian liars."

That great scene: he's got to tell where Slater and Patricia Arquette are hiding—

Or that they're gonna torture it out of him. And so, knowing that he's got to get him mad enough to kill him . . . I mean, Tarantino is such a *schmuck* 90 percent of the time. But ten percent of the time, I've seen genius shining off the guy.

But that scene: It's convincing heroism, in a way that almost never comes through in movies.

But then the weird touch of having the name on the refrigerator the whole time. (Smiles) That's so—

Did you see The Last Boy Scout?

Is that Bruce Willis? Is that where he does the jig at the end? Huh. I don't—I didn't watch it paying much attention. I think I saw it on a VCR at somebody's house.

I really like Bruce Willis. Ever since *Moonlighting* he just had me in the palm of his hand, I really liked him in *Pulp Fiction*.

• • •

BACK IN THE CAR
ALL AT ONCE

DAVE: (Complains) I'm so fucking passive.

• • •

AT EXXON STATION

DRUNKEN GUY AT PUMPS: You guys weren't at the game by any chance, were you? Hinsdale?

Missed it.

[And then we leave the gas cap sitting on top of the pump. Which the National Rent-A-Car people aren't tremendously understanding about.]

• • •

BACK IN THE CAR
I-55

[I ask David to drive.]

Satisfy my curiosity. During that big bewildering party you had for the book at Tenth Street Lounge, when you went to the bathroom, you were looking in the mirror, right? That's what you went for?

When?

When you went to the bathroom. We were talking, and you went to the bathroom. The kind of thing where you would touch one side of your hair, push it back a little bit, and just look in the mirror. I guess I was wrong?

I went to the bathroom to take my tobacco out. As a matter of fact, I think I made it a project *not* to look in the mirror during that party. Because I knew that a lot of other people were looking at me, and if I thought about what I looked like, I was going to go crazy.

But it must have been a bewildering . . . I mean, you didn't even interact with anybody at that party . . .

(Testy) Sure I did. I didn't—I spent half that party in the office up above, with first Charis and then Mark Costello. And there was a great little like *nook*. Where we could look out at everybody talking, it was an enormous amount of fun.

[At wheel] This is nice, I get to drive a car with more than one operable cylinder. A good road-trip car.

[Break]

Michael—I'm not going to pronounce his name correctly—and it's not Michael, it's the Asian tennis player at Enfield . . .

Pemulis. He's not Asian.

No, not Pemulis.

Oh, oh, oh. LaMont Chu.

Why I brought the book into Denny's, although we didn't get around to it. The character, LaMont Chu, he has a complex response to fame. Which he goes to Lyle about.

Heh heh heah.

[He's pleased. He's been waiting for *someone* to do this.]

Tell me about that. You know why I'm asking the question, that's why you're laughing. So tell me.

Sure. Nah, it's just this whole, um—yeah, that's a lot about what it's like to be kind of a young, grad-student writer. Who really reveres certain older ones. You suffer from a delusion that, for all the pain of your envy, there's this inverse, satisfied feeling. Which is the pleasure of *being* envied by you. And that that— and then I can remember bein' a tennis player. And havin' exactly the same feeling about older, successful tennis players, and it's just . . .

But now you're in the inverse spot, actually.

Mmmmm. Really?

Yes.

Well, then I can tell you, from authoritative firsthand experience that there's nothing like—there's no *keen*, exquisite pleasure that corresponds with the keen exquisite pain of envying somebody older. Who's written something, or won some tournament, that you particularly admire.

Let's talk about the simple brute thing . . .

Just tell me where the rear window defogger is here.

Um, as I was reading it, and marking it, and knowing it had to come from your reading of other people, while you were having trouble doing your own work.

Heh heh heh heh. (Dark, exposed laugh, with the pleasure of being discovered)
      It's like, only a writer under, like, thirty would have known that that was . . . That it came out of *bitter* truths. That's actually—that's a scene that was *much* cut down by Michael. 'Cause it went on and on and on, with a whole lot of fame theory, and delusions about it, and stuff like that.

You were talking about guys who found black gold while they were out shooting game, right? And you were talking about writers who'd found that, I thought?

Oh, you mean like younger writers our age or something? It was more like the older—like that there was a feeling that went along with having your picture in a magazine. You're right—there's some delicious ironies to this whole process that I haven't even . . . This is one reason why I need to go home and *quiver*. Is 'cause I haven't thought about any of this stuff.

I'm going to begin reading to you now. I've gotta find the interior lights in here. So I can begin reading to you some quotes . . .

Let me just . . . Oh, "South," "Joliet . . ."

That's the prison, right?

That's one of its charms.

Blues Brothers?

Yeah. It's also the setting of the first part of *The Sting.*

George Roy Hill . . . great director . . . that great comedy about hockey.

Hockey—Oh, *Slap Shot?* Yeah, that was pretty good.

. . . I love the Hanson brothers.

Yeah. Yeah, "You better watch out for the kid, he's going to have somebody's dick in his mouth before you can say Jack Robinson."

There's this fascination with homosexuality in the script, which is very odd and mean.

Yeah. It's kind of a *nasty* movie, but it's very funny. [A set of taillights crosses into our lane.] This guy is a *true* asshole.

It's truly funny, it knocked me out as a kid. Then his career ended.

How did it end, by the way?

He made—Funny Farm was the last movie he made. Chevy Chase, a splashy bad real estate purchase. Strange, biggest director in the '70s . . . A Little Romance . . .

He made *A Little Romance?* It was a great movie.

The Sting and Butch Cassidy . . . huge seminal hits . . .

How did his career go away like that?

I think he just stopped doing hits . . . Diane Lane in A Little Ro-
mance . . . wonderful.

Broah! Oh yeah! I know, I'm agreeing. Not to mention the fact that
she grew up into, to just be a fucking *angel*. She was in *The Cotton*
Club, but she's been in hardly anything else.

. . . also in Streets of Fire . . .

I hate this: "Vehicles are closer than they appear."

So you thought this was coming, right?

What?

That someone was going to read these things to you . . .

Read as much as you want, as long as I don't have to respond.

You had to know that somebody would ask you about that . . . that's the
kind of thing you write . . . When you write a scene like the one with that
kid, and Lyle talking about wanting to be famous. You know that some-
one's going to come back and ask you about those things.

Except only another writer would. That's the good and bad thing
about choosing you to do this. I'm serious, man, if you—like this
would have been over a *day* ago if you hadn't been somebody who
writes novels.

Well, I appreciate that . . .

I can be very *tough* when I have to be. It's actually—it's the way to get me. Is get me to like the person, and I'll like become *way* more passive and worry about their feelings and all this stuff.

. . . have you been worried about my feelings?

It's part of, you know, this *mélange* of various things. It's one reason this is tiring. Yeah, and also, I had this incredible—I mean I'm rubbing my hands together so I can call you in six or seven months. I can't wait till *you* like have somebody, you know, hanging around. Wanting to hear your—it's all so interesting.

Nothing, the kind of thing that's happened to you happens to young writers once every five or ten years.

It may not be something of this length. But you know enough about how—I mean this—some version of the dog-and-pony show goes along with having a book come out.

No, that's true. But the kind of attention that you've gotten . . . maybe happens once in a decade to someone our age. . . .

No, this is like—this is like two things. This is the thing in *The New York Times Magazine* and the thing in *Rolling Stone*.

[Slightly disingenuous]

I follow, for better or worse . . . writers. When they break into certain kind of levels of success, when books get certain kinds of attention . . . and this kind of stuff happens very, very rarely.

Huh!

Oh, you know it too. Come on—you're smiling! You know you know it too. You follow this crap also, come on.

I follow the crap. But I struggle much harder against the *temptation* to follow the crap. And I follow it from much more of a distance— and yeah, I have some sort of idea of it. But have some compassion. I mean, I've already told you that, like, I gotta be *very* careful about how much of this stuff I take inside. Because I go home, and I spend a month getting this manuscript ready. And then I got to start working on something *else*. And the realer this shit is to me, and the more I think about it—and, of course you're holding the tape recorder so that I will end up *reading* what I've said in this article. That will *feed* the self-consciousness loop. (Laughs) That like, I *need* to be—so I'm not just, I'm not fucking around with you, and I'm not playing you like you're stupid.

You've just gotta realize that, that I've gotta be real disciplined about how real I make this stuff to me, and I also don't want to overblow it. I think something—the truth is somewhere between what you're saying and something about what I'm saying. I mean Amy Holmes is doing a tour for *The End of Alice* that's bigger, and involves more interviews, than the tour I'm doing. You know? So it's maybe like ten books a year, ten literary books a year by young, by young writers are—

Publishers want it to happen. They bait the hook in various ways. And they'll bait it with a lot of horsemeat—or whatever they bait it with—or a small amount of horsemeat—

Conch, I think, is what cuts up nicely, into cubes.

I was thinking of a kind of big fleshy thing, sure.

Huh!

But they throw it out there, and it doesn't always get a strike. I mean, they throw it out there, and they don't know who or what's gonna bite.

So there's been a strike this time?

A marlin.

The rod is bowing way down. Bowing.

A huge marlin. A marlin of, like, prehistoric proportions . . .

Ah-huh. [Trying to control pleasure]

Which happens very very rarely.

But it might be one of those fish that you get all happy, then you lean over to gaff it and it takes your arm off.

Yeah, but in this case, it's been gaffed, and it went fine . . .

Uhhhh, let's—Why don't you call—I'll tell ya, here's what would be real interesting, you can find him. Why don't you call Jay and ask for *his* take on this book. McInerney.

[Who gave the book a mixed review. Samples:

> "I felt a . . . feeling of admiration alloyed with impatience veer-
> ing toward strained credulity . . . If Mr. Wallace were less talented,
> you would be inclined to shoot him—or possibly yourself—some-
> where right around page 480 of 'Infinite Jest.' In fact, you might
> anyway."]

OK. I will ask, and I will call him. But here's the thing: Do you know how many times Rolling Stone has done a young writer, a profile, in the last ten years?

Uh-uh.

Zero.

Really.

I checked, zero.

Except let's *realize* that, OK, right; I think I wrote a good book. And I think for some reason—like the timing was right or whatever. But one reason *Rolling Stone* is interested has very little to do with me or the book, it's this kind of miasma of hype around the book, that feeds on itself.

Well, no, but it's just, it's—I mean, you're talking—you want to know what this *tour* was like. Forty percent of the interviews were interesting, and 60 percent were very charming people. Who you know, "I gotta admit, it's such a big book, I've only read five pages. But what I'm really interested in, is, what do you make of all this attention?" You know? And I'm just—the phenomenon is not lost on me. And given that fact. *Plus* the fact that I got a serious investment in having a certain amount of detachment from this . . . So all I'm trying to do is explain to you that—Yeah, if I'm playin' a little dumb I'm not, I'm not trying to condescend to you or act like you're stupid. It's just I don't, I don't want to *feel* every edge of this quite yet.

Got it.

Because, because, you know, I'm thirty-four. And I've *finally* discovered I really love to write this stuff. I really love to work hard. And I'm so terrified that this—that *this* is going to somehow twist me. Or turn me into somebody whose hunger for approval keeps it from being fun, you know?

[Reason for it]

I want to be able to—I mean, you know, I think *Infinite Jest* is really good. I would hope that if I keep working really hard for like the next ten or twenty years, I can do something that's *better* than that. Which means I've gotta be *really* careful, you know? About, you know, you know, I don't want to end up being somebody on *game* shows. And you've talked about it, it was when the tape recorder was on, nobody's done, nobody's taken this well. I mean this has never helped *anybody.* Anybody's writing future. So I would be an *idiot,* you know, if I were not playing various psychic games and erecting defenses.

This is very smart. You say something that gets a rise out of me, and I begin talking, and it's good because I like you, so I'm talking to you. But the tape recorder's on . . .

But I was thinking, you were talking about your passion for the work. There's a scene in one of Updike's essays in Self-Consciousness, he says—

He's got an essay called "Self-Consciousness"?

He has a book called that.

I thought it was called *Getting the Words Out.*

No, "Getting the Words Out" is one of the essays . . .

Boy, if nothing else you've given me six things to read. Renata Adler, "Anonymiad," Nabokov's letters—

I'm not sure you're running that risk, because you're a much more centered person . . . I'm sorry to use a word like "centered," you don't think—you were shaking your head when I said "centered." You don't see yourself that way?

No, I don't.

Why not?

I see myself as somebody who's been *unbelievably* burned by no one other than me. Through *not* being centered. I have an *enormous ambition* to be centered. But I don't—I don't perceive myself as that way. And I wouldn't be so careful about this kind of stuff, if I felt very much confidence that I could handle it well. And I'm aware that this makes very good copy, and this will be a neat part of the article. But it's also really like—you know, I feel like we've sort of become friends and . . . understand that. I mean this stuff, it's *really* scary. And I think if we were in exactly the opposite situation, you'd be saying a lot of the same stuff. It's great. But it's also, it's also really scary at the same time. 'Cause I've gotta—you know, I've got what I *hope* is like forty more years of work ahead of me.

Hah. Do you have a huge ambition in general, or no . . . ?

Yeah, I think I do. What it's been about has changed a whole lot. I mean I really, I'm now so scared of having the ambition be, to be regarded well by other people. Just cause it's—it landed me in a suicide ward.

That it's now, except for making vague, pretentious statements about art, I couldn't really name what it is.

Is there someone then who's better prepared for this than someone who was in a suicide ward about it?

I think somebody who's been in a suicide ward is either way better prepared or way *less* well prepared. Because I mean, I don't think we ever *change*. I mean I'm sure there are still those same parts of me. I've just got to find a way to not let them *drive*. Could I also have—if I can have my Diet Pepsi. [For drinking and then spitting]

You said you're hardwired for addictive behavior. You were able to train yourself out of it, you don't drink programmatically. Don't you think you can train yourself . . . ?

That's safe to say. Except I would, I don't like the word "program-matical."

[Road quiet now. Just the rush of tires over cement, that slightly sibilant, airplane-y sound of the air we're cutting through with the fender and windshield.]

I'm going to say, in the piece, that I noticed that you don't drink . . . there are places where we ate when I would have ordered like a beer or something but didn't.

You can order whatever you want.

My friends who have been through the program, they say that they've always been very conscious—'cause when they first went in the program they didn't want people to drink in front of them, and so I've always since not . . .

Well, I'm not any sort of authority on any sort of program. But from my very limited outside understanding of the program, people who have been in it for a while and are fairly—are fairly nice where they're at: you could snort cocaine off the back of your hand next to them. And as long as they have a reasonably *decent* reason to be with you, you don't have to worry.

  Can I turn this off, or . . . ? [The interior light] Boy, it's easy to speed in this thing.

Seventy-five though is fair. You can hit cruise control . . .

Yeah, cruise control makes me nervous.

You killed off Michael Chang, too, I saw. In the book.

[He laughs.]

OK, here's the first quote, "The obsession with future-tense fame makes all else pale." You don't drink anymore, keep TV away from yourself . . . you had to train yourself away from it, but you know that being exposed to it might be harmful.

Ah-huh. [His debatable: Ah-huh.]

Similarly you had to train yourself away during a very painful period from thinking about attention, right? And now it's being pushed at you whether you want it or not.

Right.

What about that . . . ? Everything else you were able to regulate and control how much you got; not this.

Well, notice that it's not exactly like I'm a paragon of self-control. I've got a *raging* nicotine problem. That like that I really need to quit, at least the chewing tobacco. It makes your fucking jaw fall off. You know? I've got a sugar problem and I like, you know, I have a pretty hard time with girlfriends. I mean it's not like, you know, I'm not like . . . And no, no, no, no—but I'm just saying, you know, it's not like, it's not like . . . but yeah, this stuff, this stuff's really scary. And it's really confusing, because if I had totally eschewed all of it, then I think I really would have *fucked* over Little, Brown, who took a huge chance. *But* there's also—that could be a really great excuse, 'cause there's a little part of me of course that *loves* this, you know?

That a major magazine would pay all this money to send you— who are not an idiot or an unbusy man, to come repeat stuff I said into a tape recorder? I mean, it gets *very* confusing.

And I'm trying to make these decisions about "Do this, don't do this, what are my reasons for this, what are my reasons for that?" It's one reason I want this phase over. It's *extraordinarily*, it's very hard work inside your head. And I think it's one reason I'm like, you know, smoking three packs of cigarettes and chewing two cans of tobacco a day. (Laughs) It's just—it's fine. But one reason it's fine is, it's going to be *over*. Like starting some time tomorrow. And I've already got assurances from Little, Brown, there's no more of this. That like—that I've been a good little trouper, and there's no more of this.

What's scary to me is, I'll bet two weeks are going to go by. And I'm going to wish you were back with your tape recorder—you know what? Then I'm going to have to like, you know, um, then I'm going to have to like *decompress* from getting a whole lot of attention. Because it's like getting *heroin* injected into your cortex. And where I'm going to need balls is to be able to sit there and, and go through that. And try to remind myself that, you know . . . And you know it's the same. That what the reality is, is being *in* a room with a piece of paper. And that all this, this is tangential stuff, and some of it feels real good and some of it doesn't. But this is all—that's—*that's* what's real, and the rest of this is just conversation around it.

It is frightening, as I think about it. Must be like an astronaut stepping back to his house: He's been directed by people in a different state, shot up somewhere, outside people planning everything. And then he drives home. And his life has been invaded to some degree, and it's suddenly uninvaded. And then you have to go back . . .

Yeah, it's been invaded. That, that's less troubling to me than to what extent have I been a willing accomplice in that invasion, you know? To have written a book about how seductive image is, and how very many ways there are to get seduced off any kind of meaningful path, because of the way the culture is now. But what if, you know, what if I become this grotesque parody of just what the book is about? And of course, this stuff drives me *nuts*.

To get back to addiction metaphor for a second. You're someone who had to fight an addiction to being interested in approval, the same way you fought connections to substances, or to television.

Yeah.

And you've solved those problems by trying to keep those things away from your sideboard, and yet—

Sideboard?

Keep it off your table, so it wasn't within easy reach. And this has been put on your table. And I wonder if you're afraid that the part you trained away will jump back in, the same way that alcoholics are afraid that they'll go on a bender if they drink just one glass.

I'm worried a little bit. But you know it seems like taking this stuff off your sideboard, its location is less, is less important than getting in the psychic space where you're willing to take it off your sideboard. You know what I mean? So the next level of complication is, do I congratulate myself on my worry and concern about all this stuff, because it gives a sign that I've *not* been seduced about it? And of course then if I get *happy* about *that,* then I've lost the edge—I mean, there's just no end to the little French curls of craziness you can go through about it.

The thing that I like about it is that—is that Little, Brown is fairly *decent.* They want money and they want the book to be a big deal. And me doing a certain amount of stuff about me helps the book, and that's cool. But they've already like, you know—they're not like "Oh, the book's really hot, we've been in touch with ISU, you have the semester off, you're going to go on a whirlwind tour of *Europe,*" you know? I mean they're like, they're halfway cool. And you know, I've talked to a couple of people and they're like, "You're right. You know, you gotta teach, you got to get this manuscript ready for Michael, enough of this."

Really?

Yeah. Yeah. Which—so everything's real complicated. They're not saints, 'cause you know they would prefer to have me be in *People* magazine or whatever. But they're not, they're not *assholes,* either. Who just want to like burn me out, and use up this thing, and get their cash while they can and then fuck you. I mean, nothing's ever that simple.

So you acknowledge the book as a big deal?

What do you mean?

Is it a big deal?

To whom?

Has it been received as a big deal . . . I just wanted to have you saying that. Is this why you live in Bloomington?

Why I live in Bloomington is I got a job that I turned out—I'll tell you what. It ups my—I feel real lucky living in Bloomington. It's way better for me to be living in Bloomington.

Why?

Because every time I go to New York, I get caught up in—what do you call it? Now, see, then you're gonna make it *my* phrase—what you have called?—

What's your phrase?

I just—I just think of this enormous *hiss* of egos at various stages of inflation and deflation. It's just this whole—like I remember bein' in New York and Will Blythe's thing in *Esquire* came out. And *just* being, you know, wanting to cry. Wanting to run over and punch him in the nose. "How could he do this to me?" When I got home and a week later realized that, You know what? He wanted to do—

the hype thing pissed him off, he wanted to do something about it, ran into this problem of actually kinda liking the book, so what's the poor guy going to do? But when I'm in New York, it's all about me-me-me-me. And how could he do it and where do I—you know, is he ridiculing me in the red hot center of the artistic cosmos, and all this, and uh—

Esquire.

Excuse me?

Esquire. You remember, that phrasing is from that article in Esquire, with the Literary Universe.

Yeah, you would have been like an *infant* when that came out! I was at Yaddo when that came out. It was all like, "Who is on the horizon!" "Who is in the Orion constellation?" This whole like—um, God, what *craziness.*

So actually you really were a student of this?

What do you mean?

You were paying real close attention to the vacillations of literary fame.

That was in 1988—no, '87. That the *Esquire*—no, as a matter of fact, I know *exactly.* It was in July of 1987, 'cause I remember me and Lorrie Moore and Jay McInerney [Transcriber didn't know these names: the true parameters of literary fame] were all at the same table, all looking at our own little *Esquire* that summer. And I didn't go to—at Yaddo—and I didn't go to Yaddo till 1987.

You were in there.

I was "On the Horizon." (Smiles) I was on the horizon.

How did that feel to you . . .

Oh, I remember, it was absolutely *exhilarating*. It was absolutely exhilarating. But of course I forget who it was—oh, it was Alice Turner.
It was like, "OK, kid, now you're on the horizon, now we'll see what
you can do."

[The tape side runs out.]

So you felt thrilled seeing that?

Yeah.

[Windows closed: we're back to smoking, chomping, sipping.]

. . . Lorrie and Jay also . . .

Yeah, I recall they were *somewhat more prominent*. Can you hit that
thing that will *crack* this just a tiny bit? *Thank* you. How about we
turn this off unless you're absolutely quoting, because it makes it
hard to steer? No, you want something more interesting about that.
I remember—I mean that's a good example of why, like you know,
I mean, I—you know, I probably like that stuff as much as the next
person. But it was really *awful* because there was this whole—let me
see, it was thrilling and really scary at the same time. Because it's
like, "Oh, no, that means the *next* time this thing comes out, I need
to be, you know, three inches closer to the sun." And God forbid,
you know, any of the other On-the-Horizon people are closer to the
sun and I'm not. And it's this whole—
     And I don't think it's any different if you're like an *accountant* for
Andersen & Andersen, you know? Some big accounting firm and
that you know four or five other junior accountants get promoted
ahead of you. Or the guys who got out of law school with you make
partner before you do. I mean the *craziness* is exactly the same. I
mean, I *don't* think—I don't think it's really sort of any different.

It might be a little bit more powerful if it's taking place in *Esquire,* you know? And it's unavoidable. I just—what I'm saying isn't that dramatic, I've just *learned* that the farther away I can stay from it, the better it is for me.

I'd be awfully surprised if it wasn't the same for you, unless you're just a *tremendously* strong person.

[Flirting]

. . . people I know who've gone through this have had a very hard time with transition . . . and then—

And then, what's the next thing? And what's going to make the next thing as good as it can be? This stuff is not going to help me. [Break]

. . . I'm way into—I've decided that I need, I really need to find a few things that I believe in, in order to stay alive. And one of them is that this is—that I'm *extraordinarily* lucky to be able to do this kind of work. And that along with that luck comes a tremendous obligation to do the best, to do the very best I can.

Which means that I have to *structure* my life, you know, sort of like anybody who's dedicated to something. To maximize my ability to do good stuff. And it's just like, and it doesn't make me a *great person.* It just makes me a person that's really exhausted a couple other ways to live, you know? And really taken them, taken them to their conclusion. Which for me was a pink room, with no furniture and a *drain* in the center of the floor. Which is where they put me for an entire day when they thought I was going to kill myself. Where you don't have anything on, and somebody's observing you through a slot in the wall.

And when *that* happens to you, you get *tremendous*—you get *unprecedentedly* willing to examine other alternatives for how to live. (Laughs in satisfaction)

We're rushing. You're at Amherst and while you were in Arizona it gets published.

No, it came—yeah, it came out in the winter of my last year at Arizona.

So then you go to Yaddo the next summer, and find yourself in that list, right?

Interesting. Yeah.

Then take me through from then until the room with the drain on the floor.

I'll try my best, believing in your talent for compression. 'Cause I can't be—we can never be linear about ourselves.

It'll end up being radically compressed, with some nice sound bites coming from you.

[We'd almost run out of gas before, when we stopped at Denny's. That's how focused on the talk we'd become.]

Uh-oh—what is that, do you suppose?

I think someone's trying to build a scale model of the set from Blade Runner as a hobby.

(Laughs) Either that or Fritz Lang is alive and well in the heart of Illinois. [Break] He has his *Unforgiven*, David Webb Peoples's movies in general.

I didn't want to ask about Blade Runner. Too obvious and embarrassing. I mean: everyone loved it.

Godfrey, who wouldn't? Although Pauline Kael didn't like *Blade Runner.*

Yes, she didn't.

[Break]

About heroism and redemption in a corporate culture. I mean that's what makes it a great movie. Is that the machine thing is the barest and most skeletal of metaphors in that; Rutger Hauer is *us*. It's sort of like, I don't know, now you've got me thinking—there's so much beauty and profundity in all kinds of shitty pop culture all around us.

Like living in Bloomington: one of the things that I do, I mean, you have to listen to a lot of shitty country music. 'Cause that's like pretty much all there is on the radio, when you're tired of like, listening to Green Day on the one college station. And these country musics that are just so—you know, "Baby since you've left I can't live, I'm drinking all the time" and stuff. And I remember just being real impatient with it. Until I'd been living here about a year. And all of a sudden I realized that, what if you just imagined that this absent lover they're singing to is just a metaphor? And what they're really singing is to themselves, or to God, you know? "Since you've left I'm so empty I can't live, my life has no meaning." That in a weird way, I mean they're incredibly existentialist songs. That have the patina of the absent, of the romantic shit on it just to make it salable. But that all the pathos and heart that comes out of them, is they're singing about something much more elemental being missing, and their being incomplete without it. Than just, you know, some girl in *tight jeans* or something.

And it's so weird. It's like you live immersed in this stuff, it's very Flannery O'Connorish. And then every once in a while you realize that it's all the same, and it's all about the really profound shit. And that it's adjusted in various ways to talk to various demographic groups for commercial reasons. But that if you cock your ear and listen real close, it's—that it's *deep*, you know?

Where else do you see that kind of nice stuff rising out of shit pop culture?

Wow. Oh, God, everything. I mean even—we were making jokes about *Love Boat* and *Baywatch*. These *really*—the *really* commercial, *really* reductive shows that we so love to sneer at. Are also tremendously compelling. Because the *predictability* in popular art, the *really* formulaic stuff, the stuff that makes *no* attempt to surprise or do anything artistic, is so *profoundly* soothing. And it even, even the densest or most tired viewer can *see* what's coming. And it gives you a sense of order, that everything's going to be all right, that this is a narrative that will take *care* of you, and won't in any way challenge you. It's like being wrapped in a chamois blanket and nestled against a big, generous tit, you know? And that, OK, artwise maybe not the greatest art. But the function it provides is *deep* in a certain way.

That all this stuff is like deadly serious and really deep all the time. I mean, it doesn't mean that you should go around being some kind of scholar of pop culture and dismantling all the stuff. But that it's—that we find, that *art* finds a way to take care of you, and take part. Kind of *despite* itself. And that's one of the cool things about Kael. Is Kael, Kael writes about the miracle of . . . all the odds are stacked against, you know, the profundity. You know? Writing about the Hollywood system and stuff. And like crabgrass, or like Jeff Goldblum says in *Jurassic Park,* "Life finds a way." You know?

That like, the cool stuff and the magic stuff, it comes out all the time. The trick—you know, if there's one thing that the serious art can do, is that it can try to put you in places where you're more alive to hearing that. You know? That it can seduce you into paying attention to stuff in a way that's hard to pay attention to.

[Pleasant sound of tires over asphalt roadway. Now with like semiregular chunks, like rolling a pin over dough on a counter. We keep hearing the tires changing sound on different surfaces, and the car slightly sways. . . . It's cold now, as usual, from cracked open window. And with the air leaking in, noisy.]

. . . example . . . ? Movies or TV shows? Both were moved by that Blade Runner scene.

Well, we were talking about—we were talking about that scene in *True Romance*. Which it would be *easy* to see as high camp. You know: What an idiot, he fucking kills himself and then that number is on, and then that number is on the refrigerator. That's really this incredibly existentialist thing. It means—it means that the goal of protecting the son was never about that. That it was about the heroism. And choosing how you die. And the incredible sadness in his face as he went through this incredible, this really sad—I mean, it's about *everything*.

What's amazing, you can see it. He picks up that Chesterfield, he knows it's his last cigarette. And he smiles at it.

And he *enjoys* it. He draws the smoke in and holds it like a bong hit. A little extra time, you know, knowing it—that you know, that colors got brighter for him right then, and that sounds got sharper and he was starting to . . . One reason I think you'd like *Angels* is right at the end, this guy's going to the gas chamber. And he just talks about, you know, wanting to—he's looking out his prison cell at the clouds and realizing how cruel it is that the day is so precious to him on this, his last day. But also realizing that if it *weren't* his last day, you know, it wouldn't be so precious. It's just all—it's just all real *true*. It's not a great book, but *Angels* is full of moments like that.

And things that are less deliberately high culture . . .

Tell you what, turn the thing off for a second and let me think—
[Break]

[He asks me to prompt him: from a list of movies we've talked about.] *Last of the Mohicans. My girlfriend always mocks this part, Daniel Day-Lewis is escaping, by leaving Madeline Stowe high and dry . . . "Whatever happens stay alive. I will find you." . . . I find that moment very moving . . . And the guy who's been kind of a prick, the British officer, the Redcoat who's also in love with Madeline Stowe . . . They get captured by the bad Indians, someone has to die—*

And he does it. And I'll tell you, that change is plausible in a way Schindler's wasn't. There was something I bought, somehow. That he and Natty had been through enough, and earned enough of each other's respect, so that this man *became* enough of a man to realize that he deserves, that *Natty* deserved to live, and he didn't. Yeah, I found that *tremendously* . . . I don't know—and then the mercy of Natty, killing him, with his long rifle. No matter how *blunt* the phallic symbol, you know? I mean it's weird that it can be cheesy and—

For example, you didn't like that movie *Always*. You know? But there was—I myself found that metaphor of his appreciating Holly Hunter at just the time that she can't see or hear him anymore, is such a great metaphor for not appreciating something that you've got, you know? Loving somebody who's absent, you know? Their presence didn't satisfy but you feel their absence so much more *keenly*. And how the pain is more exquisite than the pleasure always is, because it's got that keener edge.

Or, I don't know, there's a moment—there's that movie *Broadcast News*. Which is in many ways a really—James L. Brooks is a, has the heart of a *whore*. But there's, Albert Brooks has that marvelous scene where he talks about William Hurt being the *devil*. And Holly Hunter says, you know, "Oh, what do you mean?" He goes, "Well, who do you think the devil's going to be? Somebody with"— you know, I only saw this once, but I've never forgotten it. "What's he gonna be, in a red cape? Whooo! No, the devil will be a very nice, very likable guy. Who very gradually lowers our standards of what's good, you know? And that'll be his job. And he'll get all—"

"The great women."

Right. Which of course James Brooks can't resist. He can't resist the sappy Albert Brooks's own agenda in it. You can't let Brooks have unalloyed passion, nobody in a James L. Brooks movie can do that.

So it's weird. It's like how the, like—I mean it really is, you know. You've got this enormous lump of shit, and then a rose growing out of it. And then you realize that the more *rank* the shit, the more, the more *saprogenic* the shit, the more fertile it is too. And it's not like "Oh, pop culture's great, we're surrounded by this beauty all the time." But the trick is that—is if you can *get* the right arrangement in your head. And get kind of in the right spirit to really try to pay attention, and *do* the work, to like see what's beautiful in it.

The paradox is that the popular stuff is training you *not* to do the work. It's telling you, you don't *have* to do the work.

[Break]

[We talk about *Glengarry Glen Ross*—"another absolutely great movie of the last ten years," he says—Anthony Minghella's movie of *The English Patient*.]

Have you read that book by the way?

. . . not completely my cup of tea . . .

No, Nan Graham [Scribner's editor in chief] sent it to me saying it was like the best thing published in the last twenty years. I haven't started it yet but I'm going to.

. . . read the first few pages . . .

It's not domestic? I would have thought it was very—

[Break]

. . . I make people watch the film with me . . . True Romance . . . see if they were struck by that moment of incidental niceness . . .

And we're also—we're being incredibly Pauline Kael-ish here too. 'Cause this is her whole sensibility. Is that what keeps her going, is looking for the little flashes. I'll tell ya, we talked about *Schindler's List* and I wasn't crazy about that. But that whole—that *incredibly* seductive way he tries to get Amon Göth to stop killing, by appealing to his megalomania. And indulging his forgiveness. And then that scene where—I'm sorry—Ralph Fiennes looks in the mirror, and tries to *see* himself as a forgiver. And is looking in his face, and that moment—that could so easily have been played for laughs—"Nah, I'll go kill the guy." But it's, he looks into his eyes and his soul, and *sees* that that's not him, you know? And *sees* how pathetic he is. And then can't tolerate *that,* and *that's* why he goes and shoots the boy. I mean there's so much stuff going on just in that little ten or fifteen seconds. Inside of a movie—inside of a movie whose central project ended up being, you know, dishonorable and cheating. But *that's* the neat thing about—I mean that's probably ultimately why novels and movies have it over short stories, as an art form. Is that if the heart of the short story is dishonest, there aren't enough of the little flashes to keep you going. Whereas in a novel or a movie, even if the central project doesn't work, there are often ten or fifteen great, great, great things.

. . . I love in Jaws . . . with the kid at dinner, where Roy Scheider—

Where they're making faces at each other? Yeah. Except you can really sense that Spielberg *knows* it's brilliant. And you can *hear,* like *grinding* character development going on in the chief. It's at that moment that you know the chief won't get eaten.

. . . because why? He's too likable . . .

Yeah, I mean that—there was this way, when I was talking with you in *Broken Arrow*—I mean, 'cause we're a lot the same—I mean I think we were watching that movie in a way that nobody else there . . . Maybe Julie was. But it's sort of like this *game* you play, we've seen so many of them. And we've seen, you know—we're viewers where you know if you've got Tom Sizemore, that you've ruined the movie for us. And it's, there's this, these whole other ways to kind of watch movies, and sort of fence with the director.

But it adds this whole other level of suspense: Is the director going to cheat or not? How can he—is he going to pull this off? Like the way we both *groaned* when we—when the fistfight came at the end, oh, with the twenty-dollar bill. You know, we're like—

... That was by the way why I loved Seven ... last half hour ... new kind of genre.

Yes. Although totally gratuitous stuff with Blythe Danner. I *knew* when Blythe Danner had that conversation with—that she was going to die and so was the baby. I mean emotionally a whole matrix of—

No, of course. But then ... the thrill of being surprised by having the movie change its tack like that.

Yeah. It's weird, that movie didn't do very well, did it?

No, it was a huge hit.

Was it?

... Toy Story.

[Break]

And—what was that Grisham thing?

The Firm.

Yeah.

... too broad for me ...

You're a smart movie watcher.

[After talking about Alec Baldwin and Jennifer Jason Leigh liking each other in *Miami Blues* helps *us* like them too . . .]

I love in . . . Jaws . . . it's the normal guy who got the shark . . .

Big difference in the book. Did you ever read the book? The book is a really terrible *Moby-Dick* remake.

. . . brings me close to tears, him having to pull off heroism . . . he hates the water . . .

But it's so sad, because seeing Scheider, you know, perched in that same crow's nest in *Jaws II*, I don't know, it's ruined. And it's also then seeing Spielberg milk the exact same thing in *Arachnophobia*. Or also, he milked it in *Raiders of the Lost Ark* when Harrison Ford hates snakes.

. . . he has that self-parodying repeating gesture . . . [in Jaws] people reaching out their hands to each other . . .

What do you mean reaching out—

. . . where someone's going to fall . . .

Oh, right.

. . . Close Encounters . . . falling down the hill . . . Melinda Dillon runs down . . . pulls him . . . I find that incredibly moving . . .

And I think the frame's chopped, so that we just see the hand when he's rescued? It takes us a beat to realize it's her hand. Why do you—because you know about this stuff—why does Spielberg have this fetish for putting other directors in his movies? Truffaut, who's the guy in *Jurassic Park?*—Richard Attenborough?

. . . Attenborough's always acted also . . .

So you think Attenborough, like, read for the part? What else has Attenborough been in?

. . . Séance on a Wet Afternoon . . .

Did you ever see a movie called *The Hit* with John Hurt and a very young Tim Roth? Terence Stamp. How old is that movie? Why is this guy blinking his lights at us?

. . . Terence Stamp . . . doesn't want to face death . . .

Yeah, that's very odd. I like that the woman *lived*. Tim Roth was a great—Tim Roth is another one. He's a little annoying. I think I was the only person in America who liked *Four Rooms*, just because of Tim Roth. Who, he was *completely*, he was so over the top that he couldn't even look down and *see* the top. And I saw that movie *twice*. And the second time I couldn't even get anybody to *go* with me, 'cause the word was out. I don't know what I liked, very difficult to figure out why we like stuff.

. . . smart director . . . same deflating and inflating gag in Reservoir Dogs as in True Romance . . . Tim Roth . . . about to make contact as undercover guy with the criminals. . . . He's been building his cred, working up his alias, now he's going downstairs, looks at the poster . . .

He looks at what poster?

Silver Surfer. Then he looks in the mirror, tells himself not to worry . . . then crossing street, the voiceover . . .

We see him walk out through the point of view of the cops who are—

Right, in the car behind. And the cop says, "A guy's gotta have rocks in his head the size of Gibraltar to work undercover. You want one of these?" "Yeah, I'll take the bear claw." It so undercuts the heroism . . .

But it's also very reductive of—there's a whole TV humor device which involves the person like, you know, "God, I'd never sell myself so cheaply. Oh, ten dollars? Sure." And then the audience—you know, it like happens ten times in every sitcom.

. . . had other characters do it . . .

True.

Tarantino as an example of self-parody . . . he then gets paid $200,000 to do . . . rewrite of Crimson Tide . . . all he did . . . add pop culture and comics references: an argument about the Silver Surfer.

That also had that actor who, "you got a lot of heart, kid" from *True Romance,* he played one of the—the weird thing about that movie is that movie could have been so great. If it had been left a little more ambiguous that Denzel Washington was right at the end, that sort of orgiastic vindication of his chest-thumping thing. But that could have been so—that could have been so *true* to how messy that situation really could have been.

I don't know, Denzel Washington's another one, I don't know whether I like him a whole lot. But God, you talk about star presence, he's just like—you're just, your *eye,* he fills your eye no matter where he is on the screen.

I read they were saying they couldn't bank on him in a movie . . .

Wait. He's been a leading man in *tons* of movies that have done well. Oh, come on—this was a period—people don't see history movies anymore, people don't see like a *noir* movie with a black man as the hero. I mean it's an enormous risk.

. . . Glory . . .

Glory was a great movie.

That moment: Matthew Broderick saying good-bye to his horse . . .

Yeah. Talk about something that *could* have been cheap, they had the *balls* to, like, do something that could have been really cheesy. And that ends up just—and it's ingenious in so many ways. *Ferris Bueller*'s essential woodenness works perfectly for a young man, you know, prematurely elevated to a position of that kind of power.

Callow.

Callow youth, you're right. He's *callow* in this.

Best battle scenes . . . that first scene at Antietam . . . people say best battle scenes . . .

Braveheart's got some pretty fucking *good* ones.

. . . where Broderick's a coward, he faints . . .

And it gives him—and it also, it's ingenious. Because otherwise there's *no* motivation for the assault on Fort Wagner, you know? "Sir, give us the opportunity to die gloriously." It's like that would be—that would be nothing but surface, if we hadn't seen how he'd been at Antietam.

. . . intensely moving . . .

Yeah, it really is.

. . . music . . .

Oh— [Hums it: he knows the *Glory* theme; impressive.] It's a very intrusive soundtrack. But it works with this thing. I don't know, there's a whole real interesting essay to be written about the psychodynamics of melodrama in that movie, and why *that* movie allowed melodrama to work when—I mean, there's *never* been a time in serious art more hostile to melodrama.

. . . themes that deserve the most dramatic treatment.

Yeah. And it was also very safely set in the far, far, far distant past, you know? A mythic American time.

. . . Morgan Freeman . . . walking through Charleston . . . "That's right. We run off slaves, but we come back fighting men . . ."

He was *great* in that. I haven't liked him in much else, but he was great in that.

He was Easy Reader.

On *Electric Company?* Yeah. Can we turn the *heat* up a tiny bit? I also—I wonder, we've got to be fairly close.

. . . I'm worried about your dogs, too. Isn't it funny, we're two people who are used to working alone. And we speak more comfortably looking out the window in the dark as opposed to looking across the table. It's not surprising, but it is funny.

It is, it's very interesting to me the ways, I don't know, we sort of converge and differ. It's real interesting just to hear what actors you like and don't like, and all about reading. I don't very often—there's a couple writers that I know really well who I've known for years. But this is just weird 'cause I like only met you a couple days ago. It's kind of *intense.* I'll be following your career with great interest too. If only just because now I feel like I know what you're *like* a little bit.

Let's talk about music for a second. What kind of music do you play . . . ?

I have the musical tastes of a thirteen-year-old girl.

I mean, I will find one or two songs—I listened to "Strange Currencies" over and over again all summer. Right now I'm listening—

Can we turn the light back on . . . ?

Sure. I knew this would come. Because of the *Rolling Stone* thing. I'm just—and now I've taped these two Bush songs off the radio. One's "Glycerine," and I don't even know what the other one's—it's that one, "I don't want to come back down from this cloud." "Glycerine," by the way, is a complete rip-off of Brian Eno's "The Big Ship," the *entire* bass line. Here, I'll even, when we get back I'll play "The Big Ship" for you and then "Glycerine." And it's just—it's sort of like Eric Clapton's "Cocaine" is a total rip-off of a Tommy Bolin song called "Post Toastee." Litigation. [I check; he's absolutely right.]

It's weird, I know—I know little esoteric bits. I listened to a lot of fusion in high school, and listened to like an enormous amount of, like, Pink Floyd and weird psychedelic shit. And then I know a fair amount about like esoteric Australian music, 'cause my sister lived in Australia for two years and sent me these tapes. But I don't have any kind of comprehensive, you know. . . . Like I'll read *Spin* or another magazine's record reviews. And I'll be like, I won't recognize three-quarters of the records they're talking about.

But then I'll happen to hear Alanis Morissette. On the radio. And you know just for some reason—that squeaky orgasmic quality in her voice will just *hit* me. And so I'll go like listen to nothing but Alanis Morissette for two months.

Why? I saw her on the wall.

[Left Alanis poster and *Cosmo* magazines out for me to find.]

I don't know what it is. She's simultaneously *so* erotic and *so* human and she can't sing all that well, and she's got that squeaky quality. I don't know *what* it is but there's something—I can't say anything interesting about it.

Did you like that song?

Which one? "I Want to Tell You"?

No, that's O.J. Simpson's I'm-on-Trial book. . . . Would be great if O.J. had sung "You Oughta Know" . . .

"I Want to Know," yeah, that one was all right. You know what? I could—the one, the only one I really *don't* like is that "I'm high but I'm grounded, I'm . . ." You know, that Gen-X anthem shit. But the *new* one—the one that, that's, but here's what's weird. If it was anybody else, I wouldn't forgive it. I *like* that she's trying too hard. For instance, Sheryl Crow made me want to vomit, from the very beginning. And there's not really a—they're sort of functioning in the same kind of role. And you can see Joan Osborne on deck, swinging two baseball bats, ready to have her fifteen minutes after Alanis Morissette.

What similar role are all of them playing . . .

My guess is—my guess is it's some kind of, there's a ditsy overearnest quality, where we can sneer at them a little bit. Which allows—we can stand to *hear* things from them that we couldn't stand to hear from a more hard-rock band. Because there's a ditsy flaky granola-crunchy quality about like . . . *Tch tch tch tchoo. . . .* For instance: I mean a seriously political like halfway-deep singer-songwriter like, what's her name, Natalie Merchant. Who used to be with 10,000 Maniacs. Is like—her career trajectory is entirely different. I mean she's—

she's got sorta small solid hits time after time. But these are different figures. Let me see, first Sheryl Crow—well, first there was Joan Armatrading for a while—not Joan Armatrading. Tracy Chapman. And lately there's been first Sheryl Crow and then Alanis Morissette and then you can see Joan Osborne—

Edie Brickell, too.

Well, see, here's what's weird: I'm really a bad person to ask about it. Because it just happens to be, like, you know, for a year I'll listen to country on the radio, and then for a year I'll listen to like shitty alt. And so now that I'm in the shitty alt phase a little bit, I'm a little more alive to the stuff. It's more like—

. . . more seasoned . . . What stuff can they say?

I'm trying to think. I mean imagine if—I don't know, the "God" song, "What If God Were One of Us." Let's try to imagine that being sung by, I don't know, R.E.M. Not an unearnest or an unpretentious rock band. But there's some sort of *waifish* quality about them. And we know the egg timer's running on their career, we know that they're like the 10 CC of 1996 or something like that. And that allows—it gives them a weird kind of freedom.

What I would love, and there maybe have been articles like this. But I would love profiles of the men involved, and the decisions about who gets not just record contracts, but who gets serious radio play, you know? Because it's real clear that Sheryl Crow with that "I Just Want to Live in L.A."—and then Alanis—are in lots of ways media creations. And it's probably five or six, I would imagine, guys in Ray-Bans and suits, have decided not just that they're good, but that they're *sellable*. And that there's a market. Has there been stuff like that, that I'm just too ignorant to have seen?

I don't think so . . . But it's not just those guys in suits . . . when "All I Wanna Do" came out . . . feel it in your belly somebody somewhere say-

ing, "We've got a hit." [Break] *Thinking this way: What about on a series, what you see on TV is not the characters, but just the actors straining to get their own pilots and series. . . .*

That's been what's excruciating about *Saturday Night Live*.

. . . Do you feel that ever listening to music? Like in Alanis Morissette . . .

No, I don't think so. And again—I'm very ignorant. My musical tastes are so eclectic and so involved, it's like what students have given me. I mean I didn't even, I hadn't even *heard* of Nirvana until after that man died.

What do you make of them?

I think it's absolutely incredible. But *unbelievably* painful. I mean if you, you know, all the stuff that I was groping in a sorta clumsy way to say about our generation? Cobain found, Cobain found incredibly powerful upsetting ways to say the same thing.

You wrote a whole book about rap. Why?

No, I—Mark and I wrote a book-length, a long essay that was originally going to go in a magazine called *Antaeus*. That turned, was turned *into* a book. [David's third book, *Signifying Rappers*.] That was about—why we and a lot of other white people like us, found ourselves *obsessed* with listening to black, to serious black political rap. That was thoroughly suffused with hatred for all things white. And watching these bands then get captured by white labels, and watching the hip-hop phenomenon get digested by Madison Avenue. And it wasn't—it wasn't about rap. I don't know that much about rap.

Also, I was terrified to write fiction. And Mark thought he might want to try this with me. And I was so desperate to feel like a writer, and whenever I would try to write fiction it was just an incoherent mess. So I thought that we would try that.

. . . more music stuff . . .

Don't get pissed off, though, about like I know next to *nothing* about this. I mean I am like a bonehead who listens to the radio.

[Break]

[About being a writer] . . . the attempt to track. I'm not sure we're any better, but we're able to describe the attempt to track our wandering in circles in a way that perhaps somebody else can identify with. I don't think writers are any *smarter* than other people. I think they may be more compelling in their stupidity, or in their *confusion.*

. . . well said . . .

And I'm structuring it as a sound bite, that's—I *think* that's closer to what I think.

. . . You said being a regular guy was a great strength of yours as a writer; I thought it was smart, but what did you mean by that?

I think—I had *serious* problems in my early twenties. I mean, I'd been a *really* good student. I was a really good logician and semantician and philosopher. And I really had this problem of thinking I was smarter than everybody else. [Reason for faux] And I think if you're writing out of a place where you think that you're smarter than everybody else, you're either condescending to the reader, or talking down to 'im, or playing games, or you think the point is to show how smart you are.

And all that happened to me was, I just had a bunch of shit happen in my twenties where I realized I wudn't near as smart. Where I realized I wasn't near as smart as I thought I was. And I realized that a lot of other people, including people without much education, were a *fuck* of a lot smarter than I thought they were. I got—what's the word? *Humbled,* in a way, I think. And uh, and what the weird thing is, discovering—I mean if you see more heart, you know. . . . Or I don't know, the prose is prettier or it's less cold or whatever—I—

I see more of a human person's experience . . .

I doubt I'm all that different from other like you know, seriously overeducated, intellectual kids. I *really* had this—I think I *really* had a very difficult time believing that anybody else, um, was at all like me. Or was anywhere as smart as me.

And *please*, if you put this in, make it clear that I'm talking about really how I *was*, like twelve, fifteen years ago. That I mean I, that I'm real *embarrassed* by that, you know? And I'm saying it only 'cause I pray that other people will, like—that other people will have been the same way.

Before I address that . . . In Harper's pieces, you said you peel back your skull.

Yeah. It's basically, you know, welcome to my mind for twenty pages. See through my eyes, here's pretty much all the French curls and crazy circles. And the trick about that stuff is to have it be honest, but also have it be a lot more interesting. I mean most of our thoughts aren't all that interesting. They're mostly just confused. That stuff's rhetorically real interesting 'cause it's about how to be honest with a *motive*, you know?

. . . Only two more minutes to go before we change tapes. That's really well said: how to be honest with a motive . . .

Turn the tape off. [Break] . . . instead of is it true or not? You don't even have to—I mean, just go, it's in like the first twenty pages. *The Screwtape Letters* is really—it's weird cause it's a very *childlike*, simple book. But Lewis is incredibly smart.

And it's, it's weird, it's one of the things I noticed, I don't notice that you argue by analogy or whatever. But it's like, if somebody will say something to you, your reaction is very often to quote a line *similar* to it. Or to talk about whether that's—whether that's a good *line* or not. And I think the reason why it doesn't *irritate* me, but I feel it and I notice it, is that there's a similar component in me. It's a writerly type thing.

But I guess my only justification for saying this to you is that I'm like, I'm really—there's something else. There's something else besides that. There's also this, is it *true* or not. That, does it feel true, does it taste true? And like whether it's *clever,* or whether, whether it's well said, or whether it's *fresh* or not, is only part of it. It's like—ah, I don't know. It's . . . I can't quite nail down just what I'm saying.

I think you would find that book *intensely* interesting. 'Cause it's weird, I read it for the first time when I was thirty. I swear to God, I'll read Renata Adler and Nabokov's letters if you will check that out. I think you'd really like it.

[The tape side runs out.]

• • •

CAR DRIVING HOME FROM AIRPORT
AND MINNEAPOLIS/CHICAGO
EN ROUTE TO ISU

[Big build; big build plus bandanna. Like he's going to ask you to play Hacky Sack, and if you say no he could be willing to beat you up.]

Part of social strategy. There's still something basically false about your approach here. To some degree. Which is this: that I think you still feel you're smarter than other people. And you're acting like someone—you're acting like someone who's about thirty-one or thirty-two, who's playing in the kid's softball game, and is trying to hold back his power hitting, to check his swing at the plate, more or less.

You mean in the book?

No, I mean in your social persona. And you're someone who's really trying—

You're a tough room.

You make a point of holding back—there's a point, there's something obvious about you somehow in a gentle way holding back what you're aware of as your intelligence to be with people who are somehow younger or . . .

Boy, that would make me a real asshole, wouldn't it?

[He's driving.]

No it wouldn't: It would make you a reformed person . . .

The parts of me that used to think I was different or smarter or whatever, almost made me die.

I understand that.

[What he has also is a Midwesterner's shy unwillingness about standing out.]

And I think it's also, like, I think one of the true ways that I've gotten smarter is, I've realized that I'm not that much smarter than other people. Or that there are ways in which other people are a lot smarter than me. And uh, *boy:* but I am, like especially in Minneapolis, with like you and Julie and Betsy, there was no act going on. There was one part of me holdin' back. Makin' real sure I didn't say catty shit about anybody like public, that you might write down. Or that if I asked Betsy or Julie personal shit that you might . . . and that was like *it*. And part of it is I was just so tired.

But it, uh—I don't know, it makes me feel kinda lonely that you think, that you think that I . . . In a weird way, it's sort of like the lady from the Letterman show talking to her husband. [His story "My Appearance."] Like there's been certain stuff that I've told you that's really true, and it's been *brave* of me. Because if you want—and it's also a gesture of trust, because if you *want*—I've written enough of these things, and I'm a good enough writer to know, that you could present that in a hundred ways. Ninety of which I'm really gonna come off as an asshole. But it seems like your read of them is, "Huh: what an *interesting* persona Dave is adopting for the purposes of this interview." And it's really just like, *uh.* There's a couple of times I've tried to do it a little bit. And it seems like you've caught me every time, and then we've both just laughed. I forget what it was, but . . . [Flirting]

I think there are different people on the page than in real life. I do six to eight drafts of everything that I do. Um, I am probably not the smartest writer going. But I also—and I know, OK, this is gonna fit right into the persona—I work really really hard. I'm really—you give me twenty-four hours? If we'd done this interview through the mail? I could be really really really smart. I'm not all that *fast.* And I'm really self-conscious. And I get confused really easily. When I'm in a room by myself alone, and have enough time, I can be really really smart. And people are different that way. You know what I mean? I may not—I don't think I'm quite as smart, one-on-one, with people, when I'm self-conscious, and I'm really really confused. And it's why like, My dream would be for you to write this up, and then to send it to me, and I get to rewrite all my quotes to you. Which of course you'll never do . . .

So yeah, I think I'm bright, and I think I'm talented. But I also know enough, like . . . it's one reason I'm uneasy about these interviews. Is, I know that I'm a lot more talented alone, when I've got time. Than I am in the back and forth of this.

Although I'm not an idiot. I mean I know, you know, I mean I can talk intelligently with you and stuff. But I can't quite keep up with you. [Patronizing? Flattering?] Whereas if we did it through the mail, and I had access to a library, and I could go look up the stuff you're talking to. That you and I would be equals. And that's as clear and honest an explanation as I can give.

[Maybe just painfully, humanly honest.

　　Later. We're quiet.]

It's not just "aw-shucks, I'm just in from the country, I'm not really a writer, I'm just a regular guy." I'm not trying to lay some kind of shit. And I'm—

But you just did it again. You just laid it on me, I mean . . .

[We turn off the tape. He asks me to stop talking. David's driving. I start to mumble-sing R.E.M. to myself, it's so dark I forget I'm not alone. Then I'm embarrassed, and look over, and David is mumble-singing too, and we head down the road in the front of the car.]

• • •

BACK IN BLOOMINGTON
KEY IN DOOR
DOG TAILS THUMPING, BARKING
DAVID DROPS BAG, RELIEVED

[This is hello to the dogs. The dogs go crazy when Dave steps in. He kneels on the ground: they go after him like the boy in my dad's old ad. Nudging, licking, batting, sniffing.]

(Elvis voice) I'm never leaving you again, baby. I swear, I swear.

[Looks around, a little rug check, some dog staining.]

(To dogs) Nothing wrong with a little shit on the floor, you guys. Happens to the best of us, hey guys?

[Can hear ice flow in the pipes, he says. He bangs around house, checking the pipes. He runs the water out, to stop icing and cracking.
   "*L.A. Times* called" . . . on notepaper.
   "What do you know about yarn?" he asks me. I turn out not to know a thing about yarn.
   We walk dogs down street; empty, soft breezes, street iced, long views. David with hands in pockets. We're waiting on Drone's and Jeeves's pleasure.]

You get instantaneous production from the Jeevester. Drone's a much tougher nut.

[On the neighborhood] People burn leaves when they want to, there's a slaughterhouse close by, it's kind of a savage area. There's a couple trailer parks around.

[Looks for mail in box. DFW, the box says.]

Peeing in the snow, that's a good thing. [We're heading back inside; still feels weird in the legs and under the sneakers to walk, after such a long time in the car.] Now I've just gotta clean up some shit. That I can handle, cleaning up shit. God, it's good to be home. Nothing like a little excremental work . . .

[Hears voice on tape: I'm checking the last one, to see where we left off.]

God, is that what my voice sounds like?

[Tennis case: Trophies. Unpacking. His beat-up shaving case.

Like many men who live alone, has a toilet seat in the upright position in the bathroom. The toilet seat is padded.]

I should check my e-mail. Can I . . . ?

My phone line is your phone line. My fridge is your fridge. My spare blanket is your spare blanket.

[I say this, and then am sort of embarrassed, as we aren't going to do an e-mail interview. I remember our earlier e-mail conversation, when I first arrived. His reason for not having a modem in house. David: "If I can get out, they can get in." No info re who they might be.

Cans of pop by the case. Lots of vitamins on the trip.]

I end up drinking ten or twelve Diet Rites a day, and end up leaving 'em around—I used to drink Diet Cokes, but then a friend said that there was enormous amounts of *salt* in it. And that it actually made you thirstier, so I switched over to this. Which to me is a bit thin and overcarbonated, but at least it doesn't make you— [Funny, he pounds them. Two six-packs a day.]

[But he thinks he ought to just accept that his intake is massive and start buying in quantity, instead of multitrip days.]

I should buy six cases, as opposed to just buying one and constantly running out. I leave 'em around, can't tell which ones are fresh and which ones aren't.

[Tells me he read *Lord of the Rings* five times as a teenager.

Gets an idea, walks to the kitchen. "The cookies we bought the first night are still in there."]

You loved Tolkien. Is it a pleasure to have written a book long enough so readers can lose themselves in your world, same way you did in Tolkien's?

I think it's different though. 'Cause this is a harder book, and it's more in *chunks*. I mean, the thing about Tolkien is, it's a very long linear narrative, where you feel like you yourself are on a voyage. And this is much more . . .

But on the Web boards I've visited, people do speak about it as if entering a different world . . .

That would be very neat.

[We're chewing the chilly cookies, from a plastic take-out container. Jeeves pads over and drops down directly on the carpet in front of us.]

[About Jeeves] You see, Jeeves gets very obedient when there's food around. You sit, Drone. You know, it should be clear by now that you're not getting any of this. *Good* dog.

[I ask him what he listened to when writing the novel.]

In Syracuse, I didn't listen to anything, because I didn't have a tape player. But when I was here, I was listening to Nirvana, because a grad student gave me that. And then this woman named Enya, who's Scottish.

[David pulls his tapes out, fires up the stereo, sits on the floor. First he plays is Bush. "Glycerine" does come from the Brian Eno song, as he demonstrates. Dave is singing along.]

The song is "The Big Ship"; it's off an album called *Another Green World*.

You researched for about a year and a half and then you wrote for about another year and half?

Nah, I think I started researching this thing—there's a real funny thing, I don't know, did you read Sven Birkert's thing? Sven had this whole argument about how, he went back and read this *Harper's* thing that had names of characters in it, and there was clear evidence that the tennis stuff in the book was autobiographical. I can't understand why Sven would make a mistake of that size . . .

Let's go back. You saw your name on the Esquire rising-star "Guide to the Literary Universe" thing in '87.

So that was the summer at Yaddo. And that was also the summer that I—it was an interesting summer, because I wrote the first half of this novella called "Westward," which was a big deal for me. Anyway, I wrote the first half of that, and then went down to New York for this abortive *Us* magazine shoot, that's where I got to meet the fabled Tama Janowitz. And then like walked out of the shoot, it was just a terrible thing, ended up spending the night at a friend's house near Washington Square.

And my car got broken into. And the half of the thing was just all handwritten. The first half was real different. The trunk got broken into, it got stolen. It was really funny, because they clearly took this airline bag out, looked through it, and then threw it away. And I *found* actually the bag in a Dumpster, about two blocks away. The thing was gone. And I figured they used it to, I don't know, light their crack pipes with or something.

So then I'm in terrible—anyway, so I go back to Yaddo, I rewrite that thing. And then for the next two months was like typin' that manuscript, gettin' it ready. And then, when I was at Yaddo, I got a job. I got an offer to teach for one semester at the university which I'd just graduated from. So that fall I go and I live at Amherst and I teach. Very bizarre, because there were students in that class who'd been in classes with me as a student, when I was, like, a senior and they were freshmen.

Weird.

It was very weird. And then what all happened?

Wait—how is that possible? Had they taken time off?

No—I graduated in spring of '85 and taught there fall of '87. So one year had passed.

No, two.

Yeah. So they would have been freshman my last year and now they were first semester seniors.

When you were walking around looking for your bag, were you thinking, Fuck, this is what happens when I get big ideas about myself and do press appearances? Symbolic in a way.

God, no—all I could think of was: I mean, I'd spent three months writing the first half. And it's weird, I went back to Yaddo, and wrote a first draft of the whole thing in, like, a week. No, I don't think . . . I don't think I *read* my life very effectively then.

OK, in '88 I lived at home. And then I lived in a little cabin in the desert in Tucson for a while. I was rewriting—there were like three or four things that had to be rewritten for the book. [*Girl with Curious Hair.*]

And then this—there was this whole messy thing, and I don't know what you know about it. Stories that were in that book appeared in various magazines. And one was the Letterman story. Which, um, the version in the book was very different than the version that I turned in. Or that sold to Alice, had sold to Alice at *Playboy.* Because the first version had a *whole lot* of stuff that was from an actual Letterman interview. And, um, it never occurred to me to tell 'em this, I mean the whole story was structured so that you couldn't tell what was made up and what was true. But anyway, um, like two weeks before *Playboy* went to press, they reran that interview. It was one of those Letterman rerun nights. And the shit really hit the fan.

Alice had this idea that I'd like intentionally tried to embarrass her, somehow. She really went on this paranoid fantasy. And actually, the thing ended up coming out . . . meanwhile, *Playboy*'s lawyers called Viking's lawyers, and clued them in about what was going on, and then they started looking at the *Jeopardy!* story. And at "Westward," and the Johnson story, and the fact that a lot of the minor characters were real people.

And so a lot of the time in Tucson—I lived in Champaign winter of '88. And then I moved to Tucson for four months, and then I moved back to Champaign for like five months all through '88, early '89. And basically, the book got killed. Viking already put a cover—it's weird. A collector showed me, the collector's got a bound galley of the Viking version of the book. Which, you know, for collectors now apparently it's like an upside-down postage stamp, it's just worth thousands of dollars, because Viking killed it. It's weird—they didn't even think they were gonna lose, they just thought they'd get sued.

Hey, Drone! Are you gonna eat my chair?

How'd you feel?

It was a very confusing time. Because they invoked the principle of what they called the right of publicity. Not right to privacy, but a right to publicity, such that publishing the *Jeopardy!* story would be the equivalent of my capitalizing on a physical resemblance to Pat Sajak—like running around at mall openings *as* Pat Sajak, and receiving income that was rightfully his. Which seemed to me so utterly bizarre.

But of course, the letters I'm writing were legally stupid. They're these long, impassioned, rhetorical things invoking literary principles and broad social, you know: "these people impose themselves on our consciousness but we are not allowed to reconfigure them . . ."

So it was a very weird time. And this was also a time when—I really think that for me just personally, "Westward" was this real seminal thing, like I really felt like I'd killed this huge part of myself doing it.

Nabokov says same thing: you write a book to get rid of, do away with that part of yourself.

This was about a whole orientation to fictional theory. I've always wondered if Barth read it, it's simultaneously absolutely homicidal and a fawning homage.

And then during all this time, I really, I mean I was really in a *panic*. Because I didn't think I was gonna be able to write anymore. And I got this idea that I'd started while being a student, and the writing was recreation from the student work. And what I'd do is contrive a situation where I applied to Princeton and Harvard in philosophy. Got a very sweet deal from Harvard. And so went out there early in '89, and moved into Boston, moved into this apartment with my friend Mark Costello.

Let me see: well, I did a bunch of stuff while I was there. That's when he and I wrote *Signifying Rappers*. And I wrote—I never published it—wrote a really long essay about video pornography. That actually *Playboy* helped me get on these sets by claiming I was a *Playboy* writer. I have some really riveting taped interviews with porn stars, too. And uh, did that, did a bunch of stuff, the long essay about *Wittgenstein's Mistress*.

Anyway, started at Harvard. And it was just real obvious that, like, I was *so* far away from that world. They had this idea that a grad student—I mean, you were a full-time grad student. I mean, there wasn't time to write on the side, there was four hundred pages of Kant theory to read you know every three days.

[Drone's stomach goes off. Loudly.]

And then Girl with Curious Hair was resold to Norton?

What happened was Gerry Howard, who was the editor at Viking, left for unrelated reasons. Went to Norton. Somehow he really believed in the book, and convinced Norton just to buy it. And to get Viking to give like—had me change some names like Leo Burnett and stuff like that. And then published it with Norton. So it's weird. I mean, there's all this stuff about that Norton didn't publish the book well, that nobody paid any attention to it. And it's more like, Man, if it hadn't been for him, that book wouldn't've ("wouldn'ta") come out at all.

That book gets passed around a lot.

[Jeeves now going crazy; batting things, barking.]

Yeah. I think it was fairly big in a kind of underground, New York way. But in terms of like, I mean *Broom of the System* sold *way* more than that did. That just *died.* Fell stillborn from the presses, as Hume said of his book.

   Hey Jeeves! We're trying to talk, I'm going to put you in your crate. You need to *hush.*

How well did Broom sell?

I don't know. But I know they made their money back on it. And I know that Norton never made their money back—no, Norton did make their money back, 'cause of what Avon paid them for the paperback. But *Avon* hasn't made their money back yet.

   Yeah, Norton's got a new paperback, which actually . . . I *gave* them, just 'cause of Gerry. Because they couldn't really offer me money for it. But I just—that's as much Gerry's book as it is mine. So anyway, and so—that was also the fall, I mean I got to Harvard, I quit drinkin' that summer.

   And the thing at Harvard was just unbelievably bleak. [Strange. So calm about it here in his living room, his house. Willing to just talk, no chess or feints, just tell his story.] But that's the semester that I went into McLean. That's the semester that I got really worried I was going to kill myself.

And so—and it was a big deal for me, because I was so embarrassed going in. But I think it was the first time I've ever treated
myself like I was worth something. Was, I mean—having to go to
the Harvard shrink, and say, "Look, I think there's this issue, you
know? I don't feel real safe."

She had me go in, which meant droppin' out of Harvard, which
meant I had to talk to Warren Goldfarb, the chair at Harvard. And it
was just unbelievably mortifying. And I was willin' to do it. I guess
to stay alive. Which in retrospect was probably promising.

This is . . .

This is late fall of '89. And then I never went back. I mean, I got out
of McLean's fairly quickly. And uh, I never went back.

Curious Hair comes out when? Same time?

I think it did. But I didn't really notice it coming out. I mean, I think
I gave, I remember I gave one reading at the Cambridge public library. That had thirteen people in the audience, one of whom was a
schizophrenic lady who kept shrieking during the reading. (Laughs,
shakes head) It was just a *bleak,* just a bleak time.

But reviews were really strong.

The only one I remember is that somebody said it was kind of exhi-
bitionistic. And they thought it was show-offy. I don't remember—I
don't even think—did it even get reviewed in *The New York Times*? It
was a bleak time. I don't think I was payin' much attention to anything other than good old yours truly.

*Happy to see it coming out then, though? What was bothering you
at that time? Some connection between desire for approval and your
writing?*

I was just unbelievably sad. All the time. And didn't think I was going to be able to write anymore. And I think that book's coming out was sort of, seemed more like a kind of, a kind of shrill jagged laugh from the universe. About, you know, I'm done, and now this *thing*, what was it like? This thing sort of lingers like a really nasty fart behind me. You know? For like a further—you know, and if it does really well, then it's a further reminder of the fact that I'm like, that I'm *screwed*.

Because you thought you'd lost the ability to write?

Well, I just thought I'd, I just didn't see the *point* of it anymore. I mean, the stuff that I was interested in seemed—I mean, I really felt like "Westward" had, at least for me, had sort of folded it up into this tiny, infinitely dense thing. And that it had kind of exploded.

But which makes it sound like I'm talking very grandiosely about the story. And it's much more about—um, it was partly that. It was partly, I think a lot of it was I think I'd really for two or three years leaned on, ah, leaned on drinkin' hard as a way to deal with stuff. And it's real weird, you do that, and then you take it away—yeah. Things get tense. And you know, I just made *enormous* mistakes.

I think going to Harvard was a huge mistake. I was too old to be in grad school. I didn't wanna be an academic philosopher anymore. But I was incredibly, um, humiliated, to drop out. Let's not forget that my father's a philosophy professor, that a lot of the professors there were revered by *him*. That he knew a couple of them. [In a sense, the *Moby-Dick* thing again.] There was just an enormous amount of terrible stuff going on. But I left there and I didn't go back.

I remember I was so embarrassed, my mother had sent me a vegetable juicer. That had arrived in the mail soon after I'd left there. And for some reason they'd taken it into the department office. And I'd always wanted to get that vegetable juicer back. And I never had the balls to go back and get it back. Because I couldn't tell if I could face those people.

And then Mark got a law firm job in New York. So he moved away. And I lived in that apartment alone, for quite a while. Um. Yeah. Got a job teaching. That spring. Started—no, I'm sorry, that spring I worked as a security guard at the Lotus Software Corporation. Which was weird.

What'd you do there?

I have yet to integrate that into my experience. I've never worn polyester every day for three months. [Funny, my phone conversation with Amy, his sister Amy, a few weeks later: Amy's stories about David loving cotton. Purloining any shirt of hers, even the girliest, if he liked the weave.] And I had to wear polyester. And I carried what was called a service baton. And this other security guard showed me, you know, the tricks cops have. The various ways—which I wasn't great at, but I was fairly good at. And I just remember *walkin'*—my shift was, ah, it was weird, it was half third, half first. So I'd go in super early in the morning until like midmorning, and in the early morning, nobody'd be there. And I'd just walk under these fluorescent lights, twirling my baton, thinking about as little as possible.

Did you think you were done then?

Yeah. I was pretty sure life was over.

This is after suicide watch is over? [Bonnie told me when she came to visit McLean and saw him, the first thing she did was find a scissors so she could cut his hair, it looked so awful to her.]

Mm-hmm. That was actually a fairly grim—I think I was in McLean's for a total of eight days. And then, I was really there just mostly 'cause I was scared I would do something stupid. And I'd actually had a friend from high school, who tried to kill himself by sitting in a garage with the car runnin'. And what it turned out was, he didn't *die*, but it really, it fucked up his brain, sort of. It fucked up the *affec-*

tive part. So that he was in terrible pain apparently all the time. But like I was just—and I *knew*, that if anybody was fated to fuck up a suicide attempt, it was me.

Which gives you some idea of my mind-set at the time: And I'll fuck up even that, and then I'll be a quadriplegic.

[I tell him van Gogh story. Van Gogh went into a field to shoot himself, in the chest, with a single-shot pistol. And *missed*. And had to walk back through town, where everyone thought he was sort of foolish already: terminally wounded but not in fact dead.]

I didn't know that story. [Doesn't find it that funny at first; then laughs.] Yeah, like I can't catch a *break*.

You were somewhat in pain about your desire to become a sort of successful literary person?

Yes, but also an awareness—I mean, I was in my late twenties then. And you know, and I was sort of aware that that was fairly empty. But the only other thing that seemed to be pulling me was the really sort of intense theoretical interest in fiction. Which then *also* seemed empty.

Metafiction. And postmodernism. And what came after metafiction—like what would meta-metafiction be like? And what were ways to co-opt pop culture? And it's very hard to explain. I think probably the not very sophisticated diagnosis is that I was just depressed.

Do you think the person you were in 1986 and 1987 would have disliked the work you did for Harper's, for example? Because it's pretty straightforward?

Yeah. I don't think he would have hated it—I just don't think he woulda *read* it. I think he would've looked at the first two pages and gone, "Huh! Wonder who likes this kind of stuff?" And then looked for something else.

How would he have felt about this book?

Boy—that's a very good question. I think he would've admired a certain amount of it: the stunt pilotry and the humor of it. And some of the prose. But I don't think he would've got it real well. I don't think he woulda got what I would hope people could get out of it.

'Cause he thought things like character were pointless . . . ?

Not pointless but that they were *easy*. And that the hard stuff was more, you know, front of the head. It's never as stark as pointless or not pointless. It's, you know, what's interesting, what's advanced, what's *next*? It's gotta be—right? Not what's *true*, but what's fresh and novel and whatever. It's very difficult to get out of that.

[Nudging me again here; an invitation to leave that behind.]

But anyway. And then you know, the next couple of years are fairly dull. I finally got a job I think the next fall—

Let's do it chrono. It's interesting about the crap jobs . . .

OK—then I've got an even better one. You don't know what I'm going to talk about, man.

   OK, so I worked for a while as a security guard at Lotus. And then quit for the incredibly brave reason that I got tired of getting up so early in the morning.

How long?

Three and a half months.

Faulkner worked that kind of job too. When he wrote As I Lay Dying, at night . . .

How do you *know* all this stuff? Is there some like masterwork of biographies of writers that you just . . .

Yeah, there's a little baseball-card series you can collect—stats on the back—you have to subscribe to it . . .

Yeah, this wasn't great though, because you had to keep, you had to check in every ten minutes and give meaningless reports. "All clear here at this cubicle!" [He mimes a walkie-talkie.] You know, like, Lotus was incredibly paranoid about industrial espionage. But I was so new that I wasn't given access to any of the cleared areas. So I had to go around like, "This hallway looks secure." And they were incredibly—they were always worried you were gonna *not* clock in. I don't know—what was it like? It was like, um, every bad '60s novel about meaningless authority. And it was just . . .

And were you walking around thinking, "My God, I had two books come out when I was very young . . ."?

No. As a matter of fact, I remember one reason I liked that job is, I walked around *not* thinking. You know? In a really like, "Huh: there's a ceiling tile." "Huh: there's a, there's a cubicle."

[Jeeves whines; I tap him on the nose, to quiet him; Dave looks as if I've overstepped my bounds. It stops him talking.]

Sorry.

Actually, he needed it. Jeeves, see look, you're pissin' even the guest off. Even the guest is swattin' ya. He just gets upset when Drone eats his bone. Drone is kind of being a bully.

[But me too.]

All right, but anyway, I quit that job basically because I just didn't want to wake up in the morning early anymore.

Hush, sit. Sit. Sit. Sit. Good dog, now you stay, you hush.

Um, and then I got a job—this is the worst—I worked as a towel boy at something called the Auburndale Health Club in Watertown. Which was a very chichi . . . They called me something other than a towel boy, but I was in effect a towel boy. Who every once in a while was entrusted with the job of checking people in, and having them show their card, and then working out on an *unbelievably* inelegant and clunky computer system how many visits they'd had.

But anyway, OK, here's why I quit that job. Is that I'm sitting there working that job, and who should walk in, um, to get their towel, but Michael Ryan. Now Michael Ryan—who's best known now for a book called *Secret Life*, which was this kinda pretty hair-raising memoir. But at the time—yeah, not to mention as we're petting a dog [the big conversation starter of *Secret Life* is teenage Michael Ryan attempting sex with his dog. David and I are both now petting Drone]—but at the time, um, um . . .

But anyway, Michael Ryan had received a Whiting Writer's Award the same year I had, like two years earlier, in 1987. So I see this *guy* that I'd been up on this fucking rostrum with, having Eudora Welty give us this prize. And two years later, I'm like . . . And I can remember, I can see—it's the only time I've literally dived under something, to have somebody avoid seeing me. Like he came in, and I pretended, I pretended not very subtly to slip, and went under the counter, and had the lady that was there . . . And I forget: I think I lay facedown, and didn't respond. And she of course didn't want to be going, "David, what's wrong?" while a guest was there. So she gave him the towel.

And I remember, I somehow worked the rest of that day. I think I would peer around corners to see what room (small laugh) he was in, and then dash and put the towel in a towel bin. And I remember I left that day, and I, I didn't go back.

And that was in, let's see, yeah, that was in June. And then I lived on extremely meager savings for two months. But finally, a couple of friends—I don't even remember who, Mary Karr and Debra Spark—do you know who Debra Spark is? She had a book called, um, *Coconuts for the Saint* come out from Faber and Faber last fall, which was actually very good. But anyway, she teaches at Colby now. They got me this job, with DeWitt Henry, who edited *Ploughshares,* a part-time job teaching at Emerson. And I did that, I did that for the next two and a half—OK, started in the fall of '90. No, exactly two years. Four semesters of doing that. And it was probably about, Oh God, what did I do? I did the TV essay that's in the *Review.* And I lived on that.

Oh! I moved to Brighton. Oh! OK! I moved to Brighton, across from this thing called Foster Park on Foster Street. And nearby there was this halfway house, I can't remember its name. And anyway, a couple of the people I met at the Y across from the Foster Street house went to this halfway house that had some kind of free pass to it or something. I remember meeting them like in the weight room, you know? I think initially because I would—when there were these big guys in the room, I'd put too much on the bench press and it would fall on my chest and I couldn't get it off. And I'd ask these big bruiser guys. But anyway I remember meeting them, and their telling me about the halfway house. And I didn't do anything about it at the time, but I remember going, "Hmm, that might be an interesting little thing for a novel." And then that same fall—winter of '91—I had, like, three friends who I was fairly close to all go into AA. And one of them lived there in Boston. And I remember drinking a lot of coffee with them, and kinda hearing them talk about it. And then, um—

Oh, and then I hadn't played tennis for years, and I played tennis with a couple of guys. Who saw that I was good, and set me up with this friend that they had to play with. Um, at a club out in Winchester or Lexington. But this guy who had taught years earlier at a tennis academy on Long Island.

[Too neat-sounding, in a way.]

Ah! OK. Yeah, and I remember, when I was in McLean's, they were gonna put me *on* something, and I had so decided—all that stuff, I just didn't want to take anything anymore. This was antidepressants. Which they were fairly persuasive about, but I just didn't want any part of it. But I remember I'd been reading up on like tricyclics and MAO inhibitors and quadracyclics and all this stuff. And then another friend—not one who was in AA but one that was in, I forget, some kind of deal. Had gone on Prozac, and was talking about Prozac, and I remember reading about Prozac. So there was just kind of a lot of this stuff going on. But I—ah! And OK, and also one of the classes that I took at Harvard was Stanley Cavell on film. Stanley Cavell is an American philosopher who's kind of a specialist in, like, Emerson and Thoreau. But he's sort of uh—he's got a book on movies called *Pursuits of Happiness,* he's real good on, like, American film.

Mark Crispin Miller.

I think he's the best writer on television alive. Um um um um. So anyway, so all this—I mean, I was always, I was at Emerson. And Emerson had a library, and I was always in the library. And in the library, I don't know what you do, but it's mostly just kind of wandering around. And I'd started in the last year, I'd probably started two different fairly long stories, both of which were just not working. And stopped doing that. Oh, and then I wrote the Michael Martone—Michael Martone called and wanted a thing about my hometown, and growing up. He wanted a thing about the Midwest and different townships. And I ended up doing this thing about tennis and math. And um—[soft sound of brain machinery clicking: *tch tch tch tch!*]—I think that was after I'd already sort of started. I don't know: I just remember doin' a lot of reading on a lot of different subjects, and at a certain point . . .

[Nabokov: somehow grown the claws and wings of a novel]

And this was of course at a time when I'd really kind of given up. I wasn't even that upset about not writing anymore. It was just more like . . . and then at a certain point, there seemed to be some kind of system for my reading.

And I decided that maybe being really sad, and really sort of directionless, wasn't just that I was fucked up. Maybe there was, maybe it was *interesting* in a way. Because I can't really tell you about it in detail, just my friends—I just had *so many* friends, who went through terrible times exactly when I did. In so many various different ways. And so many of them seemed to have so much going for 'em. And so I think—

What kind of people?

Oh, lord. We're talking: lawyers, stockbrokers, young promising academics, poets, *tch tch tch tch.* Um . . . one guy who sold advertising for a string of television stations.

Like Billy Crystal in City Slickers.

I didn't even see that movie. Jack Palance scares me. I don't see anything with Jack Palance.

You saw Shane?

Yeah, that's why he scares me. Just those *cheekbones,* you know? Anyway, just a lot of . . .

People who were promising, who—

Just, what was Carter's word? *Malaise.* Just the very air seemed sad, and kind of jagged. And then at a certain point, I mean, I always *wrote,* sort of every day. And at a certain point, I remember writin' an early, like a very early draft of that first chapter. About somebody who couldn't make themselves understood. [Jeeves grunts.] Boy, that went through fifteen or twenty drafts.

I read that out loud to my girlfriend.

Wow!

Just really funny, a great opening.

There are little bits of my experiences with college towns in there.

We're in like extremely late—Jeeves, you know what, I'm gonna put you in your crate. Sit and hush—Jeevesmeister—Drone: Good dogs. [Swats them] Now, Jeeves, why don't you withdraw to chew on that, instead of *gloating*. You watch: he's gonna drop it, in one second, and be outraged. [Good dog psych from Dave: one second, and then—] *There* it goes.

No, that section was written between Thanksgiving and Christmas of '91, and I remember I was home with my parents for '91. And that's when—I don't even think they saw me much that vacation. Because that was when a lot of the really short opening sections were written. And then when I came back—I just, I don't know, I got really bold. I started going to a lot of places and *lurking* and doing research.

What's weird is—OK, there was one in Brighton, there was one in Somerville, there was one in Medford, these halfway houses. And we'd sit around—and it was real weird, these places. They didn't ask why you were there, they didn't much *care* why you were there. And you could sit around, drink as much coffee as you wanted. And I got to sort of *like* some of these people. And *heard* a lot of their life stories, some of which in vestigial form are in the book. But I liked them so much that I twisted everything way around.

[Dogs—Jeeves—crazy again]

I didn't like the halfway house parts as much.

It's very odd, because everybody says they either prefer those parts or the tennis parts. When of course the fantasy is that neither part is separable from the other.

I think probably on a second reading . . .

[The tape side runs out.]

[He's watching the leader on the tape: has interestingly taken this over.] You have to give it a certain amount—oh no, it's already past it.

And that's pretty much when I started it. And then—meanwhile, there's all this other stuff going on with this person I can't tell you about. And I ended up—this is just something I can't talk about, but I ended up moving to Syracuse.

Unhappy relationship?

Not unhappy. They moved away and I missed 'em, and I wanted 'em, I wanted to be able to move there. Except the thing about it is, man, I really can't use any of it because this person whose name I'm not saying . . .

Well . . .

[Shuts the tape off]

And at some point, I realized this was going to be a book, and that I couldn't both teach and work on it. It just took too much time. It was *extremely* expensive to live in Boston, I had some friends in Syracuse where—I remember Jon Franzen and I drove up there to look at places, because he was thinkin' about moving too. And I liked the area and thought it was really cheap and ended up moving there. And most of the book was written—I didn't have a job, I didn't do anything.

I took an advance and lived in an apartment that was seriously the size of like, um, the foyer of an average house. I don't know, I really liked it. It was *incredibly* tiny. You know, the front hallway that's got like a coat closet in it? I mean it was, it was very cool, because it was literally—I mean, there were so many books that you couldn't move around. And when I would want to write, I would have to put all the stuff from the desk on the bed. And when I would want to sleep, I would have to put all the stuff on the desk.

But things were so tight and so orderly. And the book was . . . I mean, there was just, I've never had to hold that much different information in my head at any one time. And it was *nice* to be in a little, a little sort of tiny—and it was *so* snowy, they got *record* snowfall that year. And it was almost impossible to go anywhere. But there was a grocery store that was close by, and I had a friend who lived very close by that I could go and spend time with.

I moved to Syracuse in, um, April or May of '92. And I'd say— no, I was at page 250, because the first 250 pages I just typed up, and had Bonnie send out to try to get money. Because I—the last money I had was gonna go for moving to Syracuse. And it was actually very exciting, I mean, it was the first time that I've ever really seriously been *poor*. And had to eat, for like a couple a' months, waiting to see if Bonnie could sell it. Like eatin' supper at—people bein' real nice and sayin', "We really like your company, you'll have to come over for supper." When the fact was they knew that I just . . . you know . . .

And for some reason I just couldn't take money from my parents. Because I was like twenty-seven or twenty-eight—no, I was *thirty*. And I . . . it was just, it was just, it would have been obscene.

Was it exciting to—what sort of advance?

Well, I mean I already told—no, I didn't tell Adam Begley. Michael didn't want me to tell anyone the advance. It was under six figures.

But not so far under?

Pretty far under. But the nice thing that they did, they didn't give it to me all at once. They split it up, like gave me part the first year and part the second, which made it way easier. And, uh, *tch tch tch tch.*

Halfway?

(Spitting slurpy tobacco) It was more than that. So once again we've closed in on figures. Which was fine. But which wasn't all that much when you're splitting it year after year.

But what I wondered emotionally was this: wasn't it nice to learn that after you thought you'd cracked up as a writer, to know that you could get what is a healthy advance for literary fiction?

[He turns off the tape again]

As a matter of fact it *wasn't* an exhilarating feeling. It was this real, um, like, I have this thing about takin' money before it was done. I felt like it was sort of, it was jumping off the bridge. Because once I'd taken money for this thing, I knew I had to finish it.

And, um, it was, I think after going into McLean's in '89, it was the bravest thing I've ever done. Because every cell in my body didn't want me to do it. But I also was just—I *knew* I was going to finish the thing. I mean, the thing was alive for me by then. But there was just this whole, um—which probably makes you think I'll take an advance for yet another thing. But the difference is now, it's like I've got this teaching income. Where I don't have to have it. [Loud crisp belch]

Anyway. [He's being totally up-front now, has dropped other stuff.] And then, you know, the bulk of it was written between . . .

Oh, wow . . .

[Drone nudged me down. I'm rolling on the ground laughing; both these big dogs are licking me, batting me over. I'm laughing on the carpet . . .]

You're gettin' the *full*—You want to know what my life is like? *That's* what my life is like.

I'm laughing because now I've become the kid in my dad's ad.

Exactly. The thing about it, here's the thing, Drone really loves to put the *weight* of his head on somebody. He really likes to rest his head on another person. Which I think is very moving in a weird way. He *really* likes you. He's never taken to a male like he's taken to you.

[Flattering me again]

I think just because I'm showing him attention.

All right. Anyway, so I lived there. No, I got part of the advance right away. They gave me half up front and half on delivery, and they split the half into two years. And that's what I lived on that year in Syracuse and then part of the next. I moved. I got the job offer from ISU in the spring of '93, and for a variety of reasons decided—for one thing, I didn't have health insurance. I was just sick of driving ten miles an hour around Syracuse, for fear I would get in an accident and my family would be wiped out. So I moved here—

Perfect detail.

I moved here—it's actually biblically true—I moved here in the summer of '93. And I remember, the book was about three-quarters done. 'Cause the reward for gettin' three-quarters done . . . Which meant finishing, there's a very long scene about a tennis match between Ortho and Hal, and Gately had been shot but wasn't in the hospital. The book was three-quarters done, and the break from it was doin' the State Fair piece. [For *Harper's*] Which I did like two weeks after I'd moved here. And did that that fall, and then started teachin' that fall, and finished the book. It was really funny because I'd have grad classes in this other house.

Who was your local correspondent?

Oh. Well, Native Companion was—yeah, Kimberly went with me to that. It's not really her voice, it's somebody else's voice, if you can get my drift. But um, yeah, she was not pleased to have somebody else's voice put in there. But all the stuff happened, like she really *did* get put in that thing called the Zipper. Nothin', *nothin'* in there is made up. That's so weird, I've never done something—well, maybe the baton twirling wasn't quite the carnage that . . . Although it *seemed* awfully dangerous at the time.

This was the stuff about texture you never had in your stuff before . . .

Well, I never would have said that it smelt *good*. I mean, I would've made fun of it somehow, you know? Like, "The smell of cowshit is everywhere. But shit was important, because shit was foul . . ."

All right, so I did that. But the neat little detail about that was, um, I developed this thing, I think it started at Lotus. I just can't *stand* fluorescent light. And as you saw up at ISU, it's a fucking fluorescent light *festival*. It started at Lotus, but even when I was a little kid . . .

Anyway, for some reason that year it was just *crippling*, and so I could only hold classes in the house. And the class would come over, and I worked in the living room, because I'd gotten Jeeves.

Here?

No—this was, I only bought this house last spring. This was actually a house that I rented through the *mail* before I moved here, up near Illinois-Wesleyan. It was very nice but it was real small, um. We would hold class and literally like, you know, people would have to *move*, you know, the *Compendium of Drug Therapy* and *Psychiatric Nursing*, you know, *The Emergence of French Art Film* over. And it was like, it was weird to be teaching.

It was really like, I could tell I was getting near the end, because all the people were comin' in, you know, and like sittin' on the stuff. And there'd be all, there'd be jokes about, you know, Mount Manu-script.

Could tell you were near the end why?

'Cause—it's probably the same for you. It's the end when like, when somebody else can . . . man, I gotta be clear about it. Be-cause I knew, like I knew what was going to happen. I knew how it was gonna end. It didn't matter if other people came in the room where all the stuff was. Because there wasn't anything that could get shaken up. I wasn't worried—well, I just wasn't worried that hav-ing other people's heads around would fuck with what it was I was doing . . . Whereas in Syracuse, I was really, except for one or two people, I really didn't . . .

[Dog rolls on back]

. . . want anyone in?

Well, nobody could *come* in, literally. I mean it was like, you know, I think my girlfriend and I maybe spent a total of two hours in my apartment, just 'cause it was impossible to be there for more than one person. But anyway, that was kind of neat. To teach, to have other people in there and to teach, in the same place where all that was going on.

And then, uh, you know, I'd gotten Jeeves, and by the last part, I had a whole bunch of handwritten drafts, I had a whole bunch of typed drafts. And then when I finally sat down and typed the whole thing, I had Jeeves.

And Jeeves had his own room in the next room. And the en-tire time would be spent with Jeeves up on his paws on this dog gate barkin' at me. And I would either have headphones on, or I bought these earplugs, you know, those foam earplugs? And then finally a friend here gave me—because even that wouldn't block it out—a friend gave me, you know, what airline workers use? Those earmuffs? That I would put on *over* the earplugs.

It's really weird to type when you can't hear the sound of the keyboard, that *anchors* you in some weird way. So it got very dreamy. And, uh, I was late. I was supposed to deliver on January 1, 1994. And I delivered June 18, 1994. And I remember being terrified that they were gonna sue me—so *naïve!*—for being late. And finally, I think Bonnie had to tell me that you know half the *planet* was always late and stuff.

What else? So I delivered that summer and then I went to my sister's wedding. And I didn't, I remember, I didn't hear from Michael for six months, and I was really mad, 'cause he said, "Deliver deliver deliver it."

And then I *did* hear from him. And he had, he'd written like a twenty-five-page letter.

What'd it say?

Well, he's just talking about having read it, and the first half was making clear that he got it. And then talking about, um, talking about *cuts,* and talking about *demands on the reader.* Oh, no—here's another funny detail.

[Have the impression now he sort of wants to write article for me, he's in the planning and sorting with me.]

Is when I first typed it up and printed it out, and I knew it was way too long. I mean, he'd sort of had like a thousand-page top.

When you first discussed it . . .

He knew it was gonna be pretty long. But I mean I would talk to him every couple of months. And I was really kind of shining him on. I wasn't tellin' him how long it was, but I remember thinking I could fool him by—I printed it out in nine-point font, single-spaced. And

I think it came to like, I don't know, 1,070 pages; well, about the length of the book.

But he called back, and this is the only time Michael's ever really gotten mad at me. Because he said he'd tried to read the first fifty pages and it just hurt his eyes and what was I doing, and did I think that he wouldn't notice how long it was if I printed it . . .

So he made me—this is the only time that he's ever like pulled, you know, authority shit on me—he made me go back and print the *whole* thing out double-spaced. In regular font.

And I remember, those three days, being just terrified at how long it would end up being. Printing it out. That poor printer, I've had that printer for eight years. And it printed out, I would say, a total of like five thousand pages of various drafts of that book. But then I printed it out, and it was more like—it was almost seventeen hundred pages, you know, so things were really grim. And then he sent me this letter. And I knew, I *knew* several hundred pages needed to go. But every cut that I would make, like I'd cut about two hundred pages before I sent it to him. But, I remember, cutting the two hundred resulted then in writing an extra hundred and fifty—you know how it is. You cut one thing, it's got implications in a hundred other places, and to patch that shit up . . .

Anyway, and he wrote me this letter. And you know, it was a hard couple of months, and it's hard to be clear about. I was worried for a while—he made a big mistake, he mentioned, "We really want to price this book at $30," it set off all these flares in my head. "Oh no, these cuts are for commercial reasons. I'm a whore if I do this." And that was right around Christmastime of '94. And I remember, I think I told you about this, just happening to run into Richard Powers at this party, and him being *immensely* helpful. And givin' it to Steve Moore to read, and Moore, Moore helped me with some structural stuff. Talkin' to a couple of people about it, gettin' letters.

I actually, there's a couple of kind of older, more established writers, that I'm sort of pen pals with. And I remember writing them, and asking them, and just getting real good advice. And I worked— that was also when I quit smoking. So it was December, January,

February, of '95, late '94 early '95, that I went back and about 350 pages got cut. And then sent that back. And that spring I was working on all kinds of different stuff, nonfiction, writing short stories.

And then I got *another* letter from Michael in spring of—yeah, this past spring. Like May. Saying, "You know what? I just, I had the feeling there was more we could cut. I went back, I line-edited again." He had another like two hundred pages of cuts. A lot of 'em being footnotes. And I didn't take quite as many of those, I ended up taking about half. So another hundred pages got cut.

So a lot of that year was like—it wasn't really—I mean, I did the cruise piece, that was kind of a vacation. But a lot of that year it was really hard to get any kind of work done. Because it was like this *thing* that just kept *following* me.

[Dogs chewing, clacking their bones]

But I knew, I knew . . . like Michael was smart. And if I believed him, and I trusted him, I took what he said real seriously. And it was hard work knowing—Do I cut this? If I don't—If I do, what do I do here?

And I just remember, like, $400 phone bills. Calling Michael like *all* the time. And at home. Gettin' to know his wife from talking to his wife when he was on the train going home. It was cool. I mean, it's the only time, I've never thought I could work well with anybody else. The thing with Mark was a joke, I mean that was like, you know, I ended up retyping the whole thing. But this thing with Michael was, I really felt like, not only *grateful* to him, but like I was bein' smart. Like there were certain things that were hard, that were unnecessarily hard. Or that were real cold, cerebral shit. And Michael being real smart about, "All right, maybe you don't cut this scene, but you take five pages off this, and it's 30 percent easier to read. And save yourself 10 percent reader alienation, which you *need* thirty pages later for this part." You know what I mean? Like *smart*. Like smart.

And that took through like May and June and July—no, May and June—more or less up to the present. I mean I worked on other shit over the summer, I went to tennis tournaments for *Details,* I went to the U.S. Open. Oh, I did a long thing on Dostoyevsky for the *Village Voice,* that took most of July. So there was busywork all summer.

And then the copyediting came.

That was a *fucking, fucking* nightmare. That came in August.

Tell me: do you sometimes hate the copyeditors?

This—let me tell ya, Little, Brown was really good. Because I had told Michael, I'd had bad experiences with them before, like copyediting it like a freshman essay. And I told him that if this happens, it's gonna be a total mess.

So they set me up with their head copyeditor. And *gave me his number.* And he and I would call back and forth about stuff. And they also—when it came time for the galleys, they hired *another* outside copyeditor. And gave me *his* number. And he and I edited the galleys like together and made sure that important shit cross-checked. Because there were enormous numbers of details to keep straight. But anyway, my understanding is that's nonstandard. Not only hiring extra people but giving you access.

I mean, they were incredibly, I've just never—and I know this sounds very like, "I want to thank the Academy." But I've just never had, I really liked Gerry, but I've never had everybody from like the copyeditors to Michael to these PR people at Little, Brown who are just (a) really smart, and (b) they're just really nice to me. You know? And did—I think when I made clear that the stuff I wanted to do, like talking to the copyeditor, would result in a better book—they just did it.

There aren't acknowledgments in the book because the list would be too long. And I had had a long list at the start of *Broom* and it looked very jejune to me. I wrote letters to—there were about ten people who were key on this. And said to them that there was just no way to do it, to thank them. And there were a lot of people around Boston, like in these halfway houses, that helped a lot who I just cannot, you know, thank.

So that was pretty much it.

The galleys were a fucking nightmare.

And then you had your sister copyedit the final part, the proofs.

She is—my mother is the best proofreader in the world, Amy's second, and I'm third, as far as I've seen. And um, paid Amy a dollar a page, and it was worth it. She bought a car.

Haven't paid her the whole thing?

She's gonna proofread the hardcover, to get mistakes for the paperback. She's gonna do that, and I'm gonna pay her for it. Oh no, I paid her up front. You don't stiff the proofreader.

How long did it take Bonnie to read it? A lot of reading.

I don't know, and I have never wanted to ask her, because I know that she would be embarrassed or feel like she had to say it was quicker. It's *weird*—Bonnie's a really good agent. Her cup of tea is not my cup of tea. I don't think, she doesn't vibrate on my frequency. She sort of goes, "Oh, I don't know what it is with David, just let him do what he does."

I send short stories to Bonnie—I trust her opinion on short stories.

I sent this to Charis Conn, sent it to Jon Franzen, sent it to Mark Costello. But also, I sent it to them—I mean, Michael was the reader on this. He did something real smart: he got me to trust him, somehow.

Publicity?

[David fully in teammate mode, wanting to get this right, switches the tape player on and off now as memories occur to him.]

There are a lot of things that if I'd been in charge I wouldn't have done. I wouldn't have done the postcard campaign. And I wouldn't have had all white males on the back of the book. I wouldn't have misspelled Vollmann's *name* on the back of the book, that was kind of a boner.

But you know how this process works. Is that, once you've turned it in you just, they're gonna do what they're gonna do. But um, and I remember feeling really weird, because like, I've got a rule, I don't blurb friends. I don't blurb much anyway, but I don't blurb friends. And when Jon said that Michael had sent him a bound galley, I told him I thought that if he didn't want to blurb it, I sure wasn't going to hold it against him. And I wouldn't've blurbed his book. And, so, that's the only thing on the back of the book that makes me uncomfortable. Like, it could be perceived as log-rolling. I mean, it's not.

It just seems like they went after people who are pretty well known in our age group, and he's . . .

Mark Childress—Bonnie is Mark's agent too. And Rick Moody is Michael's editee. And I mean Vollmann, I think Vollmann and I have been blurbing each other back and forth for years. It's very odd because we're so different, and we get lumped together. Well, our first books came out the same year.

Backwards a little bit; in six months while waiting to hear: were you nervous? Or pretty confident about this? Worry it wasn't good?

It's like I said: I worked real hard on this, and I like, there was a *weird* kind of calm that was a result of that. I was nervous because I knew it needed cuts, and I was terrified that it was gonna turn out that the cuts he wanted were gonna gut the book. And I was nervous about that. But it's weird, the year after going to McLean's, I developed this real habit of, at least for a period of a few months, I could *not* think about stuff.

I mean, I can really like, when thinking about it starts—you have an interesting little stain on your pants. He specializes in that. [Dave laughs. Drone has been snout-resting on my thigh.] He specializes in makin' you look like there's been a horrible accident. It's usually right before you go out on a date. You're sittin' there reading and you notice this.

[Drone is now licking my pocket.]

And it was a tough summer. It was very hard for me, because I would like to be married, and I would like to have children. And it was hard for me when my sister got married, who's like *younger* than me. And there was a certain amount of stuff going on in the family. And I was also, I was just *tired*. I was tired, and I had a lot of nonfiction to do.

But when did someone come to you and say, "David, you really nailed it"?

It's very odd, because Michael would say really nice stuff to me, and he'd say it in the context of having critical suggestions. So I could write it all off as you know, Well he, this is the sugar that's making the medicine go down.

And Charis liked it, but Charis likes everything I do. There was some stuff—because Mark is really good friends with Nan Graham, who knows more about the publishing industry than anybody. She's really good, I think. She was DeLillo's editor, which as far as I'm concerned does it for me. So I can remember—when they did this postcard thing, and when they wanted to do signed bound galleys and sent me boxes full of paper—my thinking, my not knowing what to make of it. And calling Mark and having Mark find out, I presume from Nan, although I don't know from whom, that this meant that they were gonna support the book, and that they were into the book or whatever. Which given that the book is a thousand pages made me think that they thought it was a pretty good book.

Relieved? Remember, this is only about four years from McLean's.

I really don't want to pump it up. It could be embarrassing, it could seem like it was entirely an emotional breakdown, and a lot of it had to do with the work, too. I guess as long you don't . . .

Um, it's hard to explain. But I sort of like, um, that book didn't get written for any of the reasons the other books did. I mean, I decided that I wanted to think of myself as a writer, which meant whether this got published or not, I was gonna write it.

Which four years ago, when I was all thinking, "Oh no, what if the next thing I do isn't as good as . . ." I mean, it would've been unthinkable. I'd really sort of *given up,* in a certain way. Given up a lot of . . . Hush, Jeeves. . . .

Became a writer while writing this, then?

Yeah. I thought, yeah. I mean, this was different in a lot of ways. This was the first thing that I ever said, "All right, I'm gonna try to do the very best I can." Instead of doing this, "All right, I'll work at like three-quarter speed, and then I can always figure that if I just hadn't been a fuckup, the book coulda been really good." You know that defense system? You write the paper the night before, so if it doesn't get a great grade, you know that it could've been better.

And this—I worked as hard as I could on this. And in a weird way, you might think that that would make me more nervous about whether people would like it. But there was this weird—you know like when you work out really well, there's this kind of tiredness that's real pleasant, and it's real sort of placid . . . ?

[Hamlet quote about buzzing . . .] *"There was in my head a buzzing that would not let me rest . . ."*

I guess . . . Yeah. So anyway. So no, I wasn't that nervous.

Like I said, it never really *felt* finished. Because it felt finished and then I had to reprint it. And it felt finished and then I spent a few months waiting for Michael's cut and then working on the cuts.

And then it felt finished but then a few months later hearing that there were more cuts. And then right after the cuts—I mean, the copy editor must have been on speed, because a month later it came in. So it just, it hadn't felt finished. And then the bound galley was such a *mess*.

Here's the deal: Is one reason I want this phase over. It's gonna feel finished when this is over. Because this has been part of a whole like unending stream, that started when I started the book. Like this feels like part of it. And when you go, and I unplug the phone for two days, that's when it's gonna to be over. And then I'll let you know. Because I think it's going to take me a day to just sort of stop quivering.

Any moment of euphoria you can give me?

I'm not sure. [Long pause]

I know we probably disagree—I think Sven's really smart, and I was really nervous. I knew two months ahead of time, but there's a last paragraph of the review that's something about . . . And I just realized that for me Sven's a big deal, and I was very scared. And I remember that last paragraph feeling, having to go *way* up into the stacks to get the magazine out. And reading it and then taking the stairs down two at a time, and walking out with this kind of wonderful . . . yeah, it felt done then. . . .

[Birkerts: "Wallace is, clearly, bent on taking the next step in fiction. He is carrying on the Pynchonian celebration of the renegade spirit in a world gone as flat as a circuit board; he is tailoring that richly comic idiom for its new-millennial uses. . . . It is resourceful, hilarious, intelligent, and unique. Those who stay with it will find the whole world lit up as though by black light."]

[Dave checks the tape.] We work real differently, man—I would never be able to boil all this down. Maybe I'm a minimalist, in a perverse way.

We're almost out. You have tapes around here?

[I check my watch.]

It's twelve ten.

That's what your watch says? It's two *twenty*, dickbrain.

[I read parts of the book to him: LaMont Chu and Lyle.]

You know how this works: sure, in one way. There's also fifty other ways.

"The obsession with future-tense fame makes all else pale." Does that . . .

Who says that?

The narrator. What does it remind you of?

I think what it reminds me of is the way that the fall of '89 felt . . . feeling like, that I was washed up, and what was painful about that is never gettin' a chance to you know be felt about the way LaMont feels about those players. And then also realizing how pathetic that was.

"To get compared to M. Chang, lately expired [He's killed off all old stars.] *. . . He confesses it to Lyle: he wants the hype . . . A couple times this year the cold clenched fear of losing has itself made him lose . . ."*

I make of that that it's very hard to talk about coherently—at ages twelve, thirteen, fourteen, when I was young and starting out and had promise, it looked like I could be very very very good. And some of that was literally how I would feel. And I remember clipping action shots of players out of tennis magazines and envying them. And you know, so there's a whole bunch of not real interesting . . .

And it seems to me that it's somewhat true of everybody from, you know, grim eighteen-year-old premeds who know that they're gonna be a leading podiatrist at thirty, and have a trophy wife and $200,000, to nine-year-old ice skaters who are skipping *Beverly Hills 90210* to practice their compulsories. That there's something real American about it.

Shut that off for one second . . .

[On the PR campaign, his fears—David: "It would get the same response hype gets from you, which is like a derisive curl of the lip . . ." If the book came to him that way, with postcards.]

The end of that reasoning—there's no such thing as bad attention, which I strongly disagree with. That was Tama Janowitz's battle cry—"no such thing as bad attention." Attention that seems to shut you down as a writer is arguably bad attention, isn't it? That's under your game show attention to it.

(More reading) *"You burn to have your photograph in a magazine . . ."*

In fact, I sort of think that's probably one facet of the great theme of sadness that's going on.

"After the first photograph . . . the famous men do not enjoy their photographs so much as they fear that their photographs will cease to appear in magazines. They are trapped, just as you are."

Sounds like a fuckin' good little bit of dialogue to me.

Extremely intelligent.

I'll tell ya, the thing that it reminds me of, is that it took me a long time to figure out what was so sad about the cruise. Have you read the thing about the cruise?

Of course.

Is that the great lie of the cruise is that enough pleasure and enough pampering will quiet this discontented part of you. When in fact, all it does is up the requirement. That's the sort of thing that it's about. And yeah, my little corner of that experience, some of this had to do with the writing, you know? I can remember being twenty-four years old and having my, you know, smiling mug in the *New York Times Magazine,* and it feeling really good for exactly like ten seconds. You know?

Magazine?

I'm sorry—*The New York Times Book Review.* Or, the big one also, some pointillist drawing of me in the *Wall Street Journal,* and some article like, "Hot Shot's Weird New Novel" or something like that. And I remember that coming out when I was at Yaddo. ("Yahdo") [He has the reformed person's apparent responsibility to feel contempt for the person he'd been then.]
    And feeling real cool, because you know all of them were reading it in the living room and stuff. But it feeling intensely good, and probably not unlike a *crack* high. You know? Intensely good for thirty seconds, and then you're hungry for more. And so that, clearly, I mean if you're not stupid, you figure out that the real problem is the discontented self. That all this stuff that you think will work for a second, but then all it does is set up a hunger for more and better.
    And that the thing that interested me, at least in the book, and I know it's less interesting for the purposes of your essay [By now calling it an "essay," which is what he writes. Interesting], is that that general pattern and syndrome seems to me to get repeated, at least in our culture, for our kind of plush middle-class part of the culture, over and over and over again in a million different arenas. And that we don't seem to get it. We do *not* seem to get it.

This is just for color; so the fact that you've gotten the readership that you might have wanted in your midtwenties ... quote from Self-Consciousness: photograph Updike sees of himself in his mother's house, as a five-year-old boy, which now looks kind of sinister. "I'm what you wanted me to be," you know what I mean? "You got me into this: now what do I do? I await his instructions." I mean, in a sense, you fulfilled the ambitions that twenty-five-year-old had in terms of the kind of impact you wanted to make . . .

You know, it may be that those ambitions are what get you to do the work, to get the exposure, to realize that the original ambitions were misguided. Right? So that it's a weird paradoxical link. If you didn't have the ambitions, you'd never find out that they were sort of deluded.

But there is, you're right, once you've decided those delusions are empty, you've got a big problem, because like you said [three days ago, in airport], you can't kill off parts of yourself. You have to start building machinery that can incorporate that part of yourself, but . . . that isn't at its mercy, you know?

Started writing fiction when how old?

Twenty-one.

Never before?

I think I started a World War Two novel when I was nine. [I laugh.]

And abandoned?

Yeah, well, it was about a bunch of people with *strangely* hyperdeveloped skills and powers, who are going to invade Hitler's bunker during World War Two. And I remember I started it after seeing something called *Kelly's Heroes,* or maybe *The Dirty Dozen* or something. And it was very much a project inspired by the experience of liking that movie. And once that . . . I mean, so yeah, I really started when I was twenty-one, and I started because—it was actually Mark kinda got me into it.

Well, I'd done some stuff—when I was in college, I'd written a couple of papers for other people. Because there were a lot of students who . . . it was kind of neat.

They were paying you to write their papers?

Well, I wouldn't put it that coarsely. But let's say there were complicated systems of reward. But—and it didn't happen a whole, whole lot of the time. But I remember one of the things that was interesting was reading two or three of their papers to learn, you know, what their music sounded like.

And I remember realizing at the time, "Man, I'm really *good* at this. I'm a weird kind of forger. I mean, I can *sound* kind of like anybody." Or I would write papers for professors that would parody the stuff that the professors had said—I mean, that'd sound just like them, only more so.

Nabokov called that the ability to do blue magic.

Yeah. And it was weird, because I remembered that I'd always wanted to be an impressionist, vocally. But I just didn't, I don't have an agile enough vocal and facial register to do it. Although I can do it.

Mark and I resuscitated an old humor magazine that had been dormant for a couple of years—

What were your impressions?

I can do, um, I can do Scooby-Doo, I can do Dudley Do-Right, and I can do a really good James Carter.

Do one for me?

How would this play in the piece?

[He does one; it's not great.]

How many papers?

I wasn't Michael Pemulis: The number of times I did this, you could count on one hand.

Was it money?

Come on . . .
   So we did this humor magazine, and I really liked it, and then Mark . . .

[The tape side runs out.
   We're out of tapes; Dave finds me one belonging to an ex-girlfriend. It's an old step-aerobics mix tape that says "Step!" We tape over.]

In this class we read *Ada,* and we read *Gravity's Rainbow,* we read a bunch of Barthelme, anyway stuff like this.
   And see 'cause, there were literati on campus, but they were these *sensitive,* you know like, politically correct—yeah, the beret guys.
   And I just—boy, I remember, one reason I *still* don't like to call myself a writer is that I don't ever want to be mistaken for that type of person . . . Uuuh! Yeah, I think on East Coast colleges, with their little campus magazines, and their little infighting about who's gonna get it, and it's just *Uh!* The vanity speaks so stark.

[One of his strengths: he judges and speaks like a Midwesterner, a kid's offhand slang, that's inside all the intelligence, it's the cement base under its field.]
   Um, but anyway, we got really into that, and then Mark, Mark had always kind of written fiction. And he wrote a thesis, he wrote a creative thesis in the English department. And by this time, he was a year ahead of me, because I took a year off from college to drive a school bus.

Why?

God. I wasn't very happy, I wasn't very happy there. And I felt kind of inadequate. And there was a lot of stuff I wanted to read that wasn't part of any reading class. And Mom and Dad were just totally cool, it was pretty clear I wasn't fucking off. They just let me take a year off, live at home and drive a school bus. And I read, pretty much everything that I've read was read during that year.

Anyway, OK, I was majoring in philosophy, and it was serious, I mean, I was on a career track.

[Wouldn't it be great to fall in through this transcript, back to that house, and tell him to live differently, explain to him how it was all going to go? It's suddenly odd that this isn't possible.]

Anyway, Mark went ahead and wrote a novel for his English thesis, and I didn't know that this was possible, that you could get *sanctioned* to actually. And there were big writers there at the time. Brad Leithauser was there. Marilynne Robinson was there. And you could get these people to read it and like help you. And Mark sort of blazed that trail.

And that spring I took a workshop—the only undergraduate one I've ever had—from a man named Alan Lelchuk. Right, *American Mischief.* Safe to say that he and I didn't hit it off. But anyway I took that class, and actually, I liked a couple of the other students, there were a couple of other students who were incredibly good, who're now, like, teaching at Catholic schools in New York and L.A. So I just kind of eased into it.

And then I thought I would just sort of do this, because the philosophy thesis I was gonna do looked really hard and I was really scared about it, and I thought I would do this jaunty thing. Kind of like a side—I figured it would be like a hundred-page thing. And *Broom of the System,* the first draft of it was like seven hundred pages long. It was written in like five months, and it was just this very weird, it was sorta like it had, I had . . .

A whole lot of stuff coming together. I mean, there was a lot more theoretical stuff in the first draft of that. That, and the mimicry, and the like, the sort of adulation I'd felt for what these guys could do that we were reading in the reading group. Oh—and there was a professor there named Andy Parker who was really into theory, and a lot of us were under his sway, and he agreed to be on my committee. And he's the one who introduced me to Manuel Puig.

It was just—a whole lot of weird things came together. And that was actually a big deal, because I was really supposed to go to philosophy grad school. And nothing had ever been said in my family, and my dad, my dad would have limbs removed without anesthetic before ever pushing his kids about anything. But I *knew* I was gonna have to go to grad school—there's no way, in my family, you *don't* go to grad school. But I applied to these English programs instead, you know. And I didn't tell anybody. In the spring.

It was weird, because the philosophy thesis, it actually went really well, we worked with this Hampshire professor. He's the one who really said, "Are you out of your mind? You can get this thing published, and you can get a *job*, while you're still in grad school. You're like totally stupid." But it was really weird: 'cause I really liked this. I mean, writing *Broom of the System* felt like it was using 97 percent of me, whereas the philosophy thesis was using 50 percent of me. It was real . . .

Surprised by ability to actually turn out a novel?

Yeah, and how fast it was, and that the professors really liked it. You jump plateaus a little bit. I mean, I got radically better, um, like the summer before my senior year, I just got *a lot* better, I don't know how. And then, it was several years before I got any better at all.

Ah—here's something you might be interested in. Part of the despair of '89 was that there was a certain way this had mirrored a tennis career for me. Which was, I started at twelve, which is fairly late, and improved exponentially. So that by the time I was thirteen or fourteen, it was not implausible that I could actually, you know, do well enough at regionals to get to nationals. You know, like really be *in* the junior show. And, but at *just* the point that it became important to me, I began to choke.

Which, I don't know if you've played enough sports to know. But in certain sports—probably baseball, basketball, where you're like shooting, or golf—where choking has this really paradoxical, the more scared you get, the worse you play. I always imagine football is the one sport where you can just develop this kind of head of testosterone-fueled rage. You know, if you're a three-hundred-pound *lineman,* do you have on games and off games? But stuff like pool, tennis, or these sort of precision things where you're really on some times and not others? Nothing keeps you from being on like this fear. And the fear for me would be a consequence of it being important to, like, my identity or whatever. And then what I saw in '89, that, "Jesus, it's the same thing all over again." That I'd started somewhat late—right? Twenty-one. Didn't know I wanted to be a writer. Showed tremendous promise. But then, the minute I felt the implications of that promise, it caved in. And I sort of saw a kind of cycle about that. And any time you've got echoes of trauma and shit from childhood going on in adulthood, that's part of the whole, "I'm trapped, I can't get out" stuff. So . . .

Kick reading reviews of Broom?

It was just—you know what, it was creepy. Just because, I'll tell you what: here's the deal. I didn't feel much of anything, except, looking back, that was on purpose. Because I was doing, I was smoking *enormous* amounts of pot. I was—it was the only time in my life that I'd like gone to bars and picked up women that I didn't even know and tried to . . . which is pretty unlike me. And a lot of that I think was just, I had enough stuff going on so that I didn't . . . And it's weird. At the time I think I would tell everybody it was really nice and I was thrilled. But it was very upsetting. It was very upsetting.

Spring of '87.

Yeah. I had started to kind of live weirdly before then.

Bad feedback at Arizona? You'd applied with Broom?

The portfolio I sent them was some fairly realistic chunks of that and two fairly long other pieces. And *Broom* was written mostly between September and February of '84, '85. So . . .

I rewrote it, I rewrote one part . . .

I workshopped a bunch of stories, maybe three or four of them—actually there was this tremendous thrill. I remember writing a story called "Here and There," which really wasn't all that good. But for Penner, that first semester, and Penner just absolutely hating it. And that I think ended up, that won um, I think that won an O. Henry. ["Here and There," *Prize Stories 1988: The O. Henry Awards.*] And it was all I could do not to, you know, send him the jacket of the book. I mean, to do something really like that, because he had hurt my feelings.

I had the same experience . . .

[Professor disliked a story, went into New Yorker, then Best American Short Stories.]

While you were in school? Then what're you asking *me* for? Just transpose your experiences onto me. 'Cause it must have been exactly the same . . .

Piece isn't about me.

Yeah, but what'd it feel like to you, I'm curious?

It felt exciting and frightening?

Now, see, if *I* were to give that answer, you would give me that kind of hurt look of, "Oh, my God, you're not giving me anything." It's hard to talk about this stuff. It's hard to talk about this stuff.

What did Penner write?

"I hope—this isn't like what was in your portfolio, I hope it isn't what you plan to do here, we'd hate to lose you."

What was the exact quote?

"We were really excited by your portfolio. I hope this isn't representative of the work you're hoping to do for us. We'd hate to lose you." (Right off the top of his head) What I hated about it was how disingenuous it was. You know, if you're gonna threaten, "if you keep doing this, we'll kick you out," say that. But this whole, complex, self-protective, "we'd hate to *lose* you." It was just representative of those guys, those guys were bitter and they were dishonest. They were helpful in weird ways. I mean they had good stuff to say. But they were . . . wait. I'm about to come up with a quote. I think it's Emerson who says, "Who you are shouts so loudly, I cannot hear what you say." You know?

But then Broom while you were there—how'd you find your agent and get the book sold?

There was a man at Arizona named Robert Boswell. Well, Boswell and I knew each other because I was frantically chasing his ex-girlfriend. He was married by this time, and he knew me as the guy who was like basically just not taking no for an answer from his girlfriend. [How Midwestern and young—the fun of being him and doing that.] And I told him that I had this thing done. And he said, "What you do is, you go to um, you go to the library and get a list of agents," because there's some agent's union book. And to send it to like the first twenty names. Not an accident that my agent, that it's Fred Hill. I couldn't find the book, so he gave me his copy. And I wrote off to the agents, and I remember, there was also . . .

Other writers: taking M.D. and law degrees, getting grants, also getting NEA fellowships—

You think it'd be a little silly not to apply while it still exists. And I've applied for a Guggenheim several times, and one of my crazy hopes is that this will help.

Boswell was like a demigod around here. . . . Robert was such a successful student, he was so successful that he was still around . . .

So I sent chapters out. And it was real interesting, the variety of responses. Ticknor and Fields said, "I think in a story, either the plot or the characters ought to win. And here neither do, so I'm not passing it on to . . ." Cork Smith, was that his name? And a lot of letters from agents were like, "Best of luck in your janitorial career." Or, "Love to read more. You do know of course that our handling fee is X," and I knew enough to know even then that that was a total scam.

I ended up getting offers, firm offers, from two. And there was this man at Arizona that I liked. He said to go with the West Coast one, because I lived in Tucson, and all those East Coast agents were whores. So I went and had lunch with Fred Hill, who I would not see again for like eight years. And that's when Fred decided my name would be "David Foster Wallace." Because "David *Raines* Wallace" wrote for *The New Yorker*. But my real agent was Bonnie, who'd gotten out of Williams the year before I'd gotten out of Amherst, and we knew people in common.

And she'd already started, like, talking like a Jewish mom to me on the phone. Which I have this thing: like, the nearest Jewish mother, I will just simply, like, *attach* myself, just put my arms around her skirt and just attach myself. I don't know what that means, sort of WASP deprivation or something. And then that was that. And Bonnie had used to work with Gerry.

And there was an auction, and I think Viking won with something like a handful of trading stamps. But . . . Tom Jenks at Scribner. I just thought he was totally cool and charming. He was a smoothie. I didn't have any idea that people were nice with any kind of agenda.

So they bought it?

They bought it, it came out. Gerry had a number of very good editorial suggestions, all of which I ignored.

How did it feel when it sold?

It was an incredible thrill. I mean, it sold for, you know, thousands of dollars. I was like, I bought a new car. I was like . . .

Not that *car.*

As a matter of fact, yeah.

[I laugh.]

For six thousand dollars, from Budget Rent-A-Car. The car I've had for . . . I remember getting a really unkind, I mean I went from you know, borderline-getting-ready-to-be-kicked-out. To, you know, all these guys—because it was such a careerist place—all these guys being, "Glad to see ya, you'll have to come over for dinner." And it was just, it was *so* delicious. I had gotten to have unalloyed contempt for them, they showed what they were like. That they didn't even have integrity about their hatred. So . . .

• • •

MORNING
WE ARE WALKING THE DOGS
HE SHOWS ME HIS NEIGHBORHOOD, WHY HE LIKES IT

[On his landscape, the long fields] When the wind blows, you can see ripples, it's like water. It's like the ocean, except it's really green. I mean, it really is. Not so much here. But you get another mile south, where it's *nothing* but serious full-time farmland and farm-houses? Sort of calm, real pretty.

There's a Mitsubishi plant, and then there's a lot of farm-support stuff. There's a lot of firms called like Ro-tech and Anderson Seeds. And State Farm Insurance.

I had a whole vampire thing when I was a little kid. Also partly superseded by the shark thing. [He likes the movie *The Lost Boys*.] You couldn't really figure out—I wasn't really confident that he wanted to switch back and forth . . .

• • •

HE'S HUNGRY

BACK IN THE RENTAL CAR

WALGREEN'S FOR SODA, THEN BREAKFAST

DOESN'T WANT A RESTAURANT BREAKFAST: WANTS MCDONALD'S

[He's the sort of rugged man of self-reliance who, faced by a reporter armed with an expense budget, is eager to pay for his own Diet Rite soda.]

(Rhapsodizes metal Savarin can) They make great paperweights, filled with pennies. The lids make good dog Frisbees for inside the house. Like Oddjob's hat. [He speaks, he says, as a fan of "movies with things that blow up."]

• • •

AT MCDONALD'S

[We order so much, he tells the counter girl, "There's a bus that we're from."]

[He makes the last nondate joke.

   She smiles at us and asks whether our huge order is to go. Back in the car, he remembers the bacon from the McD's Double Bacon Cheeseburger fondly: "Kind of rubbery, no fat involved."]

I always forget how good their fries are . . .

I don't eat there a lot.

[We're plucking fries from the bag in the car.]

Have to take pickles off: I'm what my mother used to refer to as a picky eater.

[Blanches when I write this down]

• • •

IN HIS HOUSE
BREAKFAST

[Gives food to dogs. Warns me against leaving plates, bags unattended.] You can't put it on the table because the dogs will eat it, have to eat at the table.

   I'm just worried I'm going to look like one of those insane old women who talk to their dogs. [Moans when I write down stuff about him and dogs. "The dogs will be offended." "How will your dogs be offended? Your dogs won't *read* it."]

[Asks for half my cupcake ration.]

(Bible-epic voice) "They ate. And it was good. It was *good*." Sit. Sit. [Re MacDonald's] It's bad, but in a really good way.

[On NPR, George Burns dead today.]

I wonder what George Burns died of: Maybe someone just dispatched him with a club, figuring that was the only way.

Long eulogies on the radio this morning when I was in the shower.

Saw all those vitamins in your hotel room. Where's that at?

I take a lot of C and B. I was told that if you smoke a lot, or do a lot of nicotine, you have to take megavitamins. I take between 3,000 and 5,000 mgs of vitamin C: I aim for urine the color of a legal pad, and then I figure I'm safe. I take 100 mgs of B-6. I take A, because I have bad skin. I take zinc. And I think that's it.

These are emergency reserve ones of like 500 mg: they're just a pain in the ass, you've got to drink like a whole soda pop to take one. (To dogs) We'll give 'im some right now, because he looks like he's going to start feeling a little poorly.

You give vitamins to your dogs?

No, *you*. You can't burn the candle at both ends, man. You're not getting enough sleep, you're not eatin' right, working too hard. On the go. (Laughs) Busy '90s man.

Do I just take all these?

Yeah, not all at once, else'll make you choke. Take them one at a time, in a precise little anal, philosophical way.

You'd take this many in a day? This many pills?

Yeah. It didn't hurt ya. Whatever dudn't get used gets pissed right out.

Why a thousand pages?

I don't know. I wanted to do something with a whole lot of different characters that had kind of queer, broad, slow movements. I didn't set a goal of a thousand pages.

Knew it was going to be long, though.

Uh-huh. Do you ever have an idea how long something's gonna be? I never do.

I see what you mean. But, like at the plate, you know what you're swinging toward.

That's true. Yeah, I knew this would be over five hundred. Which—I don't think I'd ever done anything over five hundred before.

Why?

[He's shower-wet now. I remember his head steaming while smoking outside the St. Paul NPR studio.]

One of the things that made me think the book wouldn't get a very good reception. Probably one answer is that I wanted something that had kind of the texture of what mental life was like in America right now. Which meant, sort of an enormous tsunami of stuff coming at you. And also—it's not entirely reader-unfriendly. Except for certain parts that are supposed to be hard in the middle. It's divided into chunks, there are sort of obvious closures or last lines—that make it pretty clear that you're supposed to go have a cigar or something, come back later.

Short chapters too.

Yeah. Especially at the beginning. A lot of them are very very short.

Hard for readers at work. All day, head home, open the door, a thousand pages a hard thing. A big thing to come home to.

Like I said, the goal was really weird. The goal was to have something that was really pretty hard, but also to sort of be good enough, and fun enough, to make you be willing to do that. And in the course of that, teach you that you were . . . more willing than you thought you were?

I'm talking about what the goal was, I'm not talking about what it accomplishes.

Tactically, though, you're right. I mean, Michael pointed out, and I agreed, that this was basically, you know, all but stomping on reviewers' feet, spitting in their eye, and daring them to be pissed off. Because I've reviewed before, I know how much you get paid for it, I know what kind of deadline you're working.

Do you think it's a hard book or do you think it's an easy book?

I think it's both. I think it can be read in a way that's somewhat easy, although there are parts in the middle that I think are fairly challenging just on a line-to-line level. The book was *designed* to be both, I guess. And for it to be set up so that—it's a very different book depending on whether you read the endnotes or not. Or whether you read them when the numbers direct you to them or afterwards, or before. There's just a whole lot of plot stuff that isn't clear, if you don't read the endnotes.

Experience of reading it hard or easy?

I don't know—I know it was excruciatingly boring for me the last two times I read it. But that was the copyediting and the galleys. That's one reason—I mean, I sent early drafts out to people. And I really, they were friends who were good enough that if they had hated it they would tell me. You know? To sort of get an idea. It was actually very heartening. They would like call me up on certain pages, chuckling and laughing. And it seemed like, it wasn't *unfun*. (Soft voice) Charis, Mark Costello, Jon Franzen.

And the book is about *fun.*

So it's supposed to be sort of fun and unfun. For instance, I like a joke that you laugh hard at, but then it's sort of unsettling, and you think about it for a while. It's not quite black humor, but it's a kind of, a kind of creepy humor.

And there's some stuff in the book that's set up to be high camp. Like the corporately subsidized years. But it's supposed to be plausible, it's not out of line with the logic of the way subsidization of various things works. Or a way to satisfy voters who demand a high level of services without being willing to pay for 'em.

Or subsidizing national debt.

I think the things that stand against it are the things that stand against, for instance, legalization of certain kinds of drugs. Do we want to be the sort of society that allows our years to be sold to corporations? I think that if things got bad enough so that sort of thing would be necessary, um, the trouble and crisis would erupt in lots of other ways first.

Can you imagine your readers? And how do you imagine them?

I think I imagine them being, uh, young enough to kind of appreciate a contemporary argot or idiom: something being *true* to the way the language works now the same way *Diner* was true to certain types of language in the fifties. And I guess I imagine the reader either being pretty well educated, or being somebody with a lot of practice reading. Because there are parts of the book that I think you've gotta sort of *know* that, you've gotta have had some practice reading hard stuff and know that there's a payoff for it.

[His sister Amy's question, similar to Michael's: How much reader irritation do you want here? Because you're gonna need . . .]

I don't think somebody whose only experience reading long stuff is Anne Rice or Stephen King will find this—I think they'll find the demands on them just unacceptable, fairly early on. I don't really have any aspirations for a truly mass audience.

Yet you have one at this moment?

Well. This thing's, what? number fifteen on *The New York Times* bestseller list? I don't know what that adds up to. I don't think there's more than like sixty thousand copies in print.

Ada went to number one . . .

There's a system of sly allusions to it in DeLillo's *Ratner's Star*—it's primarily about math, with an ending that doesn't work. I think you would like DeLillo.

Image of reader is . . . College kid? A person who might suddenly get jazzed by it?

I think probably, what I've noticed at readings, is that the people who seem most enthusiastic and most moved by it are young men. Which I guess I can understand—I think it's a fairly male book, and I think it's a fairly nerdy book, about loneliness. And I remember in college, a lot of even the experimental stuff I was excited by, I was excited by because I found reproduced in the book certain feelings, or ways of thinking or perceptions that I had had, and the *relief* of knowing that I wasn't the only one, you know? Who felt this way. Who had, you know, worried that perhaps the reverse of paranoia was true: that *nothing* was connected to anything else. I remember that early on in *Gravity's Rainbow,* and really getting an enormous charge out of it.

And I think if there is sort of a sadness for people—I don't know what, under forty-five or something?—it has to do with pleasure and achievement and entertainment. And a kind of emptiness at the heart of what they thought was going on, that maybe I can hope that parts of this book will speak to their nerve endings a little bit.

[Pauses a moment]

If you quote any of this, you'd do me a favor if you'd say that I'm talking about what I hope for the book, or what the book's tryin' to do. I don't pretend to think that it has . . .

[Watch goes off again . . .]

Was it strange then to meet your audience? You'd never been on tour before, had you?

Nope. It *was* strange. But of course I was meeting those members of the audience who had the temerity to come up.

The most passionate?

Yeah. Um, it was, there's an odd phenomenon where, I think, if you write stuff that's intimate and weird, weird people tend to feel they're intimate with you. You know? Or that to have people, I got very tired of having somebody say, "I really really really really loved this." Which for one *nanosecond* makes you feel good. But then you really don't know what to say else except, "Thank you." I mean, you could sense that they expected you to say something else. To fall into the rhythm of an intimacy that they felt. And of course there *wasn't* that there. And that, that was *sad* and unsettling. And, um . . .

It is weird, because they'd been adoring you from afar.

I don't think it works that way with writers. I mean, I think we adore . . . maybe movie stars or record people.

[Jeeves whimpers, watching us eat: his dining audience, dogs rubbernecking. They may as well be watching tennis. Fries to mouth, burger to mouth, very attentive, as if tennis balls over net.]

I think with writing it's really feeling that, their brain voice for a while becomes *your* brain voice. And that you feel—the Vulcan Mind Meld perhaps is a better analogy.

That just, they feel intimate with you, in a way. Or that you'd be, not just that you'd be somebody that it'd be great to be friends with, but that they *are* your friend. And, you know, one reason why I've got an unlisted number, and why I really try to hold down on the mail, is that, is that that stuff is difficult to deal with. Because I don't wanna hurt anybody's feelings. But it's also a delusion, and it's kind of an invasive one. But then I realize that I set it up by doing just what I did, and so it all gets very . . .

How long has the number been unlisted?

Four or five years ago. I had three or four people—I think what happened was, I had forgotten to tell my parents not to give my number out. So it was people who tracked my parents down, and um—yeah, and they were all very nice. But a lot of them were troubled and upset, and wanted to talk about, in great detail, their problems. The way for instance I talk to really good friends about it. And I just have this terrible problem of . . . um, I just really hate to hurt people's feelings. And so I did something kinda cowardly. I mean, I kinda changed my number and just got my phone disconnected, so these folks couldn't find me anymore.

Same people again and again?

There were five or six who called, who began to call a whole lot.

Once a week, once a month?

Somewhere between those two.

College kids, adults?

It ran the gamut. There was one guy who was a computer opera-tor in Vancouver, he lived in a basement. Um, who I found really moving. He was in terrible, terrible pain. But it wasn't clear what he wanted from me, and when I would sort of ask him, he'd get angry, and it got scary.

He was a sort of involuntary psychic friend?

I think so a little bit. I think one, I think one thing about probably, you can expect that somebody who's willing to read and read *hard* a thousand-page book is gonna be somebody with some loneliness issues. Or somebody who's looking, somebody like *me* or perhaps like you, who isn't always able to get the sense of intimacy they need. You know, in regular day-to-day intercourse. And is going to this. So that, I think it was really more that they were lookin' for a friend, and I don't mind bein' somebody's friend. Although there's an upper limit to that. But the weird thing was that, their, they come to you on an unequal basis.

They already feel as if they know you—which of course they don't. They know the you in the book, and it's really impossible. Julie in Minneapolis is one of the very few people I ever became friends with because she'd written me a fan letter. Y'know? As this *City Pages* editor. But Julie has also worked with a whole lot of writ-ers and knows a whole lot about the differences. And she and I dis-covered that we genuinely did kind of like each other as people, with the book not being involved.

But you'd never toured like that. You had fans.

Right.

Big line of people; some want to impress themselves on you; you can tell by how they're looking at you, or by how they're shambling back and forth. How does that feel?

[Pause] It's very complicated. In one way it's nice and gratifying. In another way it's very tense, because you feel simultaneously the obligation to have an exchange with each person, but that other people are waiting. Or somebody wants *four* books signed, but that means keeping other people waiting. Do you piss that person off or the other people off? And one of my complaints is that the bookstores aren't very helpful about it. They don't really give you advice about how to do it, you're kind of thrown in, and you have to make a lot of it up.

And it wasn't unpleasant, it was fatiguing.

[I leave for bathroom.]

Now it's just me and the tape recorder sittin' here, Drone's lookin' at the floor, I'm smokin'. Having said I wasn't going to smoke, I'm smoking. I'm just talking to your tape recorder.

You had done readings before where there wasn't enough audience to hold the reading even, and the reading was called. What was it like to go to readings where people were fighting to get in?

I'm trying to condense it into something you can use.

In a certain way it was very satisfying. I know that sounds like a cliché, but it was very satisfying. The thing about it is, I get very scared about reading. Because I get self-absorbed and worry about me. And so I remember, the two times, the two times that the reading wasn't held, I remember I felt an enormous relief, you know?

What's weird about the process is there's terrible dread beforehand, and then uh—Jeeves, shut up! And then the time that it's most fun is during. Starting with actually halfway through the reading.

All right, come on, come on. Crate. Crate. [Finally wields this threat and locks Jeeves in his crate.]

I know you're settin' me up for a nice line, and I can't think of a condensed, cool way to say it.

What was the fun part of the tour; everyone read the book, waiting to hear you read?

[He seems a man determined not to enjoy these extras, like a man attending a party with a wife he secretly plans to leave. He is determined not to enjoy the process of being celebritified.]

Except the tour started on February 18, the pub date was February 19. It was, dollars to donuts will get you, that 90 percent of the people in that room weren't there because they had read the book, they were there because of this weird sort of hype thing. Which, um, so that any kind of excitement is undercut by this awareness that there's mechanisms going on that really don't have anything to do with me.

But I'll tell you—I mean, having an audience with really really pretty girls in it, who are paying attention to you, and like what you're sayin'? Is gratifying on a fairly I think simple *mammal* level.

Why?

Oh, because I think pretty girls are what you most sort of dream and despair of ever having, of ever paying attention to you.

Trying to find my list of your tour stops. Can't find it. You didn't—

You caught me. [He laughs. Points to wall, by kitchen and wall-mount phone.]

I've got the list up there.

Mind if I take it down for a second?

Please do. I think I would take it down if you didn't.

[Loud tape-detaching sound]

When you heard how many cities it was gonna be, how'd you feel?

It's more complicated than that. I had called actually Mark and Nan to find out—I didn't want to be an asshole to Little, Brown, but I also didn't want to do this really long tour. And I found out that a small tour was eight to ten cities, and told them that I would do that.

How many did they want?

It didn't even get to that stage.

I mean, they talked about setting up a tour originally—PR departments are like anybody else: they have *first drafts* of things. Their first idea was that I and some of my grad students would go around in the Midwest in a *van*, talking to bookstore owners, trying to convince them to buy the book. And I had to have Bonnie call them and explain that I was perhaps the very last person on the list of residents of planet Earth who would make a good salesman for their own stuff.

OK: what happened in Boston? [It's the first city of his list.] *Anything funny? Anything interesting, color?*

Tch-tch-tch-tch-tch. Boston was interesting because a lot of the people I knew, including some of the folks at Open Meeting— you know, who'd helped me—were there. My best friend's parents were there, who've been very close friends of mine, but were absolutely beside themselves with joy because of the *Time* magazine picture. The *Time* magazine picture had to them signaled some kind of arrival.

It would to anybody.

You *think?* I don't know. I just remember Mark's mom, her eyes were moist. And that meant a lot to me. And my friend Gina had come down from Providence.

I'm tryin' to think: the coolest thing was, um, what started like a disaster. Because I went to Boston and I had to come back. And everything was fogged in. So they hired a car to drive me down— which was striking to me, because to me, in any other situation, I would've had to grab a bus. And the Boston to New York bus, I've done that before and it's just, it's not a pleasant way to spend an afternoon. They hire this car that shows up in like five minutes. With the squealing brakes. And it's Ash Wednesday, and it's this old Irish Catholic guy who drives me down, while, like, lecturing about Catholic lapsology the whole time. And it was real interesting.

That kind of luxe surprised you?

About landing that guy. It wudn't a limo. It wasn't one of those things with the boomerang antenna on the back, it's what's called a car service.

A Lincoln.

It made me feel important, 'cause I had to get back for the book party. And like, that I was important enough to them to spend—it was probably a few hundred dollars—it made me feel important.

Have you stayed in that many hotels before this?

No.

How was that?

That was OK—although it was a little bit like the cruise experience.

I noticed how quickly I became accustomed to the luxury, and how quickly the minibar went from a wild extravagance to just kinda part of the . . . and I notice even now I'm *pissed* that I have to go out grocery shopping. And I got used to makin' a mess and knowing that other people would clean it up. [At the Whitney, before going out, I saw him actually straightening up for the maid.] And there was also something—it wasn't a regular hotel experience, Little, Brown paid for the hotel ahead of time, and pretty much all I had to do was make sure I didn't, you know, run up extreme charges.

I was talking with Betsy about this, and I don't mind telling you about it for the essays: I had this big paranoia of like, um, trying to figure out whether to watch a soft-core porn movie, on Spectravision. But being incredibly worried that the rating or the title would appear on the bill to Little, Brown. It'd be like: "*Hot and Wet*, $8.95" would appear on the room charges. And I would have some prim spinster in the expense department of Little, Brown knowing that I had watched *Hot and Wet*. So I chickened out of doing that.

Could have paid separately.

You're right, I could've—but then you've gotta make really sure they wiped it off the computer. And that means dealing with the person at the desk, who would very quickly figure out why you were so upset. The mortification versus fun of watching it was clearly not even. [Smokes my Marlboros; he's out of American Spirit.]

New York?

New York was very interesting because my friend Erin, who's the wife of a good friend of mine here, who's a forty-eight-year-old Mennonite lady, came with me the first two days. So it was—I mean, she came with me to the reading at KGB and she'd never been to a *reading* before. And she, I think, had this idea that they really were sort of like MTV Unplugged concerts, and there were lines, you know, out the door and stuff.

So I sort of got to experience it through her eyes. And like, she stayed with me in the hotel. It was funny, we got a crazy cabbie. You know, a guy who was schizophrenic and weaving all over the road, so we had to get out of the cab. I just said, "This is close enough, this is fine"—I mean, the guy was crazy. His license was also expiring the next *day*. Clearly, there was just all kinds of bad karma.

And she almost got chain-snatched. You know: a guy came out, started the you-better-watch-that-chain-somebody'll-grab-it shit. And I got to like seem like I was a New Yorker, and y'know do this quick smooth move between her and him. Like without ever meetin' his eye and ever breakin' stride. My point is I think I felt cool about it, because having somebody even more inexperienced than me along made me . . .

Read in New York before?

Yes.

How'd it go?

It's run the gamut. I've given readings where nobody showed up. I've given readings—first reading I ever gave—at the Ninety-second Street Y, with T. C. Boyle and Frank Conroy. When I was twenty-four. And then I've given, y'know, Cafe Limbo readings, that are OK, but also people are eatin' and talkin' while you're reading.

KGB. You arrive there at what time?

We got there fairly late. We got there about ten minutes before the reading was supposed to start.

What'd you see?

Lisa Singer—who's about five two and ninety pounds—and Erin

and I all pulled up. And we thought maybe it was a building that also had a bar in it, because there were people waitin' on the *street*. And Lisa freaked.

See, this is the nice thing: you have them with you, they freak for you, you know what I mean? It's what the escorts are for too, so you can just be detached, because they'll do the worrying.

It was just funny, we just couldn't get in. I think I had a bandanna on, and at some point, people got an idea that this was actually the author on the staircase. And so various Old Testament, you know, gaps opened up at various points. It was, to be honest, it was very weird because it was simultaneously very ego gratifying and also just terrifying.

Why terrifying?

It was terrifying because the room was packed, everybody was looking right at me. Clearly if I *fucked up* a little bit, if I *didn't* . . . y'know what I mean? It felt like there was a lot at stake, socially. There was a *New York Times* lady with a flashbulb going that made it hard to read. And I had to stop, and say no to that, and worry about lookin' like an asshole.

Did you go to that one? It was like being in the subway at five o'clock. I mean, people were standin' like mashed up. . . . And the guy who read before me was the bartender, who read this thing about a Nazi conspiracy to kill Kennedy.

Actually, this was supposed to be a kind of warm-up—I mean, the real reading was supposed to be at Tower [Tower Books; also now gone], and this was supposed to just be . . . I thought this'd be good practice. And I don't think it was supposed to be publicized, it was supposed to just be a read-to-the-bar thing . . .

Everyone there from literary industry?

Yeah, I recognized a lot of people.

Asked to stop photographing?

When I was readin', yeah. Have you ever had someone—you try to read, you get that purple dot, and then you can't follow the words.

Gratifying?

Havin' a whole lot of people there, because of you: y'know? And you know it's because of you. And to see that there were that many like heavy hitters there.

Who?

I can't even quite remember. There were just all people whose faces I kind of vaguely remembered from sort of big parties and publishing things. And you can also kind of tell by the way people are dressed. I was *clearly* the least well-dressed person in the room.

Book party?

I wasn't able to talk to my friends.

Mirror? Policy not to look?

These situations where you are at least ostensibly the center of attention, it's very easy to worry about what you're lookin' like to other people. And then you can run in and check and try to compose a self. And it's just crazy—you just end up going crazy. I'm not sure I made a promise to myself. But I know that I went to the bathroom a bunch of times to take my tobacco out—I also didn't have any clean *clothes,* and I had *just* gotten off this car from Boston. I mean, I was like, I was a *mess,* and I knew if I started worrying about it, it would just be nuts.

Often best way; you looked cool, green knit polo shirt, white jeans.

If it looked right, it's one of the great ironies of life that I've learned. Had I had another hour to prepare—when I have a lot of time to dress, I end up looking ridiculous. You know? And this way, this was just, I think, the thing that had the least crusty armpits.

[Quoting from his list of cities]

Seattle?

I'm trying to think of highlights.

San Francisco?

A big one was L.A.

L.A.?

Because at this bookstore in L.A., this was Dutton's. [Also gone] And it was OK, it was just, they didn't have seats, so everybody was standing in the aisle, and I had to stand on a box. And when I read, I normally—I've got the thing they blew up, and I've made some footnotes, and there was no way to hold the book.

And then there was a serious problem with—the worst thing about the signings were the book dealers. And you've probably had—you know what I mean. They come up—I remember the first time a book dealer ever came up to me, I thought, "Wow, this guy *really* likes my work." It's sort of like [the guy in Updike's] *Bech Is Back*—because they're all carefully wrapped in plastic. But they don't want any kind of salutation, they just want it signed. And pretty soon, you figure out that it just ups the value for them.

But these guys would get in line—and there's always a type, they're always sort of the type you can imagine. Just the sorta *collector*, this obsessive, anal, unhappy, tight-mouthed person. And they've always got eight to ten books, and I think it was in San Francisco that I figured out the rule, that I'll sign two at any one time, and then once everybody's out of the line, Yeah, I'll stay around and I'll sign your books, but I'm not gonna do it while people wait.

Nice.

It's nice, but it's also smart, because it avoids some big imbroglio. But this guy in L.A., this dealer showed up with it had to've been a hundred things. Books, magazine articles, all this stuff. And there was clearly no joy in it for him and all this. And Bonnie the agent was there, and she said that I would sign twenty, and he began to make a fuss. And I lost my temper, and I said if he said one more word I wouldn't sign *anything*. And then I had anger adrenaline in me.

Iowa?

Iowa City was terrible because I ran out of money, and Western Union wouldn't give me money. Because the guy, the Western Union guy at the Iowa City bus station—a little troll-like, red-haired man—is evil and deserves to be stamped out. He—I had a *cab* waiting outside. He first claimed that he hadn't gotten the order, then he claimed that he had. Then he gave me a *check,* and told me to go to the bank, saying he didn't have enough cash. The bank was closed. I mean, and I . . . he goes . . . If I coulda gotten a lock of his hair, he'd feel stabbing in his *buttocks* right now.

How'd you run out of money?

I had petty cash. I mean I took like $500 with me, and I just spent it all on like cabs and tips. And the hotel was way outside town, and I hadn't slept, because Houston was so hot.

And then at the reading, the bookstore owner gave me Jay McInerney's review like literally two minutes before I went into the reading. And the reading turned out to be on the radio, which they hadn't told me. And there were cuss words, you know, so I ended up saying inadmissible words on public radio. Then there was a Q and A they hadn't told me about. Then at the start of the signing, a lady who'd read some catalog copy that I'd written claimed that I was incredibly insensitive to deformed children.

From Mao II, right?

["The best metaphor I know of for being a fiction writer," David writes, "is Don DeLillo's 'Mao II,' where he describes the book-in-progress as a kind of hideously damaged infant that follows the writer around, forever crawling after the writer (i.e. dragging itself across the floor of restaurants where the writer's trying to eat, appearing at the foot of the bed first thing in the morning, etc.) . . ."]

(Unhappy) Yeah. I had written this thing in an hour, about how DeLillo's analogy was correct. It was funny, but on top of everything else, I almost started to cry. That was like the nadir of the whole thing. It got radically better after that. Chicago was fine. Minneapolis was fine.

L.A. versus New York?

They seemed more like *tourists* to the book world. I mean they were dressed in like cardigans and slippers, you know what I mean? Whereas the readings in New York, you could tell, people were used to them as public events, they were there to see and be seen.

Which actually takes some of the heat off you the reader, because you feel like people are looking at each other—that they all feel they're on display too. So actually, I've figured it out now, I prefer reading in New York to anywhere else.

[We hear whining, can't identify it.]

Oh—that's Jeeves in the crate! We forgot about the Jeevester!

[We walk, Dave releases Jeeves.]

Meet with movie people out there?

No, nein.

Dinner at Bonnie's?

This friend that I'd made doing the Lynch piece, who's a unit publicist, she was there. Streitfeld was there.

[Ear-flapping sound as Jeeves shakes off]

I'm not bein' cagey or withholding anything from you, I just haven't heard anything about that.

[The tape side runs out.]

Do you wonder if books are passé? Do you worry about that? As we were talking about yesterday, Rolling Stone hasn't covered a writer your age in ten years.

I think books used to be real important parts of the cultural conversation, in a way that they aren't anymore. And the fact that *Rolling Stone,* which is a pretty important mainstream magazine, doesn't cover them that much anymore says a lot. Not so much about *Rolling Stone.* But about how interested the culture is in books.

For me—and you know this, you get together with writers, and this is a great topic of conversation, 'cause we'll all just bitch and moan. We'll talk about the decline of education and people's declining attention spans, and the responsibility of TV for this. For me the interesting question is, what's *caused* books to become kind of less important parts of the cultural conversation?

A minority taste?

Yeah, in a certain way. The thing that I think a lot of us forget is, part of the fault of that is books. Is that probably as, you know—you get this sort of cycle, as they become less important commercially and in the mainstream, they've begun protecting their ego by talking more and more to each other. And establishing themselves as this tight kind of cloistered world that doesn't really have anything to do, you know, with real regular readers.

And uh, so, so no, I don't think they're passé. I think they've gotta find fundamentally new ways to do their job. And I don't think for instance we as a generation have done a very good job of this.

Hey, Jeeves—shut that off for a second. [Jeeves whimpers, sits.]

Must find new ways to make books—what new ways?

You know what? I don't know. My guess is, it's gonna involve some way of making sort of old eternal verities and questions comprehensible—I can't think of a way to say it that isn't academic.

Could you loosen it?

(Silent verbal scowl) Well, it's not just a question of loosening up, it's that it's very hard and complicated, and to try to compress it into a couple of sentences . . .

[Tape off, break]

[We talk it out for a few minutes; then, when he thinks he's ready— and this must be what it's like to watch him go through a few drafts, as he said in the car; he's found a way to do answer drafts on the spot, by regulating the tape flow; clever—he turns the tape back on.]

I'm not sure about "give movies that" [the audience], but you're right, do you want me to just say it over? Yeah, there's stuff that really good fiction can do that other forms of art can't do as well.

And the big thing, the big thing seems to be, sort of leapin' over that wall of self, and portraying inner experience. And setting up, I think, a kind of intimate conversation between two consciences.

And the trick is gonna be finding a way to do it at a time, and for a generation, whose relation to long sustained linear verbal communication is fundamentally different. I mean, one of the reasons why the book is structured strangely is it's at least an *attempt* to be mimetic, structurally, to a kind of inner experience. And I know we disagreed in Monical's about whether experience really feels like that. I mean, I don't know whether I've done it, it's something that I'm interested in, and am trying to do.

Subject matter untackled too?

Yeah. I guess . . .
   [To tape] David is talking about today people watch more MTV and more movies and more TV, and so that the world in which readers move is very different than the world in which, say, you know our parents moved.
   I guess. Yeah, I guess my first inclination would be to say that most of that would be—to create stuff that mirrors sort of neurologically the way the world feels.

[Dogs whimpering]

[Snapping fingers] Hey, c'mere! C'mere, Jeeves.
   But you're right: and the fact of the matter is—

I was quoting you, actually—

No wonder it sounds so, so very smart.
   C'mere! You know what? You're making me nuts. Sit down! Sit down, I can't think when you're doing this.
   But I guess part of it is, it also affects the kind of inner experiences. And you know, the feelings that fiction is about. Today's person spends way more time in front of screens. In fluorescent-lit rooms, in cubicles, being on one end or the other of an electronic

data transfer. And what is it to be human and alive and exercise your humanity in that kind of exchange? Versus fifty years ago, when the big thing was, I don't know *what*, havin' a house and a garden and driving ten miles to your light industrial job. And livin' and dyin' in the same town that you're in, and knowing what other towns looked like only from photographs and the occasional movie reel. I mean, there's just so much that seems *different,* and the speed with which it gets different is just. . . .

The trick, the trick for fiction it seems to me, is gonna be to try to create a kind of texture and a language to show, to create enough mimesis to show that really nothing's changed, I think. [Different position from first interview, five days ago, when I defended the nothing-about-people-has-changed position.] And that what's always been important is still important. And that the job is to find out how to do that stuff, in a world whose texture and sensuous feel is totally different.

And what's important—you've been saying to me—is a certain basic humanity.

Yeah . . . sort of, um, who do I live for? What do I believe in, what do I *want?* I mean, they're the sorts of questions so profound and so deep they sound banal when you say them out loud.

I think every generation finds new excuses for why people behave in a basically ugly manner. The only constant is the bad behavior. I think our excuse, now, is media and technology.

I think the reason why people behave in an ugly manner is that it's really scary to be alive and to be human, and people are really really afraid. And that the reasons . . .

[As I get closer to the dogs, David likes me better too; has that pet owner's helpless, natural, unavoidable faith in his dogs' taste.

The dog keeps whimpering; David jokes he's got "Godfather

Cheeks" from chewing the tobacco. Which he's always spitting into.
things . . .]

That the fear is the basic condition, and there are all kinds of reasons for why we're so afraid. But the fact of the matter is, is that, is
that the job that we're here to do is to learn how to live in a way that
we're not terrified all the time. And not in a position of using all
kinds of different things, and using *people* to keep that kind of terror
at bay. That is my personal opinion.

Well for me, as an American male, the face I'd put on the terror
is the dawning realization that nothing's enough, you know? That
no pleasure is enough, that no achievement is enough. That there's
a kind of queer dissatisfaction or emptiness at the core of the self
that is unassuageable by outside stuff. And my guess is that that's
been what's going on, ever since people were hitting each other over
the head with clubs. Though describable in a number of different
words and cultural argots. And that our particui r challenge is that
there's never been more and better stuff comin 'rom the outside,
that seems temporarily to sort of fill the hole or drown out the hole.

Could it be assuageable by internal means also?

Personally, I believe that if it's assuageable in any way it's by internal means. And I don't know what that means. I think it's fine in
some way. [Tape off again; we keep turning it off while he mentally
drafts and redrafts answers.] I think it's probably assuageable by internal means. I think those internal means have to be earned and
developed, and it has something to do with, um, um, the pop-psych
phrase is lovin' yourself.

It's more like, if you can think of times in your life that you've
treated people with extraordinary decency and love, and pure unin-
terested concern, just because they were valuable as human beings.
The ability to do that with ourselves. To treat ourselves the way we
would treat a really good, precious friend. Or a tiny child of ours that
we absolutely loved more than life itself. And I think it's probably

possible to achieve that. I think part of the job we're here for is to learn how to do it. [Spits with mouthful voice into cup.] I know that sounds a little pious.

[We pause for a little.]

Women?

I date occasionally. I wouldn't know what to say.

Hard?

I think if you dedicate yourself to anything, um, one facet of that is that it makes you very very selfish. And that when you want to work, you're going to work. And you end up using people. Wanting people around when you want them around, but then sending them away. And you just can't afford to be that concerned about their feelings. And it's a fairly serious problem in my life. Because, I mean, I would like to have children. But I also think that the sort of life that I live is a pretty selfish life. And it's a pretty impulsive life. And you know, I know there's writers I admire who have children. And I know there's some way to do it. I worry about it. I don't know that I want to say anything much more about it—I mean, there's jokes about getting laid on tour and stuff.

It'd be nice to have someone, for example, to be sharing this with?

Yeah. I really have wished I was married, the last couple of weeks. Because yeah, it'd be nice to have somebody to um—you know, because nobody quite gets it. Your friends who aren't in the writing biz are just all awed by your picture in *Time,* and your agent and editor are good people, but they also have their own agendas. You know? And it's fun talking with you about it, but you've got an agenda and a set of interests that diverges from mine. And there's something about, there would be something about having somebody who kinda shared your life, and uh, and that you could allow yourself just to be happy and confused with.

So nice to get back to hotel and call someone?

Yeah, it's weird. You know—

I haven't had a girlfriend for quite a few months, and I haven't missed it that much. I've missed it the last couple of weeks. But I'm also—I mean, I'm aware that you don't just *get* a girlfriend, so that you can have that. [The being close, the call from a hotel.] I mean, to get somebody in that sort of position takes some work, and you have to sacrifice some of your own stuff to get close enough with them so that they could do that. So I don't really feel all that sorry for myself. But it is a problem.

Nice to have your borders redefined, though, by physical contact with another person . . . I'm not just a set of anxieties and ambitions. I'm a person confined to a limited range, realize your head is only a half-foot-long space, etc.

Yeah, there's other, I mean that kind of experience is gettable in a lot of ways. Through really hard exercise, where you learn all over again what it is to be a body. It's gettable in a piece of music that's so transcendently beautiful that you forget who and where you are.

Although, like anything else, if it's done in the right spirit and with the right head. In certain ways it can be even lonelier. If it's more like, "Oh—you know, if I do this, will it have this effect on this person?"

I remember hearing in New York, I forget who it was who was tellin' this joke: What does a writer say after sex? *Was it as good for me as it was for you?*

[We laugh: then I realize I'm not completely sure.]

And what is funny about that?

Well, why did you just laugh so hard? I think that there is, in writing, a certain blend of absolute naked sincerity and manipulation. And a certain way of trying always to gauge what the particular effect of something is gonna be.

That's a very precious asset that really needs to be turned off sometimes. And one of the reasons why I think I've had such a hard time with females, you know, when I've been doing long work like this book, is that I think I'm sort of in that head that makes it, um—where I can be both spontaneous and very very very very self-conscious.

Do you think writers make bad bed partners then?

My guess as a private citizen is that writers probably make really fun, skilled, satisfactory, and seemingly considerate bed partners for other people. But that the experience for them is often rather lonely. And if you're thinking of Orin in the book a little bit, that's fine.

Tell me about the bandanna stuff we were talking about yesterday.

I started wearing bandannas in Tucson because it was a hundred degrees all the time. When it's really hot, I would perspire so much that I would drip on the page. Actually, I started wearing it that year, and then it became a *big* help in Yaddo in '87, because I would drip into the typewriter, and I was worried that I was gonna get a shock.

And then I discovered that I felt better with them on. And then I for a while dated a woman who was—she was actually a *Sufi Muslim,* but she knew a lot about, she was like a '60s lady, and she knew all about all kinds of different stuff. And she said that there were these various chakras, and one of the big ones was what she called the spout hole, at the very top of your cranium. [He demonstrates where it is, the dolphin and whale spot.] And in a lot of cultures, it was considered *better* to keep your head covered. And then I began thinking about the phrase, Keeping your head together, you know?

I mean, I don't wear it all the time. I wear it—I know it's a security blanket for me—whenever I'm nervous. Or whenever I feel like I have to be prepared, or keep myself together, I tend to wear it. It makes me—like last night we laughed, but it made me feel kinda creepy that people view it as an affectation or a trademark or something. It's more just a foible, it's the recognition of a weakness, which is that I'm just kind of worried my head's gonna explode.

People just think it's a way you're trying to connect with the younger reading audience.

I don't know very many Gen-Xers who wear headbands. The worst thing about *here* is—I mean in the Southwest, people wear 'em all the time. And in New York, there's a certain kind of hip way to dress that involves them. *Here,* one reason I got these plain-white ones is that people thought I was a biker. Here, it spells affiliation with Harley clubs. And I just don't need that shit, you know? It's hard enough to get a cab as it is.

But people thinking it's a commercial gesture . . .

No. I don't know what to say. I guess in a way I don't even want you to have brought this up. [Like the "Borges and I" story.] Because now, I'm now worrying that it's going to be intentional. Like if I *don't* wear it, then am I not wearing it because I am bowing to other people's perception that it's a commercial choice? Or do I do what I want, even though it's *perceived* as commercial—and it's just like one more crazy circle to go around.

Another crazy circle: one of many crazy circles of this?

I guess. But once again, starting in about two hours, this is over. And I'm back, you know, to knowing about twenty people.

Do you feel your fame here? I mean, forget that I'm here, and I'm sure you felt it in New York and L.A.; but you're sitting here with your two dogs?

I think it's the sort of thing that you feel a lot more when there are other people around treating you differently. Like this FedEx guy came to the door. Whole different FedEx guy: You were maybe still in bed. To give me this *Village Voice* thing. He goes, "So how does it feel to be famous?" And *that* threw me. Because I like—this is my place not to have to deal with that stuff. So things may be weird here for a few months.

People here know? The FedEx guy knows?

Tell you man, *Time* and *Newsweek*. That's, that's—I hadn't understood this, but that's a whole different fucking level. That's not the literary world, that's the—and you know, I don't *know* when the last person from Bloomington, y'know, who got mentioned in *Time* was, so it goes through the town like wildfire. You know, all my students' parents had called them, to tell them about it . . . I mean, it was just like, your cover's totally blown.

[Starts drumming on table; this makes him anxious.]

Not people in Walgreen's or McDonald's, but the FedEx guy. Did you feel invaded somehow?

Yeah, it was a creepy feeling.

And how'd you answer him?

I said, "My dogs don't give me any more respect." The thing about it is, yeah, when people say something like that, there's this requirement always to be witty and *on*, and I feel it kinda now with *you*. Like there's this, um—people expect a kind of witty, covering answer, that will allow everyone to walk away feeling good and chuckling. And there's something, there's something I resent about that, you know? That I should get to choose, when I'm on and when I'm not. Like with you, I don't mind it, because this is all set up. But *that*, that

I minded. And I guess, I guess the solution is just to systematically disappoint people so often that they'll quit asking.

What time?

It was like ten fifteen. The guy was forty. He also said, he also said he was coming to the reading at Borders, and I panicked, because I didn't *know* about any reading at Borders. But he meant Barnes and Noble later this month.

Did he smile?

He smiled, but we were both looking down at the thing that I had to sign.

Are you at the point you wanted right now?

Expand on that.

Your book has been received well, you've gone out and promoted it. You've got other books to write. You're back at Bloomington. Your dogs are here, you're at home, about to finish your book of essays, you now are someone whose words—I mean, they've been taken seriously for years—but they're now guaranteed to always be . . .

I think I'm where I want to be because I need to—we talked about this last night. There's things about this that are good. But there are things that are hard, and things that are dangerous. And I'm gonna have to work 'em out. And I'm gonna have to work them out by myself. You know, nobody else is gonna help me work them out. And this is a good place to do it. 'Cause, 'cause I'm left alone here. And I also have a set of friends who like me for reasons that don't have anything to do with this. Which is a real precious thing. Yeah, there's nowhere else I'd rather be.

Are you pleased about where you are professionally?

I don't know, no, I'm not where I want to be artistically. I wanna—I feel like I shoulda done, I could've done a whole lot more original work in this last year, and I've been sort of jacklighted by all this stuff. I'm worried about this book of essays, and that a couple of these things are gonna have to be rewritten, or that Michael is going to have really smart editorial suggestions.

You typed this book, the whole thing, three times?

Yeah—except the first two times of typing there were also big changes, sticking stuff in.

The whole time you're doing this, you don't know how it's gonna be taken. And then everything goes about as well as it can go.

Well, the *Times* dumped on it.

Well, forgetting the Times, this is one of the few cases when the Times didn't matter—

I guess—again, my big worry, I mean, I have a problem with a diminished capacity to enjoy stuff that's goin' on. My big worry is that I won't enjoy this. But it'll just up my expectations for myself. Which . . . and expectations of ourselves are a very fine line. Because up to a certain point, they can be motivating, and inspiring, and can be kind of a flame thrower held to our ass, get us moving. And past that point they're toxic and paralyzing. And—it's another reason it's very good I live here. Because New York would not help me work this out. And you know, you can't help me work this out, nobody can.

And when I walk out of here after I pack up, you're here with the dogs, and no more touring—

Well, I've got fact-checker phone conversations, but it's essentially over.

[I want something positive from him, some sense of the achievement: he moved from football to tennis, to writing, to McLean's, to writing again, rebuilding himself, a huge thing to have brought off, and now he's become who he from now on is going to be. I can't find it. He's looking at it as a tennis player: The match is still on, it's just late in the set; he's eyeing the alleys, where the sun is shining on the court, how his serve is falling, what's on the other side of the net.]

I think it's going to be really scary. I think I've kind of unplugged myself for the last three weeks. And I'm going to have to sit and kind of feel it. The question will be whether I have the balls to do it. I mean, I could just go to the movie theater for three straight days and just sit there. And I may do that for a while. The thing about living here, shit eventually catches up with you.

Still, this place is a nice place to be, isn't it? I mean, this house, that you own, and your dogs . . .

This is a good place. This is a good place. It's been so long since I've gotten excited—like last night when we were in the car, pulling into town, or the big thing is in airplanes coming back to Bloomington. I can remember, not since I was at college and would come home for vacations, there's this weird warm full excitement of coming home. And I feel like this place is home. And I know in so many ways I'm so lucky. I mean, if this, if all this stuff had happened five or six years ago, I think it would have torn me to shreds.

Why?

Because I didn't have a home. And I didn't have—I didn't have the equipment to treat myself even marginally like a friend. Or to take care of myself, at all. And now I have at least the rudiments of it.

[He nods and turns off the tape.]

• • •

PICKUP

TOURING HIS HOUSE

A MUSEUM TOUR OF THE WALLACE ENVIRONS

THE WALL DECORATIONS, BOOKS

LIVING ROOM

Alanis Morissette cover from Spin, her taking a photograph in a grocery aisle. Um, American flag. Some weird surrealist posters. The guest room is like a trophy room or fortress of solitude: his books in different languages and editions. Magazines where essays by him have appeared. A Swiss version of Broom of the System. Lots of big, ingot-sized copies of Infinite Jest.

A Barney towel in his bedroom.

Dog stuff. Dogs have chewed everywhere, gnawed the edges off chairs and tables. Fur, crap stains on the carpet, crate for the dog. Chewed-up stuff all over the place. A shark doll—he's a great white fan—on the bookcase. Globes from old cartography thing. Three bookshelves. Um . . . low chandelier he keeps bumping his head on when he forgets to duck. How much it hurt that he refers to me on the phone a second ago as "this guy."

[Not even the *"Rolling Stone* reporter"—"this guy is over right now."]

Photographs of the dogs. Scottish calvary charge poster on the wall: he is, after all, a proud Scot. His dad gave him that.

Some sort of coal-burning fireplace set in the living room. Brick wall. Fake wood paneling. Soda cans. It's like a frat's first floor: the bookish frat. Curtains. One-story house, five, six rooms with a basement. Postcard of Updike. A cartoon: Comparative anatomy; Brains—Male, Female, Dog. Fra Filippo Lippi painting. "Sign of the Killer Cow" card on wall.

Jeeves's throw-toys everywhere. Living room: Nothing except three stuffed, crammed bookcases and dog stuff. It's a living area for bibliophile dogs.

The Barney towel is a curtain of one window in his room. Over his head there's a photograph of some German philosophers who he says—he has German ancestry, "These guys tend to be paunchy, bearded, scowling, wooly, they resemble ways I could have turned out really badly, physically." Over his dresser, in his room, photo collage of his family. Like the kind of collage kids pin on dorm walls. Photographs of his sister and stuff like that on the wall. [His house is an exhibit of separate stages of his life: dorm stage, work stage, Illinois stage, success stage (oddly enough, the guest room). Just books and dogs. His sister is pretty, and looks like a female him.]

Clothes everywhere. The closet looks like the closet of a dorm: a lot of sneakers, stuff on the floor, warm-up stuff, rolled-up stuff. It's like the kitchen of a restaurant, at the end of a long, Friday night rush. This is the swinging door, the equivalent of the full sink, the crusted pots, the sliced chives on the floor. Things draped on things. A lot of draped stuff— draping is the best descriptor for his organizing approach, how he's keeping his clothes. Aquaish lighting: blue gray. The light comes through semiclean windows, giving everything the feel of an afternoon in winter.

Bathroom.

[He tells me, "You might not want to go in, I just wreaked a little havoc."]

The padded toilet seat. Postcards: baboons crawling. The Clintons. St. Ignatius Prayer that sounds very like the AA prayer. ("Lord, teach me to be generous. / . . . to give and not to count the cost, / to toil and not seek for rest / to labor and not to ask for reward . . .") Baby climbing up the stairs by its head.

Tapes and CDs by the stereo, and a Botticelli calendar, Birth of Venus. Gold and silver chess set.

[I walk to the garage. Dave has reverted to Illinois Dave, the Midwesterner who has a relationship with his scraper. He's chipping an entire Antarctica off his car. It's encased in ice, like something that's come packed that way from the manufacturer. I mean, it's total.]

It's my poor, shitbox car.

What's the make on this? It's a Nissan?

(Like prisoner reciting his numbers) 1985 Nissan Sentra. I know it dudn't look like much, man, but this thing *starts*. This thing never breaks, it starts all the time. It's actually a terrible problem: 'cause I gotta get a new one. But I don't know what I'm gonna do. I *can't* junk this.

Why?

Because it's like, it's my *friend*. I've had this thing all . . . but I can't really leave it in the garage, I mean, that's just *sick*.

 Although riding in *that*—[He indicates my forest-green Pontiac Grand Am—like Tower Books, Dutton's, the book circuit, the Whitney Hotel, a car that also no longer exists]—made me realize that I'm, that there are whole vistas of driving experience that I am not getting.

[He did the driving home and to McDonald's.]

The feeling of *gliding* when you're driving, instead of . . . I mean my car dudn't even have shock absorbers, it's like riding a power lawn mower.

A pile of the tobacco things against the window . . . [Gives me a level look; I'm still saying things into the tape machine, which makes him laugh, then me.]

 Who drew the kid's drawing? On the shelves: the "chickenhead David Wallace"?

Um, one of my friend's daughters calls me Chickenhead, and I call *her* Chickenhead. This is her latest *salvo* in the war.

[There was a poster—written schedule—of tour in Eastern Europe.]

You went to Eastern Europe?

No. My parents are there right now.

They gave you an itinerary? That's cool.

Yeah.

[Surrealist image, floating and piping: bent over, sort of Rasta hair, flute.]

That's that Hopi flute god. Um, that my parents have statues of. And then a friend sent me that postcard. I keep trying to get *Harper's* to run that painting. I think it looks good.

Paradox: Do you think that kind of attention comes to people who want it very much. Or do you think that it comes paradoxically when you've ceased trying to get it . . . ?

I don't know, because you know there are real good writers who I think have always wanted to be—I mean, I think Mailer wanted to be superfamous. And he *did* become . . . It's just, I think part of it just has to do with your constitution. I think if you're not a real strong person, it's pretty hard to get any work done, you know, when you want that, because there's not room for anything else. I mean, do you want to be famous?

[He's neatening up. We've walked back in the house.]

I'd like to have the widest possible readership.

Well, that's a kind of clever answer. But I'm—but answer the question as baldly as you put the question to me.

[I turn the tape off. Which makes David laugh.

I'm younger than him, and this is, I see, paramount in my mind: that he must feel an accomplishment here, to have carried this off. I still want him to say this is as good as I imagine it has to feel.]

You said you're afraid of being unmasked or something. Isn't it reassuring that people are reading you a lot and saying they like the book, are also saying that you're a strong writer and—

It'd be very interesting to talk to you in a few years. My own experience is that that's not so. That the more people think that you're really good, um, actually the stronger the fear of being a fraud is. That the backlash or turnaround could be much more powerful. You know? And that's the worst thing about having a lot of attention paid to you, is that if you're afraid of *bad* attention. If bad attention hurts you, then you realize that the caliber of the weapon that's pointed at you has gone way up. Has gone from like a .22 to a .45. You know? But again, I know it's terrible, because it's more complicated than that: because there's also the good side of it. And yeah, I'm like you, there's a part of me that wants a lot of attention. And that thinks I'm really good, and wants other people to see it. And . . . it's this queer blend of shyness and exhibitionism that I think is part of, you know, it's one of the ways I think we're sort of alike, you know?

Because you—there's that thing of showing people that you weren't wasting your time. Staying in at night, during days, weeks, seasons, and stuff like that.

Or that you weren't wasting your time when you were doing something that's regarded by the culture as kind of odd and self-indulgent. And is not—and is really off the beaten track, you know? We could've, you know, we coulda gone premed, or gone to Wall Street. And that would have been a much more American thing. It's all, it's all tremendously complicated.

It'll be very interesting, before you leave, I really would like, if we could trade address data. Because I'll read *The Art Fair* after the Heinlein and I'll send you a note. I'm gonna be very curious to see how—to see what it's like being inside your head.

Come look at the Alanis Morissette thing for a second: I just think it's funny, and I want . . . [And finally, it works. Success: we locate a good thing about this. Entrée to a midrange pop star.]

It's silly, but I left it up when you came.

You must've thought about taking it down before I did. Why? She's pretty, I guess.

She's pretty, but she's pretty in a sloppy, very human way. There's something about—a lot of women in magazines are pretty in a way that isn't *erotic* because they don't, they don't *look* like anybody you know. You can't imagine them putting a quarter in a parking meter or eating a bologna sandwich. And *her*—even though I'm smart enough to know part of that image is crafted, the sloppiness— there's a kind of sexiness *in spite of,* that's very, I don't know. I just find her absolutely riveting.

Walking into your house there were a lot of things I expected to see, but this was not one of them.

Well, I mean, I'm susceptible like everybody else.

I'd been listening to cheesy Bloomington radio, and heard, "I Want You to Know." I never even would've known who she was. My girlfriend, who was living here over the summer, was really into Ani DiFranco and P. J. Harvey, and what's her name? Tori Amos. All of whom are—you know, they're OK. They're just . . . but Alanis Morissette. If by some paradox, this whole fuss could get me some kind of even just like a five-minute cup of tea with her, that would be more than reward enough.

Although, of course, I'd never do it. I'd be too terrified. "So, what's it like to be you?" "I don't know—shut up. Keep the fuck away from me."

But you'd go if she called? And said, "Let's have that tea, I'm gonna be at the Drake in Chicago."

Yeah—except this is gonna look ridiculous. It's gonna look, if you put this in the essay, it'll look like I'm using the essay as a vehicle to try to—but you know what, I'd go in a heartbeat. Perspiring heavily all the way up there, shoving Certs in my mouth. Goin' nuts. It would cost me like a week of absolute trauma, and I would do it in a heartbeat.

[Break]

[Children are somehow on his mind: he compares raising children to raising books, you should take pride in the work you do inside a family and not from how they make out in the world. "It's good to want a child to do well, but it's bad to want that glory to reflect back on you," is what he says.

And then we're back with Alanis. I say it wouldn't be so awful to use the book to meet someone he thought he might like; that would be white magic, rather than black magic.]

My point is that it's very weird because I think, I mean, I think I'm as worried about the changing from white magic, using white magic—that's actually a nice way of thinking about it. I always think that it's just, it's leading with the karmic chin. You know, setting yourself up for shit.

But it's real weird—like a date with Alanis Morissette? Where I would clearly be on the, the power dynamics, I'd be on the downside of the power dynamics, and I would just get mostly to gawk and ogle. Doesn't strike me that way—sleeping with a groupie does. And I think it's one reason why even though I bantered to you about it, when push came to shove, I just, I just didn't do it.

It's a nice thing, a reality gauge, thinking about Alanis: in the real scale of the world, to a certain segment of the population you're extremely important. In the eyes of her or her fans . . .

And it's not even an entirely nice thing. I mean, one reason why it was so riveting when we all watched, you know, my college colleague in that HBO thing, is that I realized that more people were watching him do this than would ever, in the sum total of . . . ever read my thing.

Might not be true.

HBO's got what, five, six million subscriptions?

That's probably real interesting about *Rolling Stone.* You get to see the machine. You get to see what the real stuff looks like. I don't see how they stand it. I don't see how they stand both the good of it and the bad of it. I mean it would be like *this,* with a three-digit exponent. You know, it's no wonder it drives them mad.

[Tears down tour schedule, and throws it away.]

Are you done in the bathroom? Because I've gotta wreak some havoc in there.

[And there is something he's excited about. Tonight, a few hours after I roll away from his house, and pass Circus Video, and a beef chain called Steak N' Shake, and flip away from Phil Collins on one radio station to find him still upright and singing on another, and past the sign that lists Bloomington's sister cities—through a program called "People to People" at the State Department—as Canterbury, England, Vladimir, Russia, and Asahikawa, Japan, past a town called Money Creek, as if the surveyors ran short on names and just decided to talk turkey, David will get to be by himself for a while. And then he's going to get dressed, and go to a Baptist church. For a dance.]

It's a black Baptist church, but a lot of people come, because black Baptists can *dance.*

You dance?

I've just discovered in the last few years that I could do it, and I've discovered that I really like it. Although I'm still not very good. I tend to do the jerk and the swim. Which is the nice thing in Bloomington, you're completely hip if you do that. I don't Vogue. That's the one thing I refuse to do. I will not Vogue.

Where's the church?

Dance Night is at a thing called—this is going to sound very rural. There's the Plumber's Hall, that's out actually where we ate. And there's another thing called the Machinist's Hall. Kind of big, kinda smooth tile floors. It's cool. All the people come in, and they've all got their dancing shoes on and stuff.

[A friend just called to invite him, he's going. It's nice to think; because as much as he's talked about being alone, he hasn't been the whole time I've seen him, and for weeks, and my sense is he might not be ready for it. It's the end of the book for him, after all.]

What kind of music?

Everything from cheesy '70s disco to cheesy '90s top forty. You don't go for the music.

People from State Farm?

Nah. This isn't really a white-collar thing. Races don't always mix in this town, but when they do it's nice. There's a few of us who go to this, there's this church up near campus, and that church is kind of good friends with this black Baptist church.

So you'll have friends there?

Sure. It's put on by this, I forget what it's called, Some Number Baptist Church of Bloomington. But they—it's nice. Everybody's just, everyone more or less wants to leave each other alone.

TENNIS

The *Harper's* tennis piece—"Tennis, Trigonometry, Tornadoes"—is reprinted in *A Supposedly Fun Thing* as "Derivative Sport in Tornado Alley."

The piece about Michael Joyce—long title: "Tennis Player Michael Joyce's Professional Artistry as a Paradigm of Certain Stuff about Choice, Freedom, Discipline, Joy, Grotesquerie, and Human Completeness"; *Esquire* two-worded it, "String Theory"—also appears in *A Supposedly Fun Thing*.

The Tracy Austin piece ran in David's 2005 collection *Consider the Lobster*: "How Tracy Austin Broke My Heart." Here's how David addresses whether absolute, on-court focus takes "a kind of genius or a kind of stupidity": "Those who receive and act out the gift of athletic genius must, perforce, be blind and dumb about it—and not because blindness and dumbness are the price of the gift, but because they are its essence."

The story he discusses from *Girl with Curious Hair*—stolen in Washington Square Park, rewritten at Yaddo—is called "Westward the Course of Empire Takes Its Way." David says, "It's also a kind of sequel to John Barth's 'Lost in the Funhouse.'"

"Lost in the Funhouse," John Barth. Collected in *Lost in the Funhouse*, 1968, and one out of four college short-story anthologies.

Thief, Michael Mann, 1981.

Die Hard, John McTiernan, 1988.

David wrote about religion—"It's very hard to talk about people's relationship with any kind of God, in any book later than like Dostoyevsky. I mean the culture, it's all wrong for it now"—in a Dostoyevsky piece in 1995. "Joseph Frank's Dostoyevsky" is in *Consider the Lobster.*

The Stand, Firestarter, "Stand by Me" (as "The Body" in *Different Seasons*), Stephen King; 1978, 1980, and 1982, apparently a sweet spot for King.

David's cruise-ship piece is the title essay in *A Supposedly Fun Thing.* When David turned it in to *Harper's* in 1995, his editor Colin Harrison remembers, "It was very clear to us that we had pure cocaine on our hands."

"The Balloon" is a Donald Barthelme story. It's collected in *Sixty Stories,* 1988. In a 1996 *Salon* interview, David told Laura Miller it was "the first story I ever read that made me want to be a writer."

What David discusses about "And how much time do I spend doing stuff that actually isn't all that much fun minute by minute, but that builds certain muscles in me as a grown-up and a human being?" sounds very much like the subject of his final novel, *The Pale King,* forthcoming from Little, Brown.

Metropolis, Fritz Lang, 1927.
You can find the photo I think David is talking about as a proposed *Infinite Jest* cover at http://farm4.static.flickr.com/3271/2692735429_fa52fdda7e.jpg.

Cabinet of Dr. Caligari, Robert Weine, 1920.

Mark Leyner. *My Cousin, My Gastroenterologist; Et Tu, Babe,* 1990, 1992.
Here's Leyner from *My Cousin* describing a drive across David's home state: "Corn corn corn corn Stuckey's. Corn corn corn corn Stuckey's."

Wild Wild West, CBS, 1965–69.

Batman, ABC, 1966–68.

Braveheart, Mel Gibson, 1995.

Schindler's List, Steven Spielberg, 1994.

Always, Steven Spielberg, 1989.

The Hardy Boys, Franklin W. Dixon, 1927–2005; *Nancy Drew,* Carolyn Keene, 1930–2004. With great, reassuring covers: mysteri-
ous paintings and a bold typeface that suggested order would
soon be restored.

DAVID LYNCH
Twin Peaks, ABC, 1990–92.

Blue Velvet, 1986. (The "Frank Booth" David talks about is Dennis
Hopper playing the very scary antagonist. He keeps taking Darth
Vader–size pulls on an oxygen mask before doing rotten things.)

Eraserhead, 1978.

Brazil, Terry Gilliam, 1985.

On not having a TV: "Having to go over to friends' houses to watch
TV *works.* It's very much like taking an Anabuse or something. I
mean, it just lowers the amount that I can watch." David writes
about going to a church-friend's home to watch broadcasts on
September 11, 2001, in "The View from Mrs. Thompson's," collected in *Consider the Lobster.*

Pauline Kael. Former *New Yorker* film critic. Her two omnibuses are
5001 Nights at the Movies, 1991, and *For Keeps,* 1994.

True Romance, Quentin Tarantino (directed by Tony Scott), 1993.
The scene David discusses—Chris Walken's verbal square-off with an eventually heroic Dennis Hopper—begins at minute 45:40, ends at 56:00.

The End of Alice, A. M. Holmes, 1996.

Angels, Denis Johnson, 1981.

Crimson Tide, Tony Scott, 1995.
The "you got a lot of heart, kid" actor David noticed—spoon-size roles in *True Romance* and *Crimson Tide*—is a young, pre-*Sopranos* James Gandolfini.

Glory, Marshall Herskowitz, 1989.

Broadcast News, James L. Brooks, 1986.

The Hit, Stephen Frears, 1984.

Four Rooms, Quentin Tarantino, et al., 1995.

Blade Runner, Ridley Scott, 1981.

The Screwtape Letters, C. S. Lewis, 1942.

"Strange Currencies," R.E.M., 1994. (From the album *Monster.*)

"(What If God Was) One of Us," Joan Osborne, 1995. (From the album *Relish.*)

"Glycerine," Bush, 1995. (From the album *Sixteen Stone.*)

"The Big Ship," Brian Eno, 1975. (From the album *Another Green World.*)

The Letterman story—"My Appearance"—gets collected in David's *Girl with Curious Hair.* An actress is so nervous about appearing on the talk show she arranges for her husband to feed her answers via a hidden earpiece. The *Jeopardy!* story, "Little Expressionless Animals," and the Johnson story, "Me and Lyndon," are in the same collection.

The TV essay, "E Unibus Pluram," appears in *A Supposedly Fun Thing.*

The State Fair piece—"Getting Away from Already Being Pretty Much Away from It All"—premiered in *Harper's,* is collected in *A Supposedly Fun Thing.*

The Dirty Dozen, Robert Aldrich, 1967.

Kelly's Heroes, Brian G. Hutton, 1970.

Gravity's Rainbow, Thomas Pynchon, 1973.

Ada, Vladimir Nabokov, 1967.

David wrote about the Guggenheim Grant in "Death Is Not the End," the second story in 1999's *Brief Interviews with Hideous Men.* The main character is America's most successful poet, "known in American literary circles as 'the poet's poet,'" with a bucketful of grants and prizes, including a Nobel. Here's the quote:

> "Never the recipient of a John Simon Guggenheim Foundation Fellowship, however: thrice rejected early in his career, he had reason to believe that something personal and/or political was afoot with the Guggenheim Fellowship committee, and had decided that he'd simply be damned, starve utterly, before he would ever again hire a graduate assistant to fill out the tiresome triplicate Guggenheim Foundation Fellowship application and go through the tiresome contemptible farce of 'objective' consideration ever again."

Ratner's Star, Don DeLillo, 1976.

Diner, Barry Levinson, 1982.

"Here and There," the O. Henry story David's professor disliked, is collected in 1989's *Girl with Curious Hair.* That's the book David read aloud to thirteen people, including one continuous shrieker, at the Cambridge Public Library.

Secret Life, Michael Ryan, 1995.

David filled in Gerry Howard on his Auburndale job. "I contemplated the circumstance that the best young writer in America was handing out towels in a health club," Howard says. "How fucking sad."

Bech Is Back, John Updike, 1981. (The first chapter's early pages have the book-collector stuff.)

Mao II, Don DeLillo, 1991.

David, having had years of experience with the Q & A format, did terrific work with it in the 1999 collection *Brief Interviews with Hideous Men.* In the story "Good Old Neon," he writes about the back-and-forth pros and cons of being able to both anticipate what people are going to next say and steering them toward a congenial square. ("Part of the shyness for me, is, it's very easy for me to play this game of, What do *you* want? What will the effect of this be on *you?* It's this kind of mental chess. Which in personal intercourse? Makes things very difficult. But in *writing* . . .") It's collected in 2004's *Oblivion;* it's an astonishingly good story.

The long quote about getting people out of your house comes from "Authority and American Usage," collected in *Consider the Lobster.*

"You Oughta Know," Alanis Morissette, 1995.

acknowledgments

This book is almost entirely a product of David Wallace's generosity and openness about his thoughts, his work, his experiences. He was a warm and gracious host, even at those moments when (his dog, the car) I was a less than ideal guest. Working on the book has left me flattered and grateful.

David's parents, Jim and Sally Wallace, and his sister, Amy, share his qualities of charm, warmth, and great intelligence. They were extraordinarily patient and generous with me during an impossible time. As with David, the book literally would not exist without their assistance.

David's agent and friend Bonnie Nadell, and his friends Mark Costello and Jonathan Franzen, were warm and helpful under exceptionally trying circumstances. The writers and editors Charis Conn, Colin Harrison, Gerry Howard, Mary Karr, and George Saunders were also kind enough to answer long questions with delicacy and grace.

At Random House, Susan Kamil and Tim Bartlett have been steady advocates. Broadway Publisher Diane Salvatore sets an extremely high standard for intelligence, warmth, and energy. Charlie Conrad edited this book, with the sort of focus and sharp suggestions that fuel a project. David Drake, Catherine Pollock, Rachel Rokicki, and Julie Cepler—in the areas that David speaks of with intelligent misgivings; marketing and publicity—have proven to be just the sort of teammates you hope to find on the field. At ICM, Lisa Bankoff remains, as ever, a great advisor and friend.

This book began at *Rolling Stone* magazine. Jann Wenner and Will Dana have been wonderful colleagues. (Will, who assigned David a tennis essay early on, told me about a kind of nonfiction proposal the magazine gets: "Every day; 'I'd like to do a David Foster Wallace take on _____ ' ") Sean Woods, Eric Bates, Anna Lenzer, Pheobe St. John, and Coco McPherson provided invaluable assistance. Evan Wright, who was one of David's escorts (maybe not the right word) at the 1998 AVN Awards, was very open and funny about his experiences with David.

There's a saying that books have friends before they ever meet readers. This book's friends were Ryan Southerland, Darin Strauss, Ellen Silva, Evie Shapiro, Elizabeth Perella, Nick Maniatis, Pat Lipsky, Deborah Landau, Rich Cohen, Jenna Ciongoli, Matt Bucher. And Rachelle Mandik, senior production editor at Crown, who devoted many hours to proofing this book, worked with me by phone for what seemed whole days, and who (in this era of electronic data transfer) I still, as of January, 2010, have yet to meet in person. Rachelle's kindness to this book had very little to do with me and everything to do with her love for David Wallace's work. In a way, she stands for the whole experience. People were patient and generous with me because of the great affection it was one of David's gifts to inspire—another thing I am grateful for to David.